MAKING MEDIA WORK

CRITICAL CULTURAL COMMUNICATION
General Editors: Sarah Banet-Weiser and Kent A. Ono

Making Media Work

Cultures of Management in the Entertainment Industries

Edited by Derek Johnson, Derek Kompare, and Avi Santo

NEW YORK UNIVERSITY PRESS

New York and London

NEW YORK UNIVERSITY PRESS
New York and London
www.nyupress.org

References to Internet websites (URLs) were accurate at the time of writing.
Neither the author nor New York University Press is responsible for URLs that
may have expired or changed since the manuscript was prepared.

LIBRARY OF CONGRESS CATALOGING-IN-PUBLICATION DATA

Making media work : cultures of management in the entertainment industries / edited by
Derek Johnson, Derek Kompare, Avi Santo.
     pages cm
 Includes bibliographical references and index.
 ISBN 978-0-8147-6469-5 (hardback : alk. paper) -- ISBN 978-0-8147-6099-4 (paper : alk.
paper)
 1. Management--Cross-cultural studies. 2. Mass media--Management. 3. Cultural
industries. I. Johnson, Derek, 1979- editor of compilation. II. Kompare, Derek, 1969- editor
of compilation. III. Santo, Avi, editor of compilation.
 HD30.3.M3445 2014
 302.23068--dc23
                              2014004213

New York University Press books are printed on acid-free paper,
and their binding materials are chosen for strength and durability.
We strive to use environmentally responsible suppliers and materials
to the greatest extent possible in publishing our books.

Manufactured in the United States of America
10 9 8 7 6 5 4 3 2 1

Also available as an ebook

CONTENTS

Introduction

Discourses, Dispositions, Tactics

Reconceiving Management in Critical Media Industry Studies

DEREK JOHNSON, DEREK KOMPARE, AND AVI SANTO

As represented in popular media, management is that force in our collective work worlds that renders labor inefficient, pointless, or suspect through its bureaucratic hierarchies, authoritarian mechanisms of control, and often the corrupted or inept personalities of those who rise to the position of manager. In the British workplace sitcom *The Office*, manager David Brent plays the fool, more concerned with his own ego than the productivity of workers under his employ. In the cult comedy *Office Space*, manager Bill Lumbergh plays the overbearing villain, a source of conflict who repeatedly tells the protagonist, "Yeah, I'm going to need you to go ahead and come in on Sunday." And when we consider the self-reflexive popular texts that the media industries produce about their own work cultures and managerial class, the management of the media is made comprehensible in the same kinds of terms. Films and television programs like *The Player*, *Get Shorty*, *Californication*, *Entourage*, *Studio 60 on the Sunset Strip*, and *30 Rock* frequently position network executives, studio developers, talent agents and market researchers alike as "suits" who oppose the more productive forces of creative talent by shaping productions to meet the needs of advertisers and corporate shareholders.

Despite such caricatures, real media management is seldom located solely in the practices of a specific, fixed category of media workers—managers—who stand in opposition to the managed. Instead, management is an unevenly distributed but nonetheless omnipresent dimension of media work in general. Thus, management must be understood as a much wider network of cultural power, negotiated by participants at all levels in institutional hierarchies. Management, in this sense, is not the province of a specific class of facilitators and bean counters at the top (or even the middle) of media production hierarchies, but is instead a culture of shifting discourses, dispositions, and tactics that create meaning, generate value, organize, or otherwise shape media work throughout each moment of production and consumption.

For this understanding of management, we draw from organizational sociology and critical theory to explore how historically situated *ideas* about management operate as contested modes of managerial (and non-managerial) identity formation that in turn codify "commonsense" managerial practices. Instead of seeing management as an inflexible or even stagnant occupational category, we argue that the various meanings that become attached to "management" come into existence only through exchanges of discourse wherein "truth" about the category is constantly being (re)constituted. Michel Foucault (1972) explains that discourses are abstract constructs that can be assigned meanings through the use of signifiers (words, images, actions) that communicate specific relations between subjects, objects, and statements. Thus, "management" as discourse within media industries is repeatedly evoked through various representational and performative strategies that in turn help to explain relationships between the numerous above, below, and "across the line" laborers (see Johnson 2013) working on particular products/productions and the industrial organization that assigns them those roles. Lara Lessa (2006) expands Foucault's definition of discourse to include "systems of thoughts composed of ideas, *attitudes, courses of action, beliefs and practices* that systematically construct the subjects and the worlds of which they speak" (emphasis added, 285). Lessa proposes a mutually constitutive relationship between meaning-making, perception (of self, of one's role within a designated field, of others' "value" within that field), and selected policies and modes of conduct. In other words, managerial dispositions and tactics are both shaped by and actively contribute to ongoing efforts to construct knowledge about management. Conversely, historically situated discourses about management also inform managerial identities, which in turn generate an array of tactics designed to enact and make sense of said ideas and identities. We expand upon this tripartite definition of management as discourse-disposition-tactic below.

Management as Discourses, Dispositions, and Tactics

In conceiving it as a set of discourses, we situate management within a Foucauldian framework for categorizing and organizing knowledge. In his seminal essay on authorship, Foucault recognizes the category of "author" as serving to unify and give meaning to a broad set of works and activities. According to Foucault (1969/1979), in the contemporary era, "author" is a category of power and distinction claimed by many but validated only through conferral by peers, critics, and reading publics. Though equally powerful, the category of "management" does not typically carry the same stature and claim to validation as does the "authorship" discussed in detail by Foucault. Nonetheless, "management" produces meanings that not only refine how "authorship" is understood (often as its presumed opposite), but also how cultures of production operate. The invocation of "management" conjures up images, imagined actions, and interactions for individuals on all sides of the creative labor divide, from executives and support staff to above-the-line talent and below-the-line craft. To either claim or be assigned the label of management depends on particular ways of constructing knowledge about industrial practices, creativity, and consumers.

Moreover, as a discursive category, management is constantly subjected to competing forces vying for definitional power over its meanings, functions, and representations. Understandings of management— of what it means to manage or be managed, of what managers "do" or how they "act"—change according to socio-historical and industrial contexts as well as the relative power of those media workers engaged in this discursive categorization. The same holds true for how those in management positions make sense of their work: the projects, peoples, and processes being managed. In conceiving of "management" as a discourse, we seek to move past debates over what managers (should) "do," and instead address how "management" is understood within industrial and academic settings (which, in turn, inform the actions taken by media industry workers who identify as "managers" as well as those who self-identify as "managed"). Within various media studies subfields, including auteur studies, creative industry studies, cultures of production, media management, political economy, and production of culture, "management" has been theorized as a category of labor bearing a particular yet ever shifting relationship to "creativity," "commerce," and "audience" (alternately understood as "citizens," "consumers," "fans," "users," or some combination thereof). Typically, managerial discourses within cultural industrial contexts have been understood as functioning to enable (Caves 2000; Bilton 2006; Deuze 2009), broker (DiMaggio 1977), negotiate (Davis and Scase 2000; Deuze 2009; Lampel et al. 2000), rationalize (Bilton 2006; Ryan 1992), constrain (McChesney 2008; Wollen 1972), and monetize (Bilton 2006) the contributions of artistic and autonomous labor.

Such discourses work as "linking pins" (see Havens in this collection; Turow 1992; Likert 1967) that connect productively charged sites of encounter within media culture: art and commerce, public and private interest, producer and consumer. Though these pairings are often discussed in antagonistic terms as sites of struggle (see Hesmondhalgh and Baker 2011; Negus and Pickerling 2004; Banks 2007) or cooptation (see McChesney 2008), management could also be constructed as facilitating and inspiring new modes of dyadic collaboration, such as the hybrid modes of "produsage" described by Axel Bruns (2008) wherein production and consumption are not so diametrically opposed. Ultimately, managerial discourses change according to the ideological perspectives and relative positions of authority held by those engaged in the construction of "truth" about management's function. What remains constant, however, is the impulse to deploy "management" as a means of making meaningful and connecting together dimensions of the cultural industrial landscape that might otherwise seem discordant.

Though all such meanings coexist and compete with one another for definitional power, hegemonic managerial discourses are continuously reformed in relation to shifting industrial and social norms. In such a context, Chris Bilton's (2006) approach to "creative management" as enabling, tracking, and monetizing a network of dispersed and diverse stakeholders (ranging from creators to consumers, but all conceptualized as potential sources of labor) is not merely a new way of theorizing the roles management ought to play in organizing creativity, but a managerial discourse made possible/plausible only within particular historical circumstances. Creative management theories emerge in response to technological changes that have allowed for the decentralization of production, promotion, and distribution. They also follow industrial reconfigurations that have elevated intellectual property (variously understood as "brands," "content," and "franchises") above particular media formats as the primary business of cultural industries. At the same time, creative management manifests in negotiation of attitudinal shifts within industrial cultures that now recognize multiplicity and divergence (ironically fueled by technological and industrial convergence) as valuable forms of research and development and ways of combating segmentation within brand communities. Mark Deuze has also foregrounded the importance of creative management, arguing that the "creative industries approach to sites of cultural production also focuses our attention on the seminal role that (the management and organization of) creativity plays in any consideration of media work" (2007: 250). Deuze creates an opening for us to consider how discourses of creativity and management are mutually constitutive. Alternately, both Paul du Gay (1997) and Graeme Salaman (1997) have pointed to changes within post-industrial cultures wherein management has attempted to redefine how employees understanding the meanings of "work" and their relationships to their employers by reinventing corporate cultures through discourses that align the workplace with both the private sphere ("we treat our employees like family") and sites of leisure ("working on the weekends can be fun"), all in an attempt to improve organizational performance and cultivate loyalty and devotion from employees.

One of the most significant interventions made by several authors in this anthology is to situate management as both a function of "intermediaries," borrowing the term from Pierre Bourdieu (1984), Paul du Gay and Stuart Hall (1997), and Keith Negus (1999), and as a site of intermediation. du Gay and Hall suggest that cultural intermediaries perform the "symbolic work of making products 'meaningful'" (62). Elsewhere, du Gay (1997) describes cultural intermediaries as "play[ing] a pivotal role in articulating production with consumption by attempting to associate goods and services with particular cultural meanings and to address these values to prospective buyers" (5). Although such figures are typically associated with promotional fields like advertising and entertainment journalism, which translate the artistic and social value of cultural commodities for consumers, Negus (1999) argues that cultural intermediaries also exist within organizational contexts and engage in the symbolic work of constructing knowledge both about consumer tastes and about the very processes of creating and organizing media products. Managerial discourses, then, might best be understood as forms of intermediation that media industry professionals (and scholars) use to explain how forces often designated as contradictory, oppositional, and irreconcilable—like creativity and commercialism—communicate, asymmetrically influence, and place pressure upon the other.

Importantly, rather than relegating cultural intermediation to a particular field, Negus identifies its presence across multiple occupational sectors, including those rarely associated with cultural production, like accounting. Similarly, we recognize management as a site of cultural intermediation occurring within media industry structures, traversed by varying populations, from "suits" to "talent." We position management as both a form and site of this kind of intermediation, reframing that intermediation as a process linked to management and not as an occupational category in its own right.

Negus also suggests that cultural intermediaries form their understandings of how the market operates in part through their memberships in particular communities defined by class, race, gender, sexuality, and nationhood, as well as in relation to the socio-historical contexts in which they operate. He states, "production does not take place simply 'within' a corporate environment structured according to the requirements of capitalist production or organizational formulae, but in relation to broader cultural formations and practices that are within neither the control nor the understanding of the company" (19). Thus, management as site of cultural intermediation is tasked with making sense of these broader formations and practices even as it is constituted within them.

While discourses of management circulate in myriad ways amongst cultural workers, and are shaped by—while also shaping—industrial, political, economic, and social structures, media management must also be conceptualized as a set of learned performances into which an increasingly diverse set of social actors are interpolated and governed. Building on Judith Butler's account of "performativity" (1999), Nancy Harding (2003) has argued that first and foremost managers manage themselves by internalizing a set of ideological positions deemed intrinsic to managerial life. Linking the socialization of managerial identity and masculinity together, Harding claims, "management in post-modern capitalism is an epistemological performative endeavor, where management is the discursive space within patriarchal manage-rialism into which the manager climbs to be subjectified and subjected" (17). While Harding's assessment denaturalizes both patriarchal identity and managerial practice, it also points to the ways in which perceptions of management amongst managers—learned through formal schooling and informal encounters with popular culture—in turn shape manage-rial purviews and produce particular managerial dispositions.

Pierre Bourdieu's (1993) work offers a flexible and historically grounded model of how occupational identity and norms are formed within cultural industrial settings. Bourdieu sees an integral relation-ship between disposition—or one's perception about and attitude toward his or her occupational subfield—and one's position within the field of cultural production, understood both in terms of hierarchy and degree of autonomy possessed within an otherwise heteronomous institution (subject to both market and political forces). As position changes, so does disposition, and vice versa. Managerial dispositions are therefore formed based on the relative yet variable positions of authority held by particular occupational subfields. Bourdieu argues that self-perception as a member of a particular labor subfield—one's sense of the expected and potential roles a group might play in shap-ing cultural output—is predicated in part on the positions of author-ity and autonomy possessed by that occupational group. Moreover, in Bourdieu's model, position and disposition work together to inform position-takings, or the actions a particular subgroup is willing and able to take in order to fortify, enhance, refine, or justify its place and role within the cultural production hierarchy.

Unlike those who take purely structuralist approaches to power wherein position dictates attitudes, behaviors, perceptions, and actions, Bourdieu sees position and disposition as mutually constituted, meaning that cultural and social beliefs also work to shape societal structures and occupational positions. Bourdieu (1979/1984) and Negus (1999) assert that certain subfields attract and/or are populated by particular social groups with shared socio-economic backgrounds, education levels, and cultural sensibilities, which in turn, inform how those subfields define their roles. Media management, like management more generally, is a profession often associated with masculinist middle-class sensibilities—imagined as rational, authoritarian, pragmatic, austere. As such, media management has tended to attract an overabundance of white, middle-class men, who in turn shape the perceived dispositions management is expected to possess. Negus further suggests that cultural production is categorized according to presumed social conventions and tastes, which in turn produce genre categories. Negus argues that popular assumptions about class, gender, and race within the music industry inform how genres are constituted, differentiated from one another, and marketed to particular consumer groups.

Bourdieu, Harding, and Negus' work complicates the functionalist and prescriptive approaches to management embraced by media management scholars, who have typically sought to teach future media managers best practices for negotiating creative, commercial, cultural, and industrial tensions within media work environments. Yet, in espousing normative strategies for effective management of media professionals, media management textbooks paradoxically seek to teach broad managerial approaches that rely heavily on case studies that marvel at the accomplishments of exceptional individuals and institutions. Unsurprisingly, these approaches have placed great emphasis on the importance of "leadership" as a quality integral to inspiring the right mix of creativity and loyalty amongst members of media organizations. Selectively defined, leadership for creative management seems to advocate for a less antagonistic relationship between the talent and the suits while also investing heavily in the Weberian (1924/1947) notion of "charisma" as essential to keeping talent in check.

As Alan B. Albarran (2010) claims, "liberating people (employees) to do what is required of them is the most effective type of leadership and management possible. . . . The leader [is] a servant in that the person removes obstacles that prevent employees from reaching their objectives" (90). Recognizing media as "fundamentally creative businesses," George Sylvie et al. (2008) argue in *Media Management* that talent need to be given sufficient autonomy to engage in divergent thinking while leadership must "[develop] a vision for the company that represent[s] a challenge to members' creativity, [provide] the resources to meet that challenge, and then [get] out of the way" (40–41). Meanwhile, in *Strategic Management in the Media*, Lucy Kung (2008) proclaims that "leading for creativity" requires managers to leverage their charisma, which is encapsulated in their vision, their demonstration of emotional commitment, and their ability to motivate emotional engagement on the parts of followers, in order to appeal to talent's intrinsic motivations, which, in turn, "promotes followers' receptivity to higher order goals and suppresses self-interest" (206–207).

In presuming that leadership qualities can be taught by studying great leaders, media management theories offer very little critical inquiry as to how great leadership qualities are constituted within particular socio-historical and political-economic contexts. For example, Kung presents BBC Director General Greg Dyke as an exemplar of how strong, charismatic leadership can transform institutional culture by offering up a new vision of its intrinsic motivations. Approaching the same topic from a cultural policy perspective, however, Philip Schlesinger (2010) situates Dyke's cultivation of a "creative ecology" at the BBC in relation to the United Kingdom's emerging investment in the creative industries beginning in the late 1990s, arguing that "at the macro level, Dyke's approach should be related to New Labour's drive to make 'creativity' a modernizing force in the UK's economy" (275). In other words, following Bourdieu (1993), it might be argued that Dyke's managerial disposition and the particular position-taking strategies he adopted were shaped by the particular position the BBC occupied as a heteronomous institution operating within the field of cultural production. Schlesinger cites Luc Boltanski and Eve Ciapello's (2005) work in asserting that Dyke's managerial style aligned neatly with a recently popular "neo-management" trend within management theory, characterized by an emphasis on "personality and personal

relations" intended to inspire, motivate, and mobilize creativity throughout the BBC (276).

On the one hand, all this suggests that managerial identities and identifications are forged within the constantly shifting relationships between
institutional, economic, and cultural structures. On the other hand,
Bourdieu's position/position-taking/disposition triad calls into question
the efforts of media management scholars to teach ahistorical "leadership strategies" to would-be managers. Bourdieu's triad helps us see that
managerial "actions" (position-takings) are always contingent upon the
degree of authority and autonomy available (position), as well as the perceived functions and value of managerial authority and creative autonomy within differentiated sites of cultural production, which in turn
inform how managerial discourses are selectively engaged (disposition).

So if media management is discursive and dispositional, it is also
tactical, in the sense that what management "does" is ultimately contingent upon socio-historical and industrial context, position, and
self-perception. For Pierre de Certeau (1984), tactics are the resistant
responses of individuals to the top-down strategies of economic and
cultural domination imposed upon them by corporations and governments. According to Michael Gardiner (2000), "strategies seek to colonize a visible, specific space that will serve as a 'home base' for the
exercise of power and domination," and do so primarily through the
panoptic tools of surveillance and quantification, whereas tactics "are
dispersed, hidden, ephemeral and improvised in response to the concrete demands of the situation at hand" (172). While management is by
no means oppositional, it does depend on interpretative practices that
can, at times, selectively translate corporate strategies to suit creative,
political, or other prerogatives. Of course, management often exercises
power through surveillance and quantification—through practices that
John Caldwell (2008) terms "giving notes" to bring producers more in
line with corporate bottom lines and measures of box office and ratings success. Yet management also involves flexible improvisation and
negotiation in dealing with creative ambitions and corporate strategies,
each of which may be diametrically opposed to the other. Management
is ultimately the tactical negotiation between institutional rules and the
agency individuals within those structures seek to assert; it is hegemony
in action, neither progressive nor regressive, certainly co-opting of

radical practices, but also essential to rendering power structures more inclusive of alternate modes of media production and consumption.

Critical interrogation of managerial discourses, dispositions, and tactics requires "midlevel fieldwork" that investigates industrial phenomena as the product of cultural forces as much as economic ones, and examines how contradictions play out in practice, where human agents work to focus and interpret those economic forces in significant ways (Havens, Lotz, and Tinic, 2009: 236, 249). As proposed by Tim Havens, Amanda Lotz, and Serra Tinic (2009)—and indeed, taken up by a number of authors in this volume—"critical media industry studies" sees "power as a form of leadership constructed through discourse that privileges specific ways of understanding the media and their place in people's lives" (237). We see management as an immensely productive site at which to conduct the critical media industry studies research that Havens, Lotz, and Tinic propose, in that we want not only to examine management as a set of tactics constituted through discourse, but also to consider how media managers—positioned between the agency of a perceived creative class and the strictures of economic institutions— embody the contradictions at the heart of such mid-level situations.

Similarly, Vicki Mayer, Miranda Banks, and John T. Caldwell describe "production studies" as a discipline within cultural studies concerned with "how media producers make culture, and, in the process, make themselves into particular kinds of workers in modern, mediated societies" (2009: 2). This concern attunes production studies to questions of hierarchy, identity, representation, and community as media workers navigate their positions within the structures of the media industries. Much like the audiences that media and cultural studies had previously privileged, producers become comprehensible in production studies as a site of meaning and interpretation, requiring anthropological methods based in ethnography, interviews, direct observation, and even participation in media production. These methods have thus far produced important work on the discourses of identity formation in production workers, often those above the line, but particularly those below the line (Caldwell 2008; Mayer 2011). However, at the mid-level range, management still remains relatively opaque and even often adversarial in this work. We should therefore heed the interventions of scholars like Denise Mann (2009), whose work in production studies has considered the meaningful intersections of management with television authorship and how producers have increasingly integrated the identities and tactics of brand management into their above-the-line creative practice.

In dialogue with critical media industry studies, production studies are perhaps best suited to the study of management as a set of tactics by which labor is organized and (perhaps even more importantly) made meaningful in the media industries. It is the aim of this book, therefore, to operate within the agenda laid out by these burgeoning subfields of media and cultural studies, as well as to offer new schema for integrating a robust study of managerial imaginaries, identities, and practices within them. In doing so, we also seek to meld production studies' grounded analysis of day-to-day negotiations and routines within media work cultures with the theoretical interventions offered by proponents of cultures of production and cultural economic research into the complex relationship between structure and agency within cultural production contexts (du Gay and Hall 1997; du Gay 1997; Negus 1998, 1999; du Gay and Pryke 2002; Hesmondhalgh 2007; Hesmondhalgh and Baker 2011).

Though management has become an increasingly important practice in the contemporary era of branding, IP licensing, and convergence, management as a discursive category of labor has existed for a long time, and it is safe to say that its functions, representations, and dispositions have changed in accordance with both industrial and cultural shifts. Hence, this anthology aims both to explore what managers do in the course of performing, imagining, and enacting management, and to rethink traditional boundaries between managerial and creative labor. This means not just considering management in terms of a traditional managerial class within the industry, but also viewing the field of cultural production and consumption as one implicitly constituted through the practices of management. In doing so, we hope to help media and cultural studies to rethink some of its assumptions about whom and where we should look to study management and managerial practice, as well as how and why investigation of management might be necessary.

Managing This Collection

It is with some sense of irony that we introduce the essays in this collection by conceding our own managerial roles as editors of this anthology.

More than merely policing the word length and citation styles of our contributors, we have understood ourselves to be engaged in the process of inspiring our authors—many of whom did not think of themselves as studying management per se until we assured them that they were—and organizing their varied approaches into a coherent conceptual whole. And it is perhaps with an even greater sense of irony that we blatantly attempt to manage how readers approach this collection. While for the sake of simplicity, we have divided essays into three sections focused on managerial discourses, dispositions, and tactics, respectively, within actual management cultures and processes of cultural management, we do not see this triad as being so easily disassembled. And neither do our contributors. Each essay in the anthology could easily have been made to fit within multiple sections. For example, Tim Havens and Laurie Ouellette's essays are as much about the formation of managerial dispositions as they are about the structuring roles of managerial discourses, while James Bennett and Niki Strange's contribution says as much about the tactical responses of various BBC personnel to the corporation's multi-platform strategy as it does about the way that strategy was situated within broader discourses of the BBC's historical mandate. We are fully cognizant that our imposed structure, while necessary, also necessarily informs how each essay could be read in relation to its categorical placement. Thus, we strongly encourage readers to approach the essays with this conceptual interplay in mind.

Leading off this collection, Amanda Lotz identifies the challenges in developing broad theoretical paradigms for studying media managers, given the lack of access scholars typically have to these professionals, the role of "spin" in framing managerial decisions, and the ever-shifting nature of cultural production, wherein project-by-project changes in players, objectives, and pitfalls require managers to adopt new managerial strategies in each new context. In so doing, Lotz grapples with media studies' need to develop a coherent set of meanings for media management (and methodologies for studying it), recognizing that while this goal is often stymied by the very managerial cultures scholars seek to explain, the project itself can nonetheless be productive in terms of generating multiple competing discourses about media management (not to mention the construction of knowledge about the role of media studies scholars in studying media management). Skeptical that a consistent methodological approach for studying media managers can be adopted, Lotz challenges media scholars to rise above individual case studies and identify the broader applicability and significance of their findings to the study of media management.

Connecting case studies to larger theoretical insights, Timothy Havens argues that media managers regularly engage in storytelling practices known as "industry lore," which not only serve as sense-making rituals in managing the circulation of culture, but also act as a means of negotiating, asserting, and rationalizing individual agency in relation to structural forces within production cultures. In particular, Havens analyzes the role of industry lore in legitimating and challenging discourses about what types of television texts can successfully circulate internationally and why. Meanwhile, James Bennett and Niki Strange detail the emergence of competing discourses among BBC creative workers over how to implement its 2006 interactive multiplatform initiative. They argue that debates over the roles multiplatform was supposed to play within the BBC's strategic mission often reproduced analog assumptions about what makes BBC content appealing to its audience.

Laurie Ouellette argues that in an era defined by neoliberalism (i.e., the liberalization of market constraints and the outsourcing/radical reduction of government social services in favor of private enterprise), citizens are increasingly asked to invest in discourses of self-branding and self-management as means of attaining resources for their success. Ouellette sees the emergence of reality television programs starring lifestyle coaches and/or featuring competitions between unpaid creative and craft laborers as part of the process of normalizing the ethos of self-governance by repeatedly demonstrating how success and failure are matters of personal choice, creativity in the face of adversity, and the ability to "sell" one's brand to clients. She demonstrates how discourses of self-management are articulated across an array of subgenres focused on gendered, racialized, and classed subjects, as well as amongst creative laborers seeking to translate social capital into real capital. Thus, Ouellette rethinks not only how managerial discourses are deployed within the media industries, but also how such discourses now permeate almost every aspect of our professional and private lives.

Significantly, all four contributions to this first section of the anthology also address the complex relationship between managerial discourses and the authority bestowed upon cultural intermediaries in rationalizing creative and economic agendas. The essays that follow in our managerial dispositions section focus less on how "management" is understood by media industry professionals, and more on how self-perception and self-identification shape managerial praxes and procedures—sometimes contradictorily—and contribute to how individuals and occupational groups are positioned vis-à-vis management. Essays in this section of the collection include Kyle Barnett's exploration of how early twentieth-century talent scouts, usually white middle-class men forced into this line of work due to economic hardships or corporate restructuring, understood their roles in identifying and evaluating the appeals of musical artists from rural, poor, and non-white backgrounds. Barnett demonstrates how talent scouts negotiated their own subject positions in relation to the talent they worked with and how, in turn, perceptions of race and class shaped how these artists were then marketed to consumers. He also addresses how decades later these men understood and sought to articulate their legacy and the methodological challenges media industry historians face in analyzing roles that individuals remember always in relation to their current positions within the field of cultural production.

Erin Hill examines how the dispositions of casting directors in Hollywood have shifted as the field has moved from above-the-line executive status during the height of the studio era to below-the-line independent contractor status in the current production climate. In particular, Hill explores how discourses of female labor have come to dominate the ways in which casting directors understand the work they do in a field where men were historically dominant. Ultimately, Hill argues that as the field's position altered, not only were more women brought into its ranks, but also the work done by casting directors was redefined in stereotypically gendered terms that focused on emotional and interpersonal management activities. This shift has proven essential to the field's sustainability, but also diminished its stature.

Focusing on the contemporary Brazilian film industry, Courtney Brannon Donoghue analyzes how studio executives in transnational, national, and independent film corporations, who must often work together to manage co-productions, seek to justify their own positions based on their supposed ability to tap into an authentic "Brazilian" identity. Brannon Donoghue explores how "Brazilianness" is articulated differently depending on the positions of the executives she interviewed. Addressing similar questions of identity, while shifting categories away from disputed evocations of the "national" to the increasingly blurred boundaries between "celebrity" and "fan," Elizabeth Ellcessor explores how actress Felicia Day manages her star persona as an authentic gamer and Hollywood outsider through social media. Ellcessor notes how Day repeatedly positions herself as a member of the communities she portrays, obscuring the labor performed by others in managing her career as well as the insider access she has gained through the success of her various web projects. Ellcessor also addresses the increased importance of self-promotion within post-industrial Hollywood, and in particular, the new ways that stars must manage their relationships to their fan bases through particular practices designed to emphasize their own fannish identities and affiliations.

Each of the four essays in the final section of the anthology approaches the tactical aspects of management somewhat differently. However, both of the first two chapters do offer analyses of the tactics by which change has been managed in moments of technological transition in the media industries. Alexander Russo investigates the transition period to format radio in the late 1940s and early 1950s and in particular, how BMI's local and regional "clinics" allowed local station owners, programming directors, and radio hosts opportunities to engage one another and propose new programming approaches. In suggesting that format radio evolved from these bottom-up tactical negotiations, Russo elucidates how management tactics are both historically contingent and site specific. Elizabeth Evans explores the development of the BBC's policies on integrating Twitter into its programming, promotion, and audience feedback strategies. Evans demonstrates how such policies tactically adapted the BBC's ongoing public service mission to meet audience expectations in an era of convergence and social media, while dutifully refusing to overstep its mandate. Evans also addresses how the BBC sought to manage both audiences and its own brand image by cultivating a more personal and responsive approach to its programming via Twitter. Evans' essay might be read in conjunction with Bennett and Strange's contribution, as both address the BBC's efforts to manage transmedia expansion as extensions of its core public service mandate. Reading these two essays side by side allows for an assessment of how managerial discourses and tactics are mutually constituted, yet can also be engaged in contradictory manners within and across the same organization.

Our final two contributors offer insights into the relationship between tactics and strategies from embedded positions within the media industries. Both straddle the academic and industrial worlds. In his previous role as Vice President of Primary Research Analytics for NBCUniversal, Justin Wyatt oversaw the development and deployment of market research projects designed to gauge audience responses to marketing for NBCUniversal programming. While Wyatt's essay lays out a strategic approach to conducting market research that benefits both clients and suppliers, he also addresses many of the tactical (if also undesirable) factors that lead to miscommunication and misrepresentation on both sides. Thus, even as Wyatt outlines how, from a strategist's perspective, an ideal market research initiative would develop, he is keenly aware of the roles that divergent interests, human error, and reputation-based economies play in muddying those waters. His contribution to the collection also offers readers a level of nuanced detail rarely glimpsed in analyzing media management practices. Meanwhile, Sam Ford, Director of Audience Engagement for Peppercomm, a strategic communications and public relations agency, offers a reflexive assessment of why media scholars should seek to combat the industries' tendencies for intransigence and fractured communications from within. Reviewing his encounters with clients who are seeking to strategically maximize their digital presence, but are often reluctant to shift tactics in how they interact with consumers or internally between different divisions, Ford both notes the error of such approaches—that digital strategies require new communication tactics that offer customers and employees opportunities to be heard—and describes the tactics he employs in trying to convince clients to rethink their approach to communication. While Ford advocates for more media studies scholars to change the existing media industry structures from within (as opposed to merely critiquing them from without), he also addresses the concerns and limitations that arise when mounting a tactical challenge of this sort. So while this book opens with Amanda Lotz identifying potential obstacles in the way of our attempts to access, research, understand, and critique the management of media culture, it ends by highlighting the ways in which those objectives might be met through direct intervention in the cultures of media management.

Covering a wide range of industrial contexts, media forms, and historical moments, the essays in this collection can be utilized in conceptualizing how managerial discourses, dispositions, and tactics function (differently) across time and space. Among the questions this anthology raises: To what other discourses, dispositions, and tactics might management be productively articulated and theorized than those featured in case studies here? If management is at some level a performance of specific identity, how might we understand that performance through closer attention to race, gender, class, age, and sexuality? If the discourses, dispositions, and tactics are as radically contextual as this volume suggests, is there a concrete means of studying media management outside of the localized case studies we have offered? Is the next step a matter of extending analysis of management in the media industries to other unexamined markets, sectors, and nations, or might there be a way to theorize management as more significantly constituted across these lines? How will the changes wrought by global, economic, and technological convergence impact the discourses, dispositions, and tactics through which the management of media culture is enacted, performed, and made meaningful? How can our conception of management continue to be useful while these shifts force its ongoing revision? To whom can these understandings of management be useful? What is our responsibility as scholars to engage in dialogue with above- and below-the-line laborers situated within the discourses, dispositions, and tactics of management? Perhaps most crucially, why will a strong conception of management continue to be important to critical media industry studies? We hope that these chapters offer several strong responses to these questions even as we recognize the value in continuing to ask them and seek new answers.

As with most collections, there are gaps. There are no essays focused on the comic book or advertising industries, nor any on management within consumer product or transmedia extension divisions. Eastern Europe, Asia, Australia, and Africa are also absent as sites of management. As no anthology can be all-inclusive, we sought cases that could be utilized as conversation starters and encourage readers to compare

and contrast the roles management plays within different media industry settings and amongst different populations (as well as ask questions,
following Lotz, about the broader applicability of these cases in formal-
izing an approach to studying media management). Future studies of
media management might confront these gaps, ask provocative questions in response, and push this work in new directions.

While it is self-serving to suggest that any such absences or indefinite
answers to key questions about management actually strengthen this
collection precisely because they encourage further scholarly inquiry,
we will note that this managerial tactic allows us to define our editorial roles as bridge-builders and provocateurs rather than gatekeepers,
and, to borrow from discourses of creative management, it validates the
enablement of divergence and disagreement amongst those invested in
studying management within media industries.

If the Suit Fits . . .

Conceptualized as a set of contentious and contingent cultural discourses, dispositions, and tactics, rather than as a stable tier or type
of labor within unchanging hierarchical structures, media management can be understood not as standing in opposition to the production of culture, but as being productive and generative of culture in its
own right. Management should be framed not merely as a work category responsible for overseeing labor, but as a kind of labor—and a
way of creating meanings and values from labor—that takes diverse
forms within the media industries. Through this approach, an opportunity arises for closer critique of the hegemonic representations of
media management we discussed earlier, as well as for directing more
attention to the discourses, dispositions, and tactics of management
within the media industries. For example, with management linked to
supposedly masculine dispositions of rationality and efficiency, self-
reflexive media representations about the perils of its own management have also often been stories about tactical negotiation of gender
roles within industrial structures. In the 2006 film *The TV Set*, the
key figure of managerial oversight is Lenny, the network president
played by Sigourney Weaver, who complains that a series pitched to
her network is "so fucking artsy and smart." This film—like many

others—represents powerful women managers as "ball busters," while depicting frustrated male intermediaries as ineffectual and unable to fulfill their creative (and masculine) roles as managers. While seizing upon post-feminist backlash anxieties about the erosion of male authority, these representations also point to the idealized masculine dispositions media workers are expected to possess to negotiate the world of media management.

Fictionalized managers aside, the labor of actual media industry workers is similarly represented as a tactical negotiation of managerial dispositions and discourses that give meaning to talent and shore up claims to creativity, originality, or authority. From 2009 to 2012, Dan Harmon served as the creator and showrunner of NBC's *Community*, a cult sitcom about a community college study group. Many in the show's small but devoted fan base recognized the program as a product of Harmon's authorial genius and individual creative expression, and this authorial discourse cohered in direct opposition to the dispositions attributed to network management. Most notably, when Harmon was dismissed from the day-to-day production of the series in 2012, NBC became the villain in much behind-the-scenes discussion about the show, which cast the bean counters as standing in the way of Harmon's personal expression (Adalian 2012; Gennis 2012; Harmon 2012; Ryan 2012). Yet from another perspective, Harmon the creative genius was also Harmon the bad manager. Given that Harmon was noted to be a control freak who often went over budget, his insistence on his own personal vision could be regarded as a tactical failure to delegate, accept compromise, and negotiate the constraints of the network system as a showrunner (Mittell 2012). In his public feud with cast member Chevy Chase, moreover, Harmon's creativity appeared to come at the expense of an ability to properly manage the talent working for him, as well his own public "self-disclosures" (Caldwell 2009). While Harmon's tweets, blogging, and other means of forging a professional identity contributed to the authorial discourse, his publicized professional disagreements with Chase and NBC suggested this authorship was unruly, unmanagable, and unbefitting a good manager. On the one hand, Harmon's talent barred him from hegemonic managerial disposition; on the other, his instability as a media manager offered yet one more example of "bad," self-defeating management from within the industry. The point here is not who or what the real site of management is—Harmon or NBC—so much as understanding both to be equally operating within discourses, dispositions, and tactics of management that shape media work. A year after his dismissal, NBC reinstated Harmon as *Community*'s showrunner, suggesting both the contingency of managerial practice as well as continued categorical tensions between authorial and managerial discourses in terms of valuing creative labor. After all, Harmon was not brought back because he had successfully completed a management seminar, but rather, because his creative vision was deemed essential for inspiring and mobilizing talent and fan labor, which NBC executives deemed essential to the network's brand image.

While we can separate managerial practices, discourses, and cultural formations from the occupational category of "managers," doing so is not meant to evacuate the term "management" of its specificity or to suggest that all media workers are equally managers. Instead, management takes on different forms and different meanings across specific contexts of media production and consumption, and is an occupational category and identity constituted, claimed, and made meaningful in complex, dynamic ways that cannot be fixed or singularly defined. This means that we might consider the whole field of cultural production and consumption as one implicitly constituted through the discourses, dispositions, and tactics of management. In this regard, management is best understood as a set of sense-making tools utilized by media industry workers—only some of whom are part of a professional class known as "managers"—for negotiating tensions inherent to cultural production.

Our goal then is not to rehabilitate media managers like Harmon and reveal them to be heroic bastions of creative energies and progressive business practices (though to be clear, we would not discount the possibility outright without investigation). Instead, we wish to challenge the assumption that the study of media management means lionizing or demonizing a single group of media professionals. We hope to offer a more nuanced understanding of management insofar as it is constituted in the processes whereby a range of media workers go about their work, talk about themselves, and insert themselves into the production process in multifaceted and culturally significant ways.

I

Discourses

1

Building Theories of Creative Industry Managers

Challenges, Perspectives, and Future Directions

AMANDA D. LOTZ

Perhaps the fictional embodiment of "Management" that best matches the underexplored aspect of cultural industries' managers can be found in HBO's relatively short-lived, Depression-era supernatural tale of a traveling carnival in the aptly titled *Carnivàle*. Here management is a never-seen, possibly mystical, force not dissimilar from the Wizard of Oz, and is referred to simply as "Management." It seems feasible that "Management" is no more than a fictitious construction invented to police the carnival crew and assert a threatening presence in a way that the diminutive carnival manager, Samson, played by Michael J. Anderson, *Twin Peaks'* dancing and backward-speaking Man from Another Place, cannot not impose himself. But through veiled and ominous threats like "Management won't like that," Samson can get anyone in line.

Unlike the possibly imaginary managerial authority in *Carnivàle*, managers do exist in the creative industries. But as this collection's editors suggest, their roles are often unconsidered and frequently assumed to amount only to that of the caricatured accountant obsessed with the bottom line and lacking any understanding of "the art." But what or who really are "managers" in the creative industries? In our course text, *Understanding Media Industries* (2012), Timothy Havens and I name "industry executives" as those participating in the creative practices component of our Industrialization of Culture framework, a model for explaining how media industries operate which identifies three intersecting "levels of influence"—organizational mandates, operating conditions, and day-to-day practices (4–5). We acknowledge "industry executive" to be an imprecise term, but generally conceive of those "who play necessary roles in providing institutional support to creators to enable the development and circulation of media products" to inhabit this role (132).

These executives help the ideas of creators—if not the creators themselves—to negotiate institutions that might produce, promote, distribute, and exhibit those ideas as commercial or public service media content to audiences around the globe. Industry managers are distinct from the individuals responsible for actual creative work such as writing or directing—although this, too, isn't always a hard and fast distinction; contemporary media industries increasingly feature a blurring of "creative" and "managerial" roles. The job titles of such managers might include Development and Programming Executive at television networks, Co-chair and/or CEO at film studios, and Managing Editor in magazine and newspaper publishing. In most cases, their continued employment depends upon achieving commercial success for an entity such as a network or studio, yet they are empowered to participate in decisions with significant creative implications.[1]

Although we may be able to define a set of jobs or roles in media industry creation as the purview of managers, our ability to speak of them as a common group is severely limited. As the range of foci in the following chapters makes clear, there is an almost incomprehensible array of conceivable managers—from talent scouts to distributors to research consultants. These individuals perform different jobs in different organizations and industries and do so with varied agency in their roles. The caricatured manager noted above is certainly common, but also must be contrasted with creative managers who "understand" and are praised accordingly, as when Emmy winners creating programming for HBO laud the premium channel for the practices that lead to its well-established reputation as an environment in which network managers remain fairly hands-off of the creators and their creative process. On some occasions, creators even commend managers for intervening and pushing them in unconsidered directions. This anecdotal range illustrates the inconsistent perspectives on creative managers.

There are likely to be good and practical reasons for the limited theorization of media executives and the underexplored nature of managers' roles in the creative industries. In no particular order of importance, it can be said that: there are enormous *methodological challenges* to researching managers; it is uncertain which of the *intellectual traditions* common to studies of media might best develop these studies; and the *broad range of tasks and agency* that managers enjoy makes it difficult to understand their experience in ways more expansive than the particular case study. Yet, some intellectual approaches to examining media industries have long overlooked the meaningful role individuals such as managers play in the production of creative goods. This essay first addresses the considerable challenges involved in studying media managers, acknowledges the uncertain theoretical base for this endeavor, notes a meaningful critique of contemporary media industry research and some routes of response, and closes with a consideration of how insight into the roles of media managers might be mined from existing work.

Challenges to Study

Perhaps the plainest reason that so little work on managers extends beyond the abstractly "theoretical" to the empirical is that there are enormous methodological challenges involved in their study. It is nearly impossible to study managers without their participation, which then confounds the research experience in whole other ways. Access to high-level decision makers is difficult to obtain for even a short interview, let alone the extended fieldwork and observation required for developing meaningful analyses. Most media managers work for highly competitive commercial entities that treat secrecy as a necessary business practice. Perhaps one of the reasons for the elusiveness of grounded studies of conglomerates—truly inveterate institutions of management that define the organization of contemporary media industries—is the difficulty of achieving the embeddedness and extent of access required to build critical understandings of how this management structure works, particularly in relation to ever-new creations of media industries. The methodological problems are not limited to access to people; concerns about competitive secrets or protecting against litigation commonly foreclose opportunities for access to documents as well. The competitive dynamics of these multi-million and billion dollar industries lead to suspicion of researchers and requirements of non-disclosure agreements for the most basic level of access.

Even when barriers to access are surmounted, the information gained is often difficult to evaluate, and its applicability beyond the case and people at hand is uncertain. As John Caldwell (2008) details, executives often engage in obfuscation and double-speak, making any information gleaned from them dubious and suspect. This is most evident in the genre of industrial biography or journalistic profile that features media managers.[2] Many of these are carefully crafted public relations vehicles aimed at the creation or perpetuation of a "great man" mythology of executives with far-reaching agency. Such profiles purport to reveal the behind-the-scenes stories of textual creation, but rarely feature critical analyses or even objective journalism.

Theoretically, the critical roots of creative industries' study lie most deeply in political economy, which has rarely—at least in its North American version—considered the micro-level of individuals' actual work in creative industries. Instead, studies typically begin by explaining how the accumulation of capital and the ownership structure of these industries might affect their behavior or the goods they create. Methodologically, this type of study draws from numerical data such as budgets, revenues, or other quantifiable measures which are rarely linked in any way with particular textual outcomes. Such a macro level focus somewhat precludes consideration of the individual case, let alone individual manager. Moreover, some researchers operating in this tradition assume that individuals have little meaningful agency and tend to operate in accord with mandate of the organization. Consequently, the strongly Marxist influenced version of political economy common in North America has rarely considered the operation of media industries to be affected by individual managers.

And yet in some ways, considerations of managers, particularly as evident in industrial biographies mentioned above, can also take on an auteurist perspective. These cases ascribe great power and influence to managers and construct them as being able to mastermind plans that might rival those of *The Simpsons'* Mr. Burns. Just as auteur theory attributes a unifying creative vision to a film director, this approach to managers ignores the myriad of creative workers who make meaningful decisions or, at the least, often narrow the universe of perceived options available to the manager as decision-maker. Such auteur-style study of managers draws primarily from interviews, often with the subject, and crafts a compelling, but rarely interrogated narrative of masterful executive plans. Though such works sometimes reveal nuggets of insight that can be useful to the critical scholar, most tend to offer description without meaningful analysis of cultures of corporations and particular managers, which in themselves vary widely enough to make theories of wide-reaching commonality among managers unfeasible.

Notably, another strand of research considers the day-to-day functioning of creative industries. The richest tradition of this work is represented by studies of the newsrooms of journalists and editors, often through extensive participant observation, as well as by analysis of both the process of media production and the media goods produced. However, such studies rarely situate their subjects in relation to the creative industries, perhaps because with its commitment to fact, the Fourth Estate would likely contest being considered a "creative" industry. Moreover, much of this work preceded the interventions of cultural studies, which are now common means for understanding the political and ideological implications of entertainment production. While Gaye Tuchman (1978), Philip Schlesinger (1978), and Herbert Gans (1979) identify the implications of decision-making models and management policies for the content of the news, the differences between fictional media and the immediacy, perceived objectivity, and political significance of journalism have made findings like theirs difficult to apply to the more brazenly commercial creative enterprises of other cultural industries.

Certainly the critical media industry studies (CMIS) approach that Havens, Serra Tinic (2009), and I advocate could provide a theoretical basis for the type of study of management called for here. Its aim of advancing studies of media that "emphasize the complex interplay of economic and cultural forces" provides a sound basis for studies of managers (235). Such an approach would likely draw from several of the methods noted above, using interviews, but interrogating the claims of interviewees and seeking cross checks, observing the process of managerial operations, and connecting these managerial practices with the cultural goods they create. Although differently named, the production studies paradigm exemplified by the work of Caldwell (2008), Vicki Mayer (2011), and others could also provide a foundation for studies of management, although these scholars have focused their attention mainly on identifying the meaningful agency possessed by those less likely to be considered "managers," such as video editors, casting assistants, and other "below-the-line" roles.

A growing range of scholarship has found ways to surmount the methodological challenges to performing such research, but this nascent area of inquiry still struggles with theory-building beyond the description and analysis of an individual case study. David Hesmondhalgh (2011) reasonably critiques the developing body of industrial and production study—including my own work—for failing to integrate into "an explanatory and normative framework of the kind associated with critical social science" (152). Indeed, some of those doing such research conceive of their studies as more humanistic endeavors and consequently, and reasonably, do not aspire to developing the kind of normative frameworks central to the intellectual pursuits of social science. Nevertheless, even studies grounded in the humanities have an interest in theory-building, and I take Hesmondhalgh's critique to suggest that the rich detail such case studies produce has not been used to suggest theories or conceptual schema for understanding phenomena beyond the individual case study at hand.

Responding to Hesmondhalgh's critique in developing theories of media managers is complicated. Research aspiring to produce normative and explanatory frameworks or theories is certainly needed, yet the feasibility of producing such work is constrained by the instability of managerial agency. Rather than aiming for specific theories of the managerial role, perhaps the most reasonable outcome, at least at this stage of knowledge-building about creative industry managers, is the development of frameworks of variables that affect the agency and ramifications of managers, typologies of managerial conditions, or concepts, perhaps drawn from an individual case, but designed to be tested and explored in other contexts. For example, Havens (2007) uses the concept of "industry lore" to address how industry workers—often managers—adopt certain presumptions about the commercial viability of different creative components. These perceptions are rarely grounded in empirical fact, but nonetheless structure the range of texts and attributes deemed likely to succeed. While Havens names and identifies the power of industry lore in research into the global animation market and analysis of how textual options are foreclosed by industry lore in this particular context, his concept of industry lore might be used to explain the forces that enable and constrain certain textual possibilities in a wide variety of instances. Industry lore is clearly conceptually plausible; building the type of frameworks Hesmondhalgh (2011) calls for requires systematic application and empirical study of industry lore.

In another case, Havens and I (2012) use the term "circumscribed agency" to explain the limited ability of managers to affect the process of production and distribution of creative industry products. To be sure, in many cases agency is extensively circumscribed, and we always regard any agency on the part of an individual as just one aspect of a broader framework encompassing the mandate of the media system and broad conditions such as technological availability, regulatory structures, and economic norms. Agency is circumscribed by the cultures within which individuals live and work (is the culture or workplace heavily hierarchical or are individualism and broad thinking rewarded?), the conventions of the particular media industry within which they work (is it heavily centralized and closely monitored or far-flung and extensively reliant on subcontractors or freelancers?), the priorities of managers and superiors (does the management style allow and reward risk-taking or is it a culture of heavy micro-management?), and the specific positions held by the individual in society (is it a workplace of meaningful diversity or do particular identity factors such as gender, ethnicity, sexuality, and age earn considerable privilege?). Conceiving of agency as circumscribed and, consequently, widely variable makes broad theorizing about the role of individuals difficult to sustain. Nonetheless, positing that individuals such as managers can play a meaningful, if varied role in media industry operation remains a significant departure from existing research based on political economy.

Finally, Jimmy Draper (2012), who examined the production of men's magazines for indications of how these processes shaped the magazines' varied constructions of masculinity, proposes the notion of "discerning savvy" to identify the informal process through which media industry workers come to understand and adopt the priorities and perceived expectations of their superiors. While discerning savvy is similar to industry lore in describing the transmission of unspoken norms, it also provides terminology that calls attention to the constructed nature of those norms and the informal but powerful processes of their transmission. Thus, whereas it is easy to see a memo from an editorial superior outlining the priorities of a publication as a vehicle for the transmission of editorial vision and ideology, Draper—like others—identifies how these priorities are not asserted in such an explicit form. Discerning savvy consequently provides a way to speak of a practice that can seem invisible and derives considerable managerial power precisely because it is obscured.

I present industry lore, circumscribed agency, and discerning savvy as nascent critical concepts relevant to theorizing the actions of media managers in ways that remain far from established theories, but offer opportunities to transcend the case study and provide the framework-building Hesmondhalgh calls for. Research that takes seriously the role of individual decision-makers within media organizations indicates an important initial step toward greater sophistication than possible when evaluating media organizations at the most macro levels of political economy. Such concepts may not yield models predictive of behavior—and indeed, many researching at the level of particular organizations or individuals would likely question whether such models are feasible. But these concepts do help establish connections among discrete cases of organizations and individuals, connections which in turn might yield opportunities for broader knowledge-building and enable scholars to more easily recognize possibilities for broader application. Indeed, none of the phenomena of industry lore, circumscribed agency, or discerning savvy are new, and antecedent illustrations likely proliferate in previous scholarship. The development of conceptual vocabulary and frameworks for explaining micro-power relations in media creation provides researchers with tools to launch subsequent examinations.

Insights into the Role of Managers in Previous Scholarship

Another inspiration for inquiring about what we might expect from the endeavor of studying managers or how concepts of managerial roles and practices affect textual possibilities, the practice of creativity, or the experiences of audiences can be found by mining existing work. A few examples of manager research in studies that do not centrally aim to investigate managers can, nevertheless, illustrate the rich insight offered by scholars who confront the theoretical and methodological challenges already discussed. The scant scholarship on creative industry managers often considers managerial input as one of a number of forces involved in creative work and is deeply contextual and case based—at least in my specialty subarea of television industry studies. Reviewing this scholarship offers lessons on the claims available to research on managers and evidence of what we might extract as broader lessons for those interested in such work.

Vance Kepley, Jr.'s (1990) "From 'Frontal Lobes' to the 'Bob-and-Bob' Show: NBC Management and Programming Strategies, 1949–65" is an exemplar of an approach to studying creative industry managers in a manner consistent with the enterprise of critical media studies. Kepley valuably combines basic economic theory regarding the behavior of a public-good industry with the particular study of a single company in a moment—or moments, in this case—of specific competitive norms. It is not coincidental that Kepley's study is historical—an issue taken up later—and that he is able to base his analysis on archived internal memos. The result is a study that provides an authoritatively informed understanding of programming strategies and the particular managers involved. The study also has continuing relevance in that a resourceful scholar might consider parallels between this innovative moment for the medium of television and contemporary media facing a comparable moment of innovation and undefined norms. Similarly, parallels may be drawn between strategies useful in shifting competitive dynamics in this era and those that have changed and still continue to change the norms of this industry.

The most compelling feature of Kepley's study is its deep context. Kepley addresses the more macro levels of competitive norms of the time—that established radio players NBC and CBS were trying to transition audiences and their businesses into the new medium of television, and that NBC had particular needs and challenges because of its corporate ownership by RCA. As a subcomponent of the broader RCA manufacturing enterprise, NBC's managers reported to RCA managers, who were more concerned with sales of television sets than with the success of emergent programming. Thus Kepley places NBC's managers within their occupational milieu, acknowledging how the composition of the broader RCA entity served to circumscribe the agency of NBC managers in ways particular to the company at the time.

But Kepley's careful contextualization also extends to consideration and assessment of the programs produced, allowing him to make connections between corporate imperatives, composition of the managerial structure, and textual outcomes which are otherwise often simply assumed in scholarship about media that never bothers to analyze actual texts. He highlights how NBC's programming strategically differed from that of CBS in these early years, as NBC endeavored to develop programming that showcased the technology RCA sought to sell and that created a strategic alternative to CBS's steady, established schedule of radio shows and talent at a time when NBC's biggest radio stars had defected to CBS. Although he doesn't engage in a close reading of particular shows or episodes, Kepley explains how NBC sought to develop programming with general attributes that connected to its institutional goal of selling more sets or created a beneficial image for NBC that would help it expand its affiliate agreements and be perceived favorably by the FCC.

This is not to say Kepley's account is without limitation. Like many other industrial histories of television, it often too easily verges into the terrain of "great man" constructs. While the management field at the time was very much dominated by men and while hierarchical theories of managerial behavior firmly structured many industries and corporations, Kepley could have at least gestured to the staffs who contributed to programming that he simply attributes to either Pat Weaver or the subsequent management team of Robert Sarnoff and Robert Kintner—though this may not be obvious in archival documents and thus a limit of method. (See Erin Hill's chapter in this volume for such an illustration.)

Certainly a consequence of building such deep context is that Kepley's case is narrow and specific, such that those seeking singular answers or broad and consistent theories about the role of managers may believe his analyses to be of limited utility. Kepley's work—with its depth of information despite lacking sustained focus on the actions of managers—is rare. More commonly, scholarship attends quite loosely to the work of managers, offering what might be considered as analysis that is cognizant of their role although not focused on developing theories of media industry operation aimed at explicating their function. Jane Feuer's (1985) inclusion of analysis of the managerial strategies of Grant Tinker and Fred Silverman in constructing an industrial context for the success of *The Mary Tyler Moore Show* and MTM Enterprises is a good example of this tactic. Research can be meaningfully informed simply by acknowledging the existence of those such as network executives, thereby reminding readers that creative work does not occur in a vacuum and that even if it is difficult to understand or consistently theorize how executives might affect the creation of cultural products, this assertion of their presence helps mitigate against narratives that too strongly affirm the creative genius of those in roles such as writers or writer-producers.

Feuer's work importantly inserts Tinker, whose role was not primarily creative, into the process of creative production. In Feuer's industrial history, Tinker becomes an inside man of sorts; where "creative" producers are typically contrasted with network "managers," Tinker was a manager on the "creative" side of the production studio, although he would eventually work as a more conventional network manager in his years as chairman and CEO of NBC. Feuer credits Tinker with insulating creative workers from the notes and meddling of network executives, thus functioning as the most clear embodiment of an "intermediary" in his ability to bring the practical, commercial concerns of the network into the writer's room when appropriate and to speak the language of network executives back to the executives in a way that explained creative outlooks. Feuer's work hints at another strategy for theory-building: identifying different types of managers and how they affect certain kinds of creative industry outcomes.

Feuer's work seeks to build an industrial context for understanding the particular commercial and creative success achieved by MTM in the mid-1970s. Although not her aim, Feuer's work—informed by business and trade press and the more popularly targeted accounts of the era such as those by Les Brown (1971) and Sally Bedell (1981) —offers a valuable case study explaining the commercial viability of "quality" television. The MTM shows were regarded as part of the turn to relevancy, which also included Norman Lear's sitcoms such as *All in The Family* and *Good Times*, and were part of a highly regarded cycle of television creativity. Implicit in Feuer's scholarship is an assessment of the type of managerial relationship that can be connected with the creation of programming that achieved both commercial success and critical regard. This case-based finding can be subsequently tested using other methods and approaches to confirm whether this managerial context might consistently explain the commercial success of critically acclaimed or otherwise uncommon texts, or whether the managerial environment was just one of many factors.

It would be interesting to know how Feuer's industrial history—constructed through trade press accounts—might compare with a similar project informed by interviews with figures such as Tinker and Silverman. Bedell had access to Silverman, his words feature prominently in her account, and she positions him as a powerful manager; in Feuer's work, Tinker is one component among many in setting up the context for MTM Enterprises' emergence and success. Importantly, we learn as much, if not more about the role of managers from Feuer's mere inclusion of this aspect of industrial context as from Bedell's focus on a particular manager because of Bedell's investment in constructing a narrative that advances a "great man" story. Bedell writes without a critical lens, which makes it difficult to assess whether it is the method or the author that might account for different views of the managerial process on offer.

Concluding Remarks

The chapter obviously considers only a few of the many pieces of media industry scholarship that reflect in some way on the role of managers. Another more recent examination is Georgina Born's (2005) richly informed analysis of the BBC and the consequences of the shift in managerial styles from those of John Birt to Greg Dyke. This work, like Kepley's article and many of the chapters here, addresses understandings of management by asking questions and exploring contexts that may not be explicitly about managers. Perhaps a meta-analysis examining media

studies scholarship that does not claim to examine creative industry managers, but does so unwittingly—as I suggest Kepley and Feuer
do—will reveal new conceptual frames or nascent theories which will
offer additional building blocks for a systematic and rigorous body of
media industry management analysis. If Kepley's article is any indica-
tion, much information might be mined from those not explicitly seeking to theorize managerial practices and roles, or might offer additional
illustrations of preliminary theory-building that is developing in other
contexts.

The study of creative industry managers is quite clearly fraught
and complicated for those utilizing a critical media industry studies approach, but the enterprise remains valuable. Kepley's study is
unusual in the explicitness of its focus upon key management figures.
Much other scholarship weaves managers into a broader story of industrial operation and creative development, and this may be one of the
more useful strategies given established pitfalls of overemphasizing
managerial style or behavior especially where manager agency can be
so variable. Attention to the role of managers more often emerges in
the context of a broader study of a phenomenon or in industry biographies or histories that are primarily descriptive. Such accounts often
provide helpful secondary source material, but encourage "great man"
approaches that obscure the complicated practices and myriad roles
required by cultural production.

Further, perhaps the component that leads to the excellence of Kepley's study is its historical nature and the type of evidence consequently
available to him. The internal memos that he draws from aren't without limitation, but they are considerably richer and more reliable than
much of the evidence available to researchers examining contemporary
contexts. Other insightful studies of managers, as can be found in Chris
Anderson's (1994) account of the negotiations between Warner Bros.
and ABC in program development in the 1950s, similarly benefit from
being written as historical studies. At the same time, these can beg the
methodological question of whether studies that take contemporary
managers as their object of analysis are so fraught as to be without use-
fulness, and to a large a degree, I suspect this is the case.

Trade press and industry lore probably lead us to overly invest in
individual managers and ascribe too much significance to personalities.

Often fascinating and compelling narratives in their own right, trade analysis, journalistic profiles, and biographies may offer enthralling stories of the visions of creative industry managers, their successes, and their failures, but the distinction of academic criticism demands more than these other forms of writing. A more critically grounded approach requires context and carefully considered evidence and aims to produce knowledge and structures of understanding larger than the case description—endeavors still very much needed for explaining the roles, opportunities, and constraints of creative industry managers.

NOTES

1. The measure of success differs to some extent in a public-service media context; here a manager succeeds according to the aim of the institution.

2. See book-length industry biographies, such as Brandon Tartikoff and Charles Leerhsen, *The Last Great Ride* (New York: Turtle Bay Books, 1992) and Sally Bedell, *Up the Tube: Prime-Time TV and the Silverman Years* (New York: Viking Press, 1981); or journalistic articles such as Lynn Hirschberg, "Giving Them What They Want" (a profile of Les Moonves), *New York Times Magazine*, September 4, 2005, http://www.nytimes.com/2005/09/04/magazine/04MOONVES. html?pagewanted=all, and Amy Wallace, "Violence, Nudity, Adult Content" (a profile of Chris Albrecht), *GQ*, November 2010, http://www.gq.com/ news-politics/newsmakers/201011/chris-albrecht-vegas-hbo-starz.

2

Towards a Structuration Theory of Media Intermediaries

TIMOTHY HAVENS

The analysis of media industries raises two important, related questions for critical theory. First, what is the impact of particular kinds of industrial relationships, organizations, and priorities on the autonomy of creative workers in the industry? And, second, what is the impact of these forces on the diversity of content that the industries produce? While related, these questions are also analytically separable: creative autonomy does not inherently lead to content diversity, and content diversity can—in theory, at least—stem from conditions of restricted creative autonomy.

This essay tackles the second of these questions, positing a theory of media intermediaries as prime focalizing sites for the transaction between industrial and representational practices. Media intermediaries serve as organizational "linking pins" (Turow 1992; Likert 1967), working across various units and holding multiple positions within the organization. For instance, at the major Hollywood studios, a president of international television also often serves as a member of the program development team, which is headed by a vice president of programming. Given their organizational boundary crossings, executives fulfilling such multiple roles offer excellent sites for examining the impact of organizational pressures, including commercialism, on textual choices in media for two reasons. First, as members of multiple organizational subcultures, they are uniquely aware of taken-for-granted assumptions that may not inhere in other subcultures. As such, they can often speak clearly and authoritatively about these forms of organizational common sense. Second, in the media industries, these intermediaries exercise some degree of control over the production of media texts. Thus, presidents of international television at the Hollywood majors can generally green-light or kill a series pilot depending upon their impressions of its global sales appeal. They can also influence choices about setting, casting, scripting, and more. Consequently, media intermediaries serve as one of the prime vehicles through which organizational priorities find their way into representational practices, specifically through organizational common sense—or what I call "industry lore"—which marks the boundaries of how industry insiders imagine television programming, its audiences, and the kinds of textual practices that can and cannot be profitable. Moreover, because of the linking-pin roles that they fulfill, intermediaries are bearers of industry lore who are often quite cognizant of that lore.

Industry lore forms but one component of contemporary managerial discourse, which several scholars have begun to explore as an active agent in producing the organizational lives of white-collar workers (Broadfoot, Deetz, and Anderson 2004; du Gay and Pryke 2002). At the same time, industry lore is specific to the cultural industries and arises from unique features of those industries—namely the unknowability of audience preferences, exorbitant costs of production, and highly unpredictable success of cultural commodities.

Most prior theorizations of media intermediaries explain their influence on content as rooted in the structural relations of the media industry. By contrast, I draw here on Anthony Giddens' post-structuralist[1] conceptualization of "structuration" as a middle-ground between structure and agency, as well as Michel Foucault's theories of power/knowledge; these allow us to examine how knowledge about the audience and the kinds of media content that might appeal to it are produced through an interaction between structural and cultural forces. This lore subsequently functions as a form of power/knowledge that makes the world of the intermediary knowable and manageable, tilling the ground from which dominant media production practices sprout, while simultaneously sowing the seeds of dissidence and change. I conclude the chapter with two case studies about the impact of media globalization on minority television that demonstrate how changing technological and market considerations have altered industry lore about audience tastes and textual meanings, creating new opportunities for the production and circulation of minority-centered texts.

Throughout this chapter, I concentrate primarily on the global television programming industry, with which I am the most familiar. This industry is in many ways distinct from other media industries. First, television tends to be corporately planned and authored far more than other media products, including films, music, and games, which are sometimes developed and produced with less direct involvement of corporate executives. But there is really no such thing as "independent" or "alternative" television, and there are very few instances of motivated, creative individuals producing "surprise hits" outside of dominant, corporate structures, as there are in other industries.[2] Moreover, the global nature of today's programming business—the financial demands for both producers and telecasters in many parts of the world to generate revenues or source programming from abroad (Havens 2006)—combined with the diversity of television cultures, languages, and media ecologies around the world, require television merchants to be particularly attuned to what kinds of programs "travel" and why. This attention, naturally, produces a good deal of industry lore that circulates through trade journals and at global television trade shows, thereby making the industry lore of global television executives uniquely prolific and available for analysis.

Nevertheless, despite the distinctiveness of the global television programming industry, I trust that my observations about structural conditions, executive agency, and industry lore have relevance for the study of intermediaries in other media industries as well. What these industries share is the production of media culture that circulates symbolic discourses to a wide population. Studying the articulations between industry lore and textual discourses provides a window into how the media industries process these symbolic forms, in a manner that I believe is more accurate and insightful than can be attained through blunter theoretical perspectives, which in one form or another, tend to overplay either the determining nature of structural conditions or the agency of intermediaries.

Intermediaries, Structure, and Agency

I consider it uncontroversial to claim that theorization about media intermediaries and the exercise of social power is minimal. The vast amount of research available comes from the "production of culture" tradition in sociology (Peterson and Anand 2004), which adopts a functionalist, micro-level approach to describe in detail how intermediaries operate within the organization, how environmental changes alter decision-making practices, and how media organizations differ from other kinds of industries. While providing far more detailed descriptions of the work lives of intermediaries than most other approaches, production of culture studies do little to examine questions of social power or the relationship between organizational practices and representational politics.

While critical approaches to media intermediaries have largely been absent, one can cite a handful of important exceptions. Todd Gitlin's book *Inside Prime Time* (1983) gave a thorough, yet critical account of the role of network programmers in the television industry, demonstrating how industry "lore" or "scuttlebutt" influences programming decisions at least as much as does audience research. At the same time, Gitlin showed how uncertainty among programmers, especially in times of change such as the introduction of cable television, can create the conditions for television programming that is more challenging and progressive than conventional fare. Ultimately, however, though he identified the central and formerly unrecognized role that uncertainty played in industrial decision-making, and the consequent reliance upon conventional wisdom among intermediaries, Gitlin did not theorize where this wisdom came from or how it was related to the structural conditions of the industry, except in cursory ways.

Conversely, the "power roles" framework that Joseph Turow (1992) developed accounts quite thoroughly for the structure of the industry and the ways in which various media organizations are able to exert power vis-à-vis one another, depending upon the institutional role they fulfill. That is, different kinds of organizations have control over different types of resources, and are able to permit or deny access to those resources in order to gain concessions from other organizations. Moreover, Turow is able to connect these power struggles to programming innovations (1981; 1985), as organizations fulfilling different power roles develop more or less power due to changing industrial and technological conditions, thus providing new organizational actors with greater decision-making power over representation. Ultimately, however, Turow locates the source of programming decision-making in structural relations of power alone, without considering the ways in which the worldviews of intermediaries and their *interpretations* of structural conditions account for their decisions as much as the conditions themselves. Put slightly differently, while Turow's framework accounts well for the industrial conditions that make programming change possible, it cannot account for the directions those changes take or how they are integrated into or depart from prior representations.

In a similar vein, David Hesmondhalgh's (2006) adaptation of Pierre Bourdieu's writings on cultural production, which is one of the most sophisticated efforts to develop a critical theory of media intermediaries, tends to privilege the structure of the industrial field over the agency and professional culture of intermediaries. Bourdieu develops an elaborate theory of cultural production that sees it as a particular field of knowledge, which is related to other fields of knowledge in society in a core-periphery relationship. Thus, certain fields of knowledge, particularly those of economics and politics, which Bourdieu's describes as the "field of power," are more central to social power, while other fields, including the cultural fields of religion, science, literature, and so forth, are more peripheral. Agency (or "autonomy" in Bourdieu's terminology) in the field of cultural production comes from the distribution of economic and symbolic capital within the field, its structural organization, and its relationship with other social fields, especially the field of power. Bourdieu distinguishes between large-scale and small-scale forms of cultural production, identifying the latter with literature and the arts, which exhibit high amounts of cultural capital, low amounts of economic capital, and smaller organizations that produce a great deal of individual and institutional autonomy. Large-scale productions, on the other hand, exhibit low degrees of autonomy due to their high levels of economic capital and low levels of symbolic capital. Bourdieu's formulation has several strengths: it theorizes the relationship between cultural production and other spheres of social activity; it plausibly explains the different degree of autonomy in small-scale versus large-scale cultural production activities; and it integrates both structural and cultural (symbolic capital) forces into its theoretical framework. Ultimately, however, Bourdieu's theory remains a structural one, where creative autonomy derives from the political-economic structures of the field of cultural production.

For post-structuralist scholars, privileging structure over culture is a mistake: while structural relations rooted in economic and political capital surely exist and shape the worlds in which we live, they cannot do so unless they are perceived by human agents—unless, that is, they first enter discourse. As Anthony Giddens explains, "Structure has no existence independent of the knowledge that agents have about what they do in their day-to-day activity" (1984: 26). Instead,

> the structural properties of social systems are both medium and outcome of the practices they recursively organize. Structure is not 'external' to individuals: as memory traces, and as instantiated in social practices, it is in a certain sense more 'internal' than exterior to their activities. (25)

Thus, while structures might exist, they cannot be known, acted upon, or act unless first represented in discourse.

For structuralist theories, then, even one as nuanced and complex as Bourdieu's, social structures have "primacy over action, and the constraining qualities of structure are strongly accentuated" (Giddens 1984: 2). Post-structuralist approaches, by contrast, retain the careful conceptualization of social structures, while placing the roles of discourse, agency, and culture on an equal plane. For Giddens, the tension between the persistence of social structures and the role of individual agency in daily life forms a "duality of structure" that accounts for both the presence and alterability of social structures. He sees the persistence of human behavior over time and across space as evidence of self-reflexive (or 'recursive') human agents engaging in meaningful activity that both derives from social structures *and* reproduces those structures and behavioral patterns anew. While human agents have the ability to change social structures, given both self-monitoring and the policing of others, most of us fall in line most of the time, reproducing in our daily lives a million mundane routines that support the status quo. Giddens refers to the process by which structures and agency are co-produced as "structuration theory."

Giddens, however, spends little time addressing the role of mass media in society, so any attempt to apply structuration theory to the mass media must selectively adapt appropriate elements of the theory. In particular, I want to focus on the duality of structure for intermediaries working in the media industries; on adapting the theory of agency to media inter-mediaries who work in particular political-economic and historical con-ditions; and on institutional structures of signification, domination, and legitimation within the global television syndication industry.

Structuration Theory and Media Intermediaries

Giddens' (1984) idea about the duality of structure suggests that social structures, including such macro-economic facts as the degree of con-centration of ownership in an industry, the conglomeration of smaller, diverse organizations into centrally owned ones, and the transnational-ization of media markets, all shape the daily lives of people who work in those organizations and are *reproduced* in their daily activities. For instance, the television executive who refuses to green-light a dra-matic series featuring an African American lead character because she knows that international sales are crucial to funding production and she believes that foreign buyers don't want minority-lead dramas, does so because of the structure of the industry and the television program markets, but in so doing also reproduces that structure.

The distinction between social structures as the medium *and* out-come of social action is, of course, unnecessary unless we introduce the idea of *agency*—that the television executive could have acted dif-ferently if she decided to, even within the restraints of these macro-economic structures and the conventional economic practices of her organization. Giddens distinguishes between intended and unintended consequences of our actions when it comes to agency: in order for us to claim agency, we must also be aware of both types of consequences. Some of the most compelling questions for Giddens lie in studying how social agents reproduce social structures unintentionally. So, to return to our television executive, she may be progressive in her racial politics, even strongly in favor of expanding the range of roles that African Americans can play on TV, but she still might quite unintentionally reproduce the structural biases against dramatic portrayals of African Americans as merely an unfortunate and inescapable fact. Tracing where these unintended consequences come from, and what sustains them as routinized actions, can lead us to an understanding of the current television industry and its relationship to the maintenance of the representational status quo.

Structuration theory was designed primarily to apply to everyday life, and not necessarily the work environment, where structural impediments are far more visible for most of us, and where conventional patterns of action and thought may be much more tightly tied to those structures than in everyday life. Giddens was, however, especially interested in the role of institutions, which he defined as sets of recurring social activity that persist across time and space. Work environments, for instance, routinize activities through professional codes, conventional business practices, executive training sessions, team-building activities, and the like and in that process reproduce the structures of the industry.

Giddens' analysis of social institutions distinguishes among structures of signification, domination, and legitimation, wherein "signification" refers to the symbolic order of society, "domination" refers to the institutions that bear the power to sanction normative behaviors, such as the government, and "legitimation" refers to those structures that make the exercise of normative sanctions seem appropriate, especially legal structures. Of course, media intermediaries face each of these social structures in their daily lives, and a full consideration of agency and structure might take into account intermediaries' daily lives as well as their work lives, but then intermediaries do face special manifestations of structure in their workaday worlds, and it is on these particular manifestations that I wish to focus.

Let us take Giddens' three structural forces in reverse order. First, while media industries intermediaries certainly face structures of legitimation in terms of laws and regulations promulgated by local, state, national, and international authorities, the business itself offers perhaps the greatest legitimating structures. I have suggested elsewhere (Havens 2003; 2011) that international television trade fairs, which take place in exotic locations around the world and feature both formal and informal competitions for recognition, function primarily as rituals of legitimation for the companies and individuals involved in global television trade. Trade journals, likewise, legitimate certain companies and intermediaries by consistently seeking them out for comment. Of course, the structures of legitimation primarily serve to legitimate the structures of domination. Again, in international television trade, these structures of domination primarily derive from the business itself, particularly the relative economic power of particular firms and nations, as well as the policing of business behavior.

Not surprisingly, the Hollywood majors wield the greatest amount of punitive power in the global television industries. If a foreign buyer violates Hollywood's copyright, Hollywood can sanction the buyer by refusing to sell further content, by convincing other Hollywood distributors and distributors around the world to follow suit, and by suing in international and national venues, as happened when the South African broadcaster Bop-TV negotiated carriage on a transnational satellite service despite having paid only for terrestrial rights for Hollywood material. While small distributors might make the same threat, they often lack the resources to follow through on lawsuits and the clout to get others in global syndication to go along with them. As this example suggests, the structures of domination are rooted in economic inequality, as well as formal and informal business sanctions. These business sanctions generally take the form of damaging someone's reputational capital, which, in turn, profoundly influences participants' chances of getting access to content or buyers. For instance, program distributors of all sizes share a "blacklist" of buyers who have not met their contractual obligations.

The reputational capital of an organization or an individual points us in the direction of the symbolic structures of the international television industry. Reputational capital, rooted in the dominating and legitimating structures of the industry, derives in part from how much economic capital an organization controls, which itself comes from the perception that companies that have been economically successful in the international television trade somehow hold the key to creating universally appealing television content (Havens 2011). Reputational capital, then, secures one's position not only in the dominating and legitimating structures of the business, but also in the hierarchy of signification. That is, an intermediary's reputation and the reputation of his or her firm gives the intermediary varying degrees of power over the symbolic structures of television trade—structures that determine which kinds of television content are generally seen as capable (and incapable) of crossing cultural and linguistic borders.

The symbolic structures of the television industry interest me most because they serve as the interface between the television industry's economic structures and practices and its representational politics. For the television industry contains not only symbolic structures that shape the worlds that intermediaries inhabit, but also the symbolic structures of society more generally. This, of course, is why the issue of diversity of media content is important. Addressing it entails several levels of analysis: first, discovering the economic and organizational structures that underlie prevalent perception among intermediaries, as well as the conventional business practices that help sustain those perceptions; second, examining how intermediaries' perceptions influence representational practices and politics; and third, exploring how changes in the dominating and legitimating structures of the transnational television industry lead to changes in both the symbolic structures and the representational politics of television content.

Symbolic Structuration and Industry Lore

One drawback of Giddens' structuration theory is that it lacks a robust conceptualization of discourse. For such a conceptualization, I turn to Foucault and to John Fiske's (1996) adaptations of Foucault's theories to media-saturated, multi-discursive societies. Foucault is often—and incorrectly, in my view—remembered as a theoretician of the "micropolitics" of discursive power, of the ways in which discourses get inscribed on our bodies and in our actions, in the smallest, most mundane ways. But throughout his career, Foucault was also a theoretician of institutional discourses, of the ways in which discourses get used tactically by powerful elites and institutions to produce pliant subjects. At the same time, as Giddens rightly notes, Foucault conceptualizes power not as *restrictive* but as *productive*: "power produces," Foucault writes; "it produces reality; it produces domains of objects and rituals of truth" (1979: 194).

Of particular interest to Foucault were the discursive resources that the eighteenth-century French bourgeoisie deployed in order to legitimate their control of French society. Foucault studied how various institutions—the asylum, the state, the medical establishment—produced specific "regimes of truth" about humanity and society that in turn led to a range of external and internal policing practices. He was especially interested in the roots of discursive change, the conditions that attend moments of social upheaval, and the discursive resources that the powerful deploy to maintain or claim power in those moments (Foucault 1979; Stoler 1995).

While specific discursive strategies that Foucault identified, including "biopower" and "governmentality," form part of the larger social contexts within which media intermediaries operate, the discursive repertoires of contemporary multicultural societies with large, often competing institutions are often more variegated (Fiske 1996). Indeed, the different practices, activities, and discourses that are enacted in distinct institutional settings are a crucial component of the efficacy of larger discursive regimes. As critical management scholars Kristen Broadfoot, Stanley Deetz, and Donald Anderson (2004) explain,

> Macro-level discourses-as-structures can be seen as existing only to the extent that they are endlessly reproduced in the language and knowledge resources deployed by individuals engaged in organizing processes. Thus, focusing on the concrete procedures, strategies, techniques, and vocabularies individuals and institutions use to construct stable, coherent, and meaningful images of reality, provides insight into the ways discursive formations become articulated, negotiated, and deployed to organize and pursue practical interests. (194)

Obviously, much of the discussion here about the relationship between discourse-in-use and discourse-as-structure within organizations resonates with structuration theory as well, and draws our focus back to the ways in which specific forms of human activity, embedded within different institutions, reproduce or challenge structures of domination.

What Foucault's ideas add to structuration theory is the recognition that it is ultimately discourse that organizes human behavior through complex, interlocking regimes that assemble a wide range of human activities and symbolic materials into coherent worldviews that serve certain interests. Discourse, thus, is *both* the expression of a worldview *and* the application of power/knowledge to human society. John Fiske (1996) explains this process clearly and succinctly when he writes that discourse refers to

> a topic or area of social experience to which sense making is applied; a social position from which this sense is made and whose interests it promotes; and a repertoire of words, images, and practices by which meanings are circulated and power applied. To make sense of the world is to exert power over it, and to circulate that sense socially is to exert power over those who use that sense as a way of coping with their daily lives. (3)

Within the media industries, of course, the "repertoire of words, images, and practices" that constitute discourse refers to those worldviews that circulate among media professionals.

I refer to these discourses that circulate within the media industries as "industry lore." The term originates with Gitlin (1983), who uses it interchangeably with other terms and does not define or theorize it. By contrast, I consider "industry lore" to be a catch-all term that refers to any *interpretation* among industry insiders of the material, social, or historical realities that the media industries face. Thus, for instance, I see industry lore as covering such diverse examples as the growing self-reflexivity of production workers in Southern California identified by John Thornton Caldwell (2008); the industrial production of musical genres and their impact on popular music studied by Keith Negus (1999); the cross-cultural negotiations of global television merchants examined by Denise Bielby and C. Lee Harrington (2008); and the predictions of the future of television unearthed by Amanda Lotz (2009). If structuration is the process whereby structure and agency get co-produced, then industry lore is the vehicle through which that process operates in commercial media institutions. Industry lore serves as a "regime of truth" that makes the chaotic waters of global cultural diversity and mysterious viewer tastes seem navigable. More than merely a set of discourses that make the social world inside contemporary media institutions knowable, industry lore also shapes cultural resources that perhaps billions of human beings draw upon in making sense of their lives and the world around them.

* * *

Industry lore, like most discourses, is often difficult to identify, in part because it forms such a taken-for-granted component of professional life that few reflect upon or even communicate a good deal of industry lore. Studying intermediaries who fulfill linking-pin roles, as I have suggested, gives us access to subjects who are likely to be the most aware of prevalent lore. Likewise, moments of significant economic and technological change permit us a window into the industry lore of the global television industry.

Such a period of economic and technological change has been active in global television since the early 1990s, and in the periods I will trace below from 2000 to 2010, those changes led to distinctly new technological realities, export markets, audience configurations, and televisual representation strategies. Moreover, because today's commercial television industry is integrated into complex media conglomerates whose ownership interests stretch beyond national borders and across media and entertainment platforms, industry lore becomes particularly visible among intermediaries who interact across business fields.

In what follows, I examine industry lore in the global television industries regarding television series with minority characters, focusing on how changes in the political economy of the media industries have prompted new forms of industry lore to develop and produced distinct representational tendencies in contemporary global television. The research on which this case study draws includes an examination of global television trade journals and interviews with dozens of global television programming executives and television producers since 1999.

Commercial Television Trade and Universal Themes

The dominant theory of cultural appeal among global television intermediaries is rooted in industry lore about "cultural universals." Powerful television executives from major television distributors and general-entertainment channels around the world share the sentiment that, in order for television to appeal across cultural and linguistic boundaries, it must possesses "universal themes" with which foreign viewers can identify. Much of the structural scaffolding that produces this stems from the political economy of the television industries, particularly in the United States, though it also draws upon structuring discourses of classical humanism and its appeal to "human nature" (Barthes 1972).

The structure of the television industries, both at home and abroad, has long favored the worldwide circulation of television programming aimed at large, undifferentiated audiences. For much of the history of the medium, the technical properties of television broadcasting, which limits the number of channels that can fit into the electromagnetic spectrum, along with FCC regulations favoring a small number of national broadcasters, combined to make mass-appeal programming the most desirable for the national broadcast networks. Abroad, most nations—particularly those in the lucrative European markets—were dominated by a single, public service broadcaster that was unable to import large amounts of television programming due to legal restrictions, different program schedules, and perceived cultural differences between commercial and noncommercial programming.

For a number of reasons, the market for global television trade changed dramatically beginning in the late 1980s. Domestically, one of the most significant changes was the 1984 Cable Act, which paved the way for several competing cable channels to challenge the traditional terrestrial broadcasters—ABC, CBS, and NBC—and led to steady declines in network audience ratings. Along with audience ratings, network advertising revenues fell and program production costs grew, as the networks spent lavishly on signature programs in an effort to stand out from their cable competitors. Decreased advertising revenues prompted the networks to lower the license fees that they paid to program producers, while increased production costs forced producers to seek greater syndication revenues from abroad (Barns 1981; Boyer 1986; Richter 1986).

Meanwhile, governments abroad relaxed restrictions on commercial broadcasting and cable television, expanding the number of international buyers for U.S. programming. Between 1984 and 1997, the number of cable and satellite channels in Europe grew from ten to more than 250 ("Europe's 'Other'" 1997: 57). Most of these startup channels depended heavily on imported programming to build audiences and fill out their broadcast schedules ("Transformation Scene" 1992: 40). Traditional public service broadcasters adjusted to this new competitive environment with an increased reliance on advertising, audience ratings, and imported television programs, which are almost always cheaper than self-produced series (Hoskins, McFadyen, and Finn 1997). This wave of deregulation and privatization quickly spread to many parts of the globe, aided by the rise of neoconservative governments that shared a disdain for the concept of public service broadcasting and preferred to place broadcasting in commercial hands (Herman and McChesney 1997: 156–58). Between 1984 and 1989, U.S. syndicators' foreign revenues nearly quadrupled from $500 million to $1.7 billion (Havens 2006).

Throughout much of the 1980s, global television syndication was a seller's market, and many import decisions were made with little careful reflection on what would appeal to viewers. However, as competition for viewers grew, and buyers began to recognize that most viewers preferred domestic programming in their own languages most of the time, the market began to equalize, requiring both buyers and sellers to consider more carefully and consciously what kinds of programs viewers might want. Out of this collective consideration, fueled by global television merchants' frequent contact with one another at executive conferences and a growing number of trade journals devoted to the trade, the industry lore about "cultural universals" grew and became dominant.

Within the American television industry, international programming executives began to move into linking-pin roles in the development process, included in decisions about what programs to produce, how to finance them, and where to sell them. As Dave Hutchinson of International Ratings Services put it in 1991, for several years,

"that funny, quirky guy in the back office in charge of international distribution at, say, Columbia or MCA, was bringing in the gravy. Everyone liked him, but no one paid him much attention. Now, . . . you can't deal with agents or producers in Hollywood without him. Foreign sales have got to be built in before anything moves ahead." (qtd. in Schapiro 1991: 29)

Acquisitions executives abroad likewise began to fulfill linking-pin roles in their organizations, where they were charged with interfacing with multiple different constituencies, including directors of programming and research within their institutions and sales executives and acquisitions executives from other markets in the global television marketplace.

The era of nationwide general-entertainment broadcast television was particularly unaccommodating toward minority television trade, in part due to the dominant industry lore about cultural universals that the broadcast system helped anchor. The drive for foreign syndication revenues, coupled with the effort to reach the widest possible nation-wide audiences, produced a conceptualization of the audience as an undifferentiated mass that could only be reached by tapping into supposedly universal human themes. As one television executive at the time explained the concept,

> "If we have a TV movie based on some very American theme, some social issue . . . we will try not to produce it. Soft pictures, cute romantic comedies are very hard to sell outside the United States. But if you have a suspense drama, an action-adventure-type drama, that sells abroad. That's the type of program we want. It's got to have that universal theme." (qtd. in Schapiro 1991:29).

Because most international television syndicators were white and the most lucrative foreign markets were also predominantly white, industry insiders tended to see unique African American experiences, cultures, and values as unsuited for international trade. According to a senior executive at a major Hollywood distributor,

> The Black American experience is unique to Black America. It's really not the same experience that Blacks are having in London or having in France. . . . So there has to be that broader sense of humanity to the show. . . . I think that there is a general sense that if it's too tied to the Black American experience, then it won't work internationally, because nobody else is having specifically that experience.[3]

The white American experience, by contrast, was rarely seen as inherently too distinct to appeal abroad. Consequently, the kinds of minority programming that did find its way into international circulation needed to fit with dominant ideals of what constituted universal values.

Cultural Universals, Family Themes, and The Cosby Show

The Cosby Show (1984–1992) provides a good case in point. It sold into nearly ninety foreign markets, undoubtedly due to the power and prestige of the American television industry in general, as well as the push on the part of Viacom, its syndicator, to establish itself abroad. At the same time, the series was widely praised for its ability to speak to universal, rather than minority, concerns. While Herman Gray (1995) identifies crucial multicultural elements in the series, not least its portrayal of upper-class African American culture and its range of black subjectivities, the setting, storylines, and values of the series also located it squarely within middle-class family concerns. Given that most European broadcasters, including public service broadcasters, conceptualized their audiences as middle-class families at the time, it is little wonder that they came to see the show's middle-classness as a form of universality. Frank Mulder, program acquisitions director for the Dutch public service broadcasting consortium NOS, explained the popularity of *The Cosby Show* in the following way: "What travels is Cosby. It's universal, I mean, it has nothing to do with America. Things that happen in every household, it happens in Cosby as well. Children *sluip* from the cookie jar or whatever."[4] Torstren Dewi, commissioner of international co-productions for German commercial broadcaster Prosieben, similarly claimed, "I think family problems are the same all over the world."[5] And Marion Edwards, executive vice president of international television at Twentieth Century Fox International Television, also asserted that "There has to be [some] broader sense of humanity to a show for it to be successful abroad, and some of the shows achieve that . . . these are like universal issues of family."[6]

Practically speaking, then, industry lore about "universal themes," rooted in particular assumptions about the audience, which were themselves built upon specific institutional priorities and political-economic conditions, served to stymie minority television trade, even African American television trade, during the boom years for American television abroad. The dominating structures of the television programming industry that made Hollywood in particular, and Western companies in general, the most powerful in terms of production budgets and negotiating authority, combined with the legitimating process of the trade journals and trade fairs that expressed and reproduced economic power relations in terms of reputational capital, were sustained and made functional by the symbolic structures of industry lore, which held that audiences would not stand for cultural dissonance, and instead insisted on "universal" values in imported programming with which they could identify.

Ironically, while the popularity of *The Cosby Show* worked to increase the number of middle- and upper-class African American television shows in the United States, abroad, the show's popularity drove sales of *white* American family sitcoms. The explanation for this state of affairs lies in the distinctly different structuration of the domestic and international markets in the 1980s. Domestically, television broadcasters continued to target national audiences, and African Americans were an important, if minor, component of that audience. Internationally, however, the Hollywood studios and large independents that produced the majority of the television programming in the United States needed to sell that programming to buyers who had few, if any, black viewers. While history might tell us that African American culture—even as expressed through television—often has a greater global appeal than white American culture (Havens 2013), the national orientation of most television broadcasters at the time prompted television merchants to think of the nation as the greatest common cultural factor, which could be subdivided into smaller, more insular subcultures. If majoritarian American television needed to universalize to appeal to foreign viewers, went the dominant thinking within the industry, then minority American television was far too culturally specific for global markets. As one American representative of a Russian channel put it, "There are white audiences in America who don't understand some Black sitcoms. So it's not a surprise that a totally foreign Russian wouldn't have a point of reference in an ethnic Black sitcom."[7]

Cultural Journeys, Minority Television, and bro'Town

More recently, the fortunes of minority programming may have begun to change, due in large measure to an altered competitive environment for smaller, niche telecasters and subsequent alterations in the industry lore of some buyers and sellers. While many of these cable and satellite channels initially operated on shoe-string budgets, those that survived their initial years went on to enjoy higher programming budgets. At the same time, of course, success begets success, and profitable new ventures began to face new competitors that either fought for the same small slice of the viewing audience or sought to siphon off smaller segments of the niche audience through counter-programming.

By the early 2000s, cable and satellite programmers abroad found themselves with more money to spend on programming, but also more competition, forcing them to think much more carefully about how to attract their desired viewers. At the same time, these programmers and smaller niche-producers moved into linking-pin roles within their organizations and the global programming industry, which led to the production of distinct forms of industry lore among cable and satellite programmers which at times differs substantially from their broadcast counterparts. Moreover, the current economics of cable and satellite programming require programmers to rely on imported television series to fill out their programming schedules, and the territorial reach of satellite channels and service means that these channels often operate in multiple territories. Consequently, their specific forms of industry often circulate transnationally.

The case of *bro'Town* (2004–2009), the first scripted prime-time series in New Zealand television history, serves a good example here. *bro'Town* was deeply rooted in Polynesian, Māori, and New Zealander culture and reflected a decidedly "brown" perspective on both New Zealander and global culture and politics. As such, it is one of several highly culturally specific television series that have begun traveling worldwide since the early 2000s, including *Chappelle's Show* (2003-2006), *Bleach* (2004-2013), *The Boondocks* (2005-), and others.

bro'Town sold to telecasters in the Cook Islands, Fiji, Australia, Portugal, Latin America, Canada, and the United States. While limited, these markets nevertheless represent a remarkable sales record for a New Zealander show. The series appealed to three different kinds of buyers: general-entertainment broadcasters in the nearby cultural-linguistic region; national and transnational cartoon channels; and alternative public service broadcasters. Each of these buyers found value in different aspects of the series, and consequently offered different reasons for why they bought it: the regional broadcasters explained their purchases in terms of cultural proximity; the public service channels viewed indigenous programming from around the world as fitting their programming needs; and the foreign cartoon channels saw the series as a reasonably priced representative of the global animation genre (Havens 2013).

I want to concentrate on the last of these buyers, foreign cartoon channels, and in particular the industry lore of the "cultural journey" that came to be expressed in discussions with these buyers. Here, I argue, we see an effort to revise the conventional industry lore about "universal themes" as the root of cultural circulation, and replace it with more fitting explanations of why a culturally specific, minority program such as bro'Town can appeal to foreign minority and non-minority viewers.

The revision of industry lore arises from changed dominating structures in the television programming industry, in which massive media conglomerates have expanded into owning both foreign and transnational niche channels that source their programming from different distributors than their general-entertainment counterparts. This structural requirement to interface with different intermediaries worldwide inevitably connects executives around the world who think of television and audiences differently. Consequently, the legitimating structures of the global programming industry have altered to include the voices of these niche-oriented intermediaries. For example, MIPCOM 2011, one of the premiere television trade shows in the world, featured an "Acquisition Super Panel" that included two buyers from niche-satellite channels along with several well-established buyers from general-entertainment broadcasters. Inevitably, the symbolic structures of the industry, in terms of industry lore, needed to change as well in order to accommodate these other altered conditions.

bro'Town's status as a member of the global animation genre was often invoked in news reports about the series' global travels, where it was frequently referred to as "The Simpsons of the South Pacific" (Lustyik and Smith 2010). In many respects, this comparison to other popular animated series is quite apt: bro'Town makes frequent intertextual references to other popular animated series; its humor is both irreverent and scatological; and it tends to attract the kind of young male demographic that cartoon channels around the world target. At the same time, bro'Town's linguistic and cultural specificity caused unique problems for buyers.

One telling instance in which the producer and buyer struggled over questions of cultural difference came from efforts to translate the series into Spanish for Cartoon Network Latin America. In particular, email discussion surrounding the translation of the Samoan word fa'afafine reveals an understanding of television viewers that is quite different from the one that industry lore about "universal themes" imagines. In Samoan cultures, fa'afafine are boys who are raised as girls and tend to live their lives as women, essentially representing a third gender category, and in bro'Town, the boys attend a school whose principal is a fa'afafine. Cartoon Network Latin America contacted the producers of bro'Town about translating the word, initially suggesting "gay." The producers, however, objected to this characterization, explaining that "fa'afafine has nothing to do with sex really" and insisting that the character in question was "definitely not gay." The representative from Cartoon Network conducted Internet research and suggested that fa'afafine are perhaps more like transsexuals, but the producer disagreed with this translation as well. Fa'afafine do not transition from one sex to another but rather see themselves as having always been culturally female. Finally, the translators decided to leave the word as is, explaining, "After all, the series is a cultural journey." In an interview, series producer Elizabeth Mitchell further explained that "we made the decision to leave Māori words 'un-translated' as they [foreign viewers] were embracing 'the cultural journey' we were embarking on."[8] What we see in this exchange is an industry lore that differs substantially from lore about cultural universals, one that recognizes that cultural differences will always frustrate both the translation and viewing processes, and that viewers have to be willing to put up with such difficulties when it comes to watching imported television programs.

I would suggest that this discourse of cultural journeys is an emerging form of industry lore that originates, in part, from efforts to sell programming originated for a particular audience segment to foreign channels targeting a similar niche audience. From an organization standpoint, we see that both producers and programmers in this niche television market have begun to perform linking-pin roles, wherein they lead production or programming within their own organization while working collectively as a group to translate from one culture or language into another.

It is difficult to specify the existence and extent of a new form of industry lore, but the phrase "cultural journey" has begun showing up more and more frequently in industry talk and publications. Perhaps most prominently, when BET Jazz rebranded itself as BET J, the executive vice president and general manager for BET Digital Networks explained, "the 'J' in our new network name is now more indicative of the complete musical and cultural 'Journey' rather than only jazz," which BET J intended to program. Programmers from the United States to South Africa use the phrase, most commonly to refer to television programming that focuses primarily on a minority or foreign culture.

To return to the question I raised at the beginning of this essay—how does the current configuration of the global television industry influence the diversity of its output?—we can see that the globalization of minority television circulation, combined with the transnationalized linking-pin roles that minority television producers, distributors, and programmers now fulfill, have led to the circulation of quite different minority television programming than we saw in the past. Hence, the industry lore of cultural journeys permits intermediaries involved in niche and minority programming to understand television content and television viewing in more complicated ways than their general entertainment counterparts.

Conclusion

The analysis here only scratches the surface of how scholarship concerned with industry lore might help address important theoretical questions in media studies today. Studies of global media conglomerates, for instance, might explore whether industry lore is imposed from above or bubbles up from below at conglomerate-owned television channels around the world; they might also examine how television coproductions or conglomerate-controlled local adaptations of television series do or do not exhibit new forms of industry lore. A comparative study of industry lore among public-service and commercial media enterprises could help determine whether and how different funding practices influence representational practices. Finally, comparative analyses of industry lore in different media institutions—or even industries—might yield important insights into whether creative workers across the media experience different degrees of autonomy, and why.

In many ways, the cases studied here point to a causal relationship between economic and symbolic structures of the industry, in which changes in the former produce changes in the latter. In practice, changes can flow either way. In the 1990s, for instance, the industry lore surrounding the suitability of situation comedies for global trade was revised due to the unexpected global popularity of a handful of sitcoms. This change in symbolic structuration led to changes in how sitcoms sell abroad and are financed. In other words, cultural markets are always imagined into existence. The daily processes of the industry, the economic power relationships among the players, the organizational structure of the media industry, and the worldviews of intermediaries constantly work together—or against one another—to produce global cultural flows. It is a mistake, then, to privilege any particular structuring site, whether the dominating, the legitimating, or the symbolic. A focus on how industry lore arises, whose interests it reflects, how it organizes intermediaries' worldviews, and how it produce particular representational forms helps us take all of these structuring processes and their interactions into consideration, and prevents us from privileging the structures of the industry over the agency of intermediaries.

At the same time, the cases examined here demonstrate that old structures and habits of thought do not easily pass off the scene. Even a minority text such as bro'Town is required to speak the supposedly universal language of the adult animation genre, in addition to its more local language, in order to appeal to buyers who work for commercially funded cartoon channels. Even as they invoked industry lore about cultural journeys to understand the appeal of bro'Town, these intermediaries understood the series as universal in terms of its generic traits.

Some of the more compelling and potentially radical uses of the series abroad came from alternative and indigenous public broadcasters in the English-speaking world, who integrated bro'Town into schedules that included both domestic and imported minority programming, thereby producing a television culture that permitted—even encouraged—minority cross-cultural dialogues. Of course, the industry lore that sustains these kinds of minority cultural flows does not integrate well with the dominating and legitimating structures of the global programming industry, and so remains at the edges of the discursive worlds that global television programmers inhabit.

Still, though the dominating structures of industry continue to marginalize the voices of intermediaries engaged in minority television trade, the cases explored here demonstrate that industry lore plays a central role in structuring their workaday worlds, shaping the representational politics of media content and the international markets for that content. Moreover, the industry lore at the center of that workaday world is continually being challenged, struggled over, and renewed. As such, industry lore is simultaneously the expression of intermediaries' worldviews *and* the fulcrum where the political economy of the industry meets the politics of representation.

NOTES

1. I use the term "post-structuralism" here to refer to an intellectual perspective that recognizes the existence of social and cultural structures, but argues that these structures shape society only to the extent that they are recognized and put into discourse by human agents. For this reason, I categorize Giddens as a post-structuralist, even though he himself has rejected the label (Tucker, 1998). Indeed, Giddens has argued that structuralism and post-structuralism share a great deal upon close examination—an argument that I consider to be essentially correct (Giddens and Turner, 1987). Nevertheless, given the strong tendency to focus on structure *over* agency in much of the critical scholarship on media industries, I choose to define both my arguments and Giddens' as post-structuralist in this essay. Furthermore, my privileging of structuration is not intended as an endorsement of Giddens's overall social theory; instead, I find the concept useful in thinking about this particular moment in media industry studies.

2. Certainly, there are "independent" television producers, many of whom have had successful shows on the U.S. networks over the decades. But even in these instances, "independents" develop only an *idea* that they pitch to the networks, which various network intermediaries alter before even a pilot episode gets made.

3. Anonymous, personal interview with author, 1999.
4. Frank Mulder, personal interview with author, 1999.
5. Torstren Dewi, personal interview with author, 1999.
6. Marion Edwards, personal interview with author, 1999.
7. Anonymous, personal interview with author, 1999.
8. Elizabeth Mitchell, personal interview with author, 2010.

3

Linear Legacies

Managing the Multiplatform Production Process

JAMES BENNETT AND NIKI STRANGE

We can deliver much more public value when we think in a 360-degree way, rather than focusing separately on different platforms or channels. So wherever possible we need to think cross-platform: in our commissioning, our marketing, our distribution.
—Mark Thompson (qtd. in Strange 2011)

The legacies that come from broadcasters are no more than the vested interests, or un-thought prejudices or world views of those who grew up in television and ruled the roost. . . . There's nothing systemic, really, about the BBC as an organization that prevents it from being effective in [multiplatform], it's just its lack of understanding.
—Managing Director, Digital Agency (2011)[1]

In 2006 the British Broadcasting Corporation (BBC) launched *Creative Future*, a five-year editorial strategy that promised the wholesale transformation of the public service broadcaster to "enable 360-degree commissioning and production and ensure creative coherence and editorial leadership across all platforms and media" (BBC 2006a). The epigraph above from Mark Thompson, Director General at the helm of the BBC, heralded the boldness of this strategy, signaling a move away from specific platforms towards a multiplatform approach that positioned audience reach at its core, whilst simultaneously enabling the BBC to fulfill a redefinition of public service goals for a digital age (Strange 2011:

151). But such institutional changes must be navigated, adopted, lived, and *managed* by a range of production cultures charged with delivering these multiplatform visions. The shift to multiplatform commissioning and production strategies not only attempted to bring together the disparate production cultures of television and digital media, but did so within a milieu that had a strong broadcasting heritage. As the second quotation above attests, such legacies bring with them vested interests, prejudices, and world views that influence the way broadcasters understand the possibilities of digital media, as well as shaping the interactions between digital and television producers.

Drawing on Philip Schlesinger's (2010) study of managerial style, creativity, and cultural change at the BBC, as well as a range of work on production cultures (Born 2004; Caldwell 2008; Deuze 2008; Mayer 2009), we ask how these varied production cultures have not only been managed in the shift to multiplatform television at the BBC, but also in turn managed the meanings and possibilities of multiplatform production itself. With the end of the five-year *Creative Future* editorial strategy, and the commencement of another marked by the publication of *Delivery Quality First, (DQF)* (2011) we are in a position to consider what impact the shift to multiplatform content strategies had on BBC workers operating at a number of levels, from commissioners, to television and multiplatform producers, to junior producers and researchers. In particular, we are concerned with how convergence culture plays out in the interactions among different participants in the multiplatform production process. Whilst Mark Deuze's study of media work argues that in the turn to "liquid life," the boundaries between types of media work have become blurred, our study suggests how boundaries between television and digital media are constantly reasserted and redrawn. As a report on multiplatform production in the UK trade journal *New Media Age* posited in 2010: "The problem is the software industry doesn't understand TV, and TV creatives don't get software." More than this, however, we argue that the baggage of broadcast production cultures often far outweighs that of their digital media counterparts, with multiplatform productions dominated by the legacies of "linear thinking." As a result, the meaning of multiplatform has shifted from the bold vision of 360-degree productions of interlinking "native" content across diverse platforms, to one in which multiplatform "became about simply delivering [linear] content across a range of different devices."[2]

Indeed, so profound has the shift away from 360-degree multiplatform production as a vision for the Corporation's creative future been that by the publication of the BBC's most recent strategy, *DQF*, the term is reduced to a single mention. As one former multiplatform commissioner noted, the new strategy entails a shift to "products," with an emphasis on the BBC's iPlayer, which places "TV first, everything else after."[3] This shift to products has involved an emphasis on implementing digital production strategies at an "enterprise" level,[4] whereby the rhetoric of creativity has been appended by a strong emphasis on digital innovation. *DQF* represented the BBC's institutional response to the newly elected Conservative government's public sector cuts in 2010, which required the Corporation to implement 20 percent cuts across the organization. The document promised to "build a shared digital public space" as one of its four strategic priorities, matched by an investment of approximately "£145m p[er] a[nnum] by 2016/17 in new content and digital innovation, creating a connected, global and continuously available BBC across platforms and devices" (BBC 2011: 14). Yet such investment and rhetoric also mask the shift away from the digital vision of multiplatform promised just five years earlier. Whilst *DQF* embraced a policy of "fewer, bigger, better," it was clear that multiplatform was not part of the "bigger and better," with the axe falling particularly heavily in that area: of the 260 jobs cut in BBC Online, over one hundred of these were in multiplatform, including all dedicated multiplatform commissioner roles.

The shift away from, and changing meaning of, multiplatform should not be read as an absolute failure of the *Creative Future* strategy, nor the result of management policies alone. As one senior multiplatform executive mused shortly before leaving the BBC as a result of these strategic changes, "it's difficult to blame strategies."[5] Rather, as Richard Sennett has argued, a "firm's culture, like all culture, depends on how ordinary people make sense of an institution, not the explanation which those at the top decree" (qtd. in Schlesinger 2010: 271). Despite the rhetoric of multiplatform transformation and creative investment at a strategic level, it has been "the social process among people within and between organizations" as much as "corporate structure, strategy, management and behavior" that influences content (Deuze 2007: 53). We argue that this "social process"—from corporate structure, budgets, and commissioner decisions through to production technologies and, most importantly, production cultures—has largely privileged the linear thinking of broadcast television's heritage. Moreover, as we'll go on to show, this is the result not just of the BBC's internal institutional culture, but of the intersection of strategy, production cultures, and wider shifts in the technological, ideological, and economic mediascape. In this sense, we understand "management" as involving not only the intersection of official policy and strategy and the production cultures charged with carrying out these policies and strategies, but also the ways in which these play out against the specific conjunctures of the wider U.K. social, cultural, political, and industrial conditions (Turner 2011). Shifts in the meaning of multiplatform, therefore, have as much to do with the need to respond to prevailing winds of neoliberalism and the Conservative government's drive against public sector expansion as issues of production cultures. Thus, we argue, it is the conjunctural nexus of these issues that has enabled the "linear legacies" of the BBC's production cultures to prevail against the official rhetoric of the Corporation's digital institutional transformation. While such legacies may produce an approach to digital platforms that the BBC is "comfortable" with, they also have the potential to adversely impact the renewal of public service broadcasting for a multiplatform, digital era.

This chapter emerges from a two-year study of the production cultures of the BBC, Channel 4, the other main U.K. public service broadcaster, and the independent television and digital media sector involved in the creation of specialist factual multiplatform content. Here we focus solely on the BBC's management of the processes of change involved in adopting multiplatform production strategies. In so doing, we also draw on our earlier research on the BBC's experimentation with multiplatform and interactive television production strategies during the early and mid-2000s, including thirty interviews with above- and below-the-line producers at the Corporation conducted between 2005 and 2011. As the BBC is not a law unto itself, we make occasional reference to a wider body of over forty further interviews conducted with the independent sector in order to understand how some of the shifts in the BBC's strategies relate to the wider U.K. TV and digital media ecology. We start by examining the context in which *Creative Future* was introduced and the managerial structures put in place to implement the move to in-house multiplatform production. We then turn to a number of key issues regarding production cultures, including the differing processes and values of multiplatform and television producers. Finally, we discuss how the varying meanings of multiplatform adopted by the different production cultures charged with managing the implementation of multiplatform were instrumental in the eventual adoption of the iPlayer as the predominant strategic innovation of the Corporation.

Methodologically, we bear in mind John Caldwell's "inverse credibility law" in reading the evidence from our semi-structured interviews. As Caldwell explains, "the higher one travels up the industrial food chain for insights, the more suspect and spin-driven the personal disclosures tend to become" (2008: 3). Thus, we test these descriptions by examining both above- and below-the-line discourse, with a particular emphasis on those intermediaries given responsibility for implementing the move to multiplatform: namely, commissioners and multiplatform producers. We further test such descriptions across a number of discursive layers and sites, ranging across the "deep texts" of industry, through to official strategy documents, and to the texts of multiplatform production themselves. We have striven to include all those voices and texts in what follows, utilizing the different interviewees' evidence to corroborate or test institutional claims but avoiding singular or lone statements. As Vicki Mayer has argued, work in production studies can be limited by the tendency for "executives to give access to researchers to emphasize commercial successes and obscure failures." As a result, it is important to locate "case studies that illustrate the times and places where the unexpected occurs and the rhetoric of achievement is called into question" (2009: 19).[6] Our study of the BBC's experimentation and consolidation of its multiplatform strategies represents just such an example, telling us much about the difficulties established broadcast institutions have experienced in reinventing themselves for an increasingly digital mediascape.

For the study of creative management, our approach insists on the need to understand management as a discursive form of power operating at a range of levels both within and outside the Corporation. From the boldness of official policy statements and structural reorganization to the external pressures of policy and economics placed on an organization, we must pay attention to management as a series of discursive layers set against the specific conjunctural nexus of production cultures, policy, and economic and technological change in play. Considered in these terms, the redefinition of multiplatform to one that is in line with the Corporation's linear legacies must be understood as part of a retreat to "safer" ground by the BBC at a time when its identity and old certainties had come under increasing threat. Such a "retreat" may not have been an official managerial strategy per se, but it can nonetheless be understood as a predominant managerial discourse that was circulated at a range of levels and sites that sought to stabilize the BBC's place in the digital era. In turn, beyond a pure economic or aesthetic analysis, such a grounded study tells us much about what the potential meanings, and limitations, of television as digital media might be.

Creative Future: Managing the BBC towards a Multiplatform Vision

Georgina Born's study of the BBC under John Birt and Greg Dyke (2004) has quickly established itself as a definitive account of the Corporation's production cultures. Her analysis points to the way in which studies of the "situated ethics and aesthetics" of producers can help us consider how the reflexivity, intentionality, and agency of cultural producers condition the creativity and innovation possible within a given medium. Although Born does not herself quite provide such a situated analysis of the texts produced, her account remains an important starting point for considering the interrelationship of BBC strategy, production culture, and public service content. Given its status, Philip Schlesinger's recent critique of Born's work is significant. Schlesinger draws our attention to the villain/hero binary that he finds in Born's account of John Birt's and Greg Dyke's tenures at the helm of the organization. For Born, "Birtist management was responsible for eroding the BBC's creativity . . . . Dyke's changes made the BBC less inhibited and more risk-taking" (Born 2004: 71). In contrast, Schlesinger suggests that both used the concept of creativity "to legitimise managerial strategies" to position the BBC in line with prevailing neoliberal economic policies, and the wider turn to the notion of "creativity" in cultural/creative industries policy in the United Kingdom (O'Connor 2007; Oakley 2009). Moreover, Schlesinger is highly skeptical that the cultural changes made to the BBC by Dyke took root in the subsequent director generalship of Mark Thompson. Although there is a continued push of the official rhetoric articulated in *Creative Future*, wherein "creativity has become one of its six fundamental principles," there remains "no independent assessment of the effects of [Dyke's] much lauded approach" (2010: 283–84).

Schlesinger's critique draws our attention to both the continuing importance of creativity as an official discourse in the BBC's strategies of digital renewal and the need to analyze the extent to which official strategies filter down, or are blocked, through the lived experiences of employees and production cultures. Creative management in the media industries, as David Hesmondhalgh and Sarah Baker have argued, must be understood as "unlike the top-down, inflexible supervision found in many other industries. It has less direction and has a 'muted and accommodating style'" (2011: 84, quoting Bill Ryan, 1992). We want to suggest how Thompson aligned creativity with digital innovation and, in so doing, positioned a BBC that paradoxically embraced digital whilst simultaneously straitjacketing its meanings because of the need to bring about change at an institutional, enterprise level into a *broadcasting* organization. Justin O'Connor charts the rise of this connection between creativity and innovation in his analysis of "new work cultures," wherein "the idea of creativity" has been linked closely to "innovation, increasingly seen as the key to economic competitiveness" (2007: 31). Similarly, Kate Oakley argues that the shift to innovation tends to state "cultural value solely in terms of economic impact" (2009: 411). For the BBC, *DQF* makes the link between innovation and digital technologies explicit, with the director general setting the organization the challenge of finding additional "savings of up to 4%" and "reinvest[ing] them in new high-quality output and digital innovation" (BBC 2011: 7). This will take the form of "products," such as iPlayer or Lab UK (a mass testing algorithm, used in programs such as *Brain Test Britain* [2009]), which operate at an "enterprise level," ensuring the BBC will "never do anything that's commissioned against a single program."[7] To understand the shifts from multiplatform to products and from creativity to innovation, we need to turn to the period immediately prior to *Creative Future*.

The shift to 360-degree productions began under Greg Dyke with the appointment of Ashley Highfield, then Director of New Media and Technology, and his polemical announcement in 2001 that the "days of commissioning programmes are over—we are now only commissioning projects that have levels of interactivity" (Highfield, qtd. in Vickers, March 13, 2001). This heralded a period of profound creative experimentation in the BBC's multiplatform strategies and textual forms which we have explored elsewhere (Bennett and Strange 2008). As Born has noted, the BBC approach during this period was informed by its relative economic stability, enabling it to "carry risks that commerce (and Channel 4) might reluctantly carry." BBC digital media executives saw the Corporation's role not only as responding to technological change and platform development, but also as driving such change to the extent that "there was a hint of techno-profligacy" (Born 2003a: 16). As Mary Deberett argues, the "BBC's role as an innovator . . . [was] reborn in the new millennium with the Government investing it with responsibility for driving digital take-up" (2010: 52). Interviews with production personnel in the period prior to *Creative Future*'s enshrinement of a multiplatform BBC revealed a culture of creative risk and innovation. We encountered a number of high profile instances where digital, web, or interactive producers were given—or took—lead editorial responsibility for a project: from the production of a docu-drama to commemorate the sixtieth anniversary of World War II D-Day landings led by the interactive TV team's collection of interviews (Bennett 2008), through to the "pegs for [a gameshow, *Celebdaq*] editorial [coming] from the website."[8] As one interviewee reflected on the period more recently:

> We've been at the cutting edge of doing this stuff for a long time . . . [led by] maverick voices. . . . So we had a huge variety of different technologies being developed, lots of different players on pages. . . . But it was done under the wire effectively . . . [but] in order to make these things work cohesively, then you have to start implementing things at an enterprise level.[9]

We shall return to this question of an enterprise level, represented by the shift to "products" under *DQF* in our conclusion. For now, we want to turn to how the managerial structures implemented as a result of *Creative Future* attempted to harness the creativity of this period of 360-degree experimentation. In these terms, it is important to understand the *Creative Future* strategy as an attempt to deal with what one digital producer termed the BBC's "'bagginess' that allows loose control," which might permit "creativity but the risk is that there's not enough direction to stop it going wrong."[10]

Creative Future articulated a central role of 360-degree thinking in the BBC's organizational and institutional structures by removing platform-specific production departments and instead creating three content production departments: Vision, Audio and Music, and Journalism. Particularly important in this restructure, as we shall discuss below, was the decision to separate these content production teams from the newly established Future Media and Technology department (FM&T), which would effectively act as technology engineers to service the creative ideas coming from Vision, Journalism, and Audio and Music. For the purposes of our focus, we will concentrate on the Vision department, within which a large team of multiplatform producers and commissioners would be embedded, and FM&T, which would house the Corporation's technical teams. The *Creative Future* reorganization undoubtedly communicated the emphasis put on multiplatform, with television no longer deemed to be of sufficient importance to feature in the BBC's manifestation of institutional self. The boldness of this strategy was matched by official rhetoric from senior producers. Thus Richard Williams, then Creative Director of Multiplatform, announced at the 2007 MiPTV conference for the European TV and digital industries that

> The assumed position of a television element with a 360-degree package is being questioned at the highest level within the BBC, with calls for big multiplatform ideas that do not involve television at all.[11]

Williams' public utterances were indicative of the BBC's discourse of creative freedom during this period.

Creative Future was implemented at a production level by the appointment of Simon Nelson as Controller of Multiplatform and his introduction of an editorial vision for multiplatform dubbed "Find,

Share, Play." Along with Nelson, a raft of multiplatform genre commissioners was introduced to sit alongside their TV counterparts. For an
area like factual television, this meant the creation of three commissioner posts with remits for specific sub-genres. From the very outset,
there was an attempt to manage the diverse production cultures that
would be charged with delivering this multiplatform vision of the BBC,
with the spatial reorganization of offices at commissioner level structured around ensuring multiplatform and television counterparts physically sat together. Announcing the strategy to in-house staff, Jana Bennett (then Director of BBC Vision) stated that there were two big ideas
behind its creation: firstly, to build a one-stop shop for multiplatform
commissioning where creative ideas could be looked at in the round
and assessed for their potential across platforms; secondly, to create a
content powerhouse bringing together four thousand program makers
in seventeen studios (BBC 2006b). Reflecting on the "Find, Share, Play"
multiplatform editorial strategy in a recent interview with the authors,
Simon Nelson suggested that the strategy had done

> pretty well. . . . The accessibility and findability of BBC content has been
> utterly transformed. . . . We launched the iPlayer, we now have a website
> for every episode for every program . . . we've opened up a huge amount
> of our data . . . we've layered a level of sociability around . . . all of our
> content.[12]

These are significant achievements. Although the iPlayer emerges as
something of a straw-man below, we want to be clear that in and of
itself, iPlayer is a significant strategic achievement for the Corporation
and will have an important role in securing the digital future of the
BBC. Yet Nelson is less forthright about the success of the strategy in
the area it was specifically designed to address, stating simply, "we've
innovated in 360-degree programs. We've done some great things,
we've done some rubbish things." More candidly, another senior executive argued, "we did end up marching people up the hill . . . before we
were ready, before the BBC had a plan."[13] Significantly, therefore, the
shortcomings of *Creative Future* need to be examined in closer detail
to understand how these were encountered at a cultural level and managed by an array of intermediaries.

The most significant of these intermediaries within television and multiplatform is the commissioner role, which has been described as the gatekeeper of production (Zoellner 2009). At the commissioner level, interviewees have described the multiplatform commissioning process as far from being a "one stop shop," and rather involving a "twin tick"[14] approach whereby a "separate sentient process" was created and "people had to speak to both [TV and multiplatform but] they stopped speaking to each other."[15] Or, as one senior television producer put it, "We had a commissioning structure that was getting in the way [of innovation]."[16] This commissioning model remained steadfastly bound to a television model, "completely weighted towards the linear schedule."[17] As one interviewee commented, this system had those intermediaries charged with implementing the multiplatform vision of *Creative Future* and Nelson's 2007 "Find, Share, Play" strategy "all fighting each other."[18] In effect, it ensured that when a TV program was green-lit, a separate round of negotiations would then have to take place with the multiplatform commissioners to decide on an appropriate interactive element to make it a 360-degree proposition. As discussed below, this created manifest problems further down the "food-chain" as producers struggled to bring the disparate production timelines of digital and television together. Moreover, this process made multiplatform commissioners and producers "feel like second class citizens," because there was a "massive disparity" between audience and budgets with "all the money [put] in the TV show."[19]

As this commissioner and others argued, this was a function not just of the commissioning structure but also the obsession with overnight rating figures, wherein little stock was placed in the audience or impact figures for non-television platforms. Producers were thus liable to remain resistant to or untinterested in multiplatform because, as one multiplatform commissioner put it, the "Channel controller isn't counting your [multiplatform] figures, they're counting my [TV] overnights."[20] As a result, rather than a "powerhouse" of creativity or an approach to considering ideas for their multiplatform potential, there was minimal impact at this key gatekeeper level. As one television commissioner reflected on his current role: "[Multiplatform] doesn't affect me at all . . . nothing has been commissioned because of its multiplatform potential."[21]

If the impact on the TV commissioning culture was negligible, equally the commissioning system made "no sense" for the web—with the approach to creating websites and applications for individual 360-degree projects contributing to a proliferation of websites that would see the BBC come under attack for market expansion and was also poorly set up to maintain and curate:

> Curating is not something the BBC is used to doing. . . . You would never put 40 percent of annual television budget to looking after last year's shows. It's very unsexy from a commissioning perspective.[22]

This led to *DQF* announcing a cull of over five hundred websites as part of the BBC's reshaping into a smaller organization. But, in truth, these were largely websites that were out of date, were no longer managed by any individual, and had very low user imprint. Indeed, in terms of rationalizing the move away from 360-degree projects, interviewees have frequently cited the number, and cost, per unique user as a failure of multiplatform production. Often projects had few users who went beyond the linear program and explored the multiplatform content. This resulted in spiraling costs per user, often "way, way over £1/unique user," according to a senior executive. This cost was contrasted against a current target of around 5p/unique user.[23] As one producer reflected prior to leaving the BBC, even when they had managed to integrate effectively between television and multiplatform teams, he wasn't "sure what we did with the [integrated] teams was any better" because "nobody's measuring."[24] Simon Nelson, then Controller of Multiplatform Commissioning, summarized the difficulties with metrics:

> [the multiplatform areas have] not properly engaged TV people with the measures of success we have. If it's purely a numbers and reach game, we lose. No question. We don't just lose against *The Apprentice*, we lose against *Flog It* [an afternoon lifestyle program]. . . . So measurement of impact, attention, overall brand value are the kind of things we need. . . . We ought to be able to bring levels of analysis . . . that are impossible with TV.[25]

Arguably the lack of clear and decisive metrics, as much as management strategy and structure, was equally as influential in the failures of many multiplatform productions during this period. The scale of withdrawal on the back of these problems has been staggering. One former multiplatform commissioner told us that the shift to "fewer, bigger, better," with its impact on multiplatform, was already well underway in 2010, with commissions scaled down "from fifty in 2008–09 to ten in 2010–11."[26] This move from "find, share, play" to "fewer, bigger, better" would be encapsulated by the primacy placed on the BBC's iPlayer and the triumph of linear legacies of production cultures, values, and processes it can be understood to embody.

Linear Legacies: Cultures, Values, Processes, and BBC iPlayer

> What is iPlayer? It's a fancy new way of delivering a traditional experience. It's not a multiplatform experience. It's linear consumption, and one of the reasons the BBC feels very comfortable with it is that it is actually a . . . very traditional experience: it shows somewhat our cultural limitations. . . . If you look at multiplatform [as] web and TV com[ing] together and merg[ing] into experiences that creatively partake in both . . . I would say that we found it tougher.[27]

The shift in the meaning of, and approach to, multiplatform has been particularly informed by the BBC's development and success of its now ubiquitous iPlayer—available on iPad, iPhone, Android, PS3, Wii, Connected TVs, and all U.K. digital television platforms.[28] Over the course of 2011, the iPlayer regularly received over 150 million "requests" to view television and radio programs each month.[29] The quotation above from Mark Thompson indicates how iPlayer was something the BBC felt "comfortable with" because of the Corporation's broadcasting culture. As one senior multiplatform producer argued, "There was a moment when Vision as a whole gave a huge sigh of relief when iPlayer came out [and they said] 'I get the web, I get it, it's like telly.'"[30] Such statements reveal how the BBC's multiplatform strategies had to move beyond rhetoric and require a more profound transformation of the cultures of production, away from broadcast linear as the default setting. Inevitably, the movement from official policy to lived experience would involve different layers of management coming into operation across a variety of production cultures, values, and processes. We explore each of these different instances of management in turn below, before returning to the question of how iPlayer further exacerbated the difficulties of creating integrated, multiplatform content.

Mark Deuze has argued that "what typifies media professions in the digital age is an increasing complexity and ongoing liquefaction of the boundaries between different fields, disciplines, practices and categories" (2007: 112) and suggested that such trends are "supercharged by . . . new information and communications technologies" (57). The BBC's adoption of a multiplatform production strategy, exemplified by the establishment of one "Vision" department—rather than distinct television and digital media or multiplatform departments—would seem to support Deuze's argument. Yet just as Deuze must himself treat game designers as "home to a distinct logic of media work," differing from film and television production, we found that boundaries between production cultures were reasserted, redrawn, and negotiated within the Vision department. As one senior television producer told us, "I actually hate the word 'multiplatform' as it reminds me of those dark days of [separate commissioners]. It's just like 'fuck off,' [multiplatform] is just the way you watch stuff."[31] For this producer, it was more comfortable to speak of multiplatform as defined by watching TV on her iPad in bed—that is, as Mark Thompson alluded, to a "clever new way of having a very traditional experience."

Although such hostilities were in fact rare, almost all interviewees have noted the difficulties inherent in the different production cultures of digital and television producers coming together. Attempts to manage these tensions were manifest at a number of levels. For example, mirroring the structure introduced at the commissioner level, certain production teams embedded multiplatform producers in the spatial organization of their team's office and production space. One can see the impact of such an integrated approach in the website for *Bang Goes the Theory* (figure 3.1), a popular science program aimed at a young audience, which had originally been commissioned as a multiplatform interactive offering that would enable audiences to "engage with real scientists and do real science" via such features as interactive tutorials for creating experiments at home or an "ask Jan" (the resident scientist) section.[32] Equally, young assistant producers (APs) were often

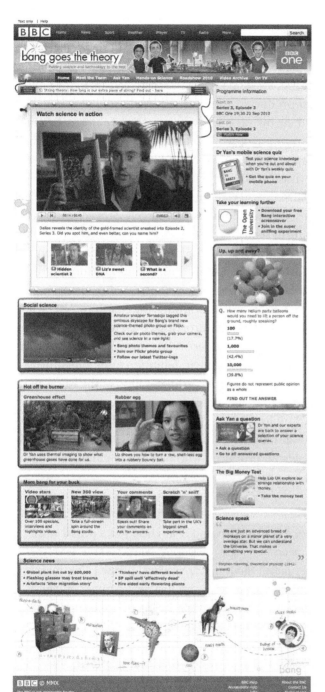

Figure 3.1. "Old" *Bang Goes the Theory* site.

encouraged to lead or take on multiplatform ideas as a way of developing their careers. Thus, one producer told us of her experience of leading the development of the use of Twitter on a major BBC One primetime science program: "It was up to me really . . . there was no extra money or time."[33] As another producer explained, the harnessing of young APs' energy for creating their own content was a classic, if informal, "management trick of turning extra work into an opportunity," which had proved important in the development of multiplatform ideas that were shared amongst television and multiplatform producers.[34]

Yet by the end of the *Creative Future* period, such attempts to manage these different production cultures had largely proved unsuccessful. As one multiplatform senior producer said, "I personally think that television don't really know what multiplatform is."[35] Indeed, even the television producer above, who had lead on a multiplatform project, understood that multiplatform was largely considered the least important element of a production and was always the first to be cut when time or money ran short. It is hardly surprising, therefore, that for many television producers and commissioners iPlayer was a key part of their immediate response when asked for their definition of multiplatform: it represented the most tangible and successful iteration of the BBC's digital strategies. However, this is not simply a case of television producers failing to understand multiplatform. Just as important were boundaries and distinctions that multiplatform producers themselves sought to establish. As one television producer, who had firmly embraced multiplatform in many of his productions, told us:

> The hardest thing I've always found is that multiplatform people tend to speak a . . . language I don't understand . . . . There was a period when the multiplatform people thought they were going to take over the world . . . where they talked about "linear viewing." [Pause.] They meant television. They had invented a new word, the only purpose of which was to be disparaging. . . . There is a slight feeling of two cultures, and one culture thought we [TV] were all dinosaurs.[36]

Similarly, a television commissioner felt that multiplatform was "'not the world I inhabit, I'm already coming to it learning to speak a foreign language." The result of such widespread differences, he suggested, was that the BBC did not "absolutely understand the potential for multiplatform as we might."[37]

To turn briefly to the question of production values, it is perhaps hardly surprising to find a disjunction between the official strategy on multiplatform and a firmly established broadcast culture's willingness to invest in this. As one TV producer explained, "multiplatform was not [the] reason I got into TV."[38] These disjunctures were clearly linked to production values within each production community. Drawing a stark contrast between digital and television production values, one multiplatform senior executive argued:

> "Beautifully shot" is a very common BBC, TV-person praise. Whereas actually if you call a website beautiful, you can't think of any other compliment to make about it. There's no value to beauty there.[39]

In turn, as Zoellner's study of professional ideology in documentary production cultures attests, notions of production value were pivotal to where producers were willing to put their efforts. As one TV producer explained in relation to her decision to refuse a multiplatform commission for a live program (in this case a thirty-minute live and interactive add-on at the end of a show wherein audiences could interact with the program's hosts and amateur contributors), "[multiplatform] could fundamentally undermine my program. By exhausting my presenters, by exhausting and frightening my contributors." For her, given the lack of comparative financial incentive to produce multiplatform content, *Creative Future* "hasn't made a fundamental difference to how I work, because ultimately I am commissioned by the BBC to make a program."[40]

The boundaries between these production cultures were further reinforced by the distinct production processes that each culture employed, causing tensions in the way teams worked together. Television producers had a long established tradition of a transmission, or "TX Culture," which emphasized working up to a final deadline whereby—via the linear process of pre-production, shooting, editing, and post-production—significant changes to a program could be made practically to the point of transmission. In contrast, "the phrase 'saved in the edit'" does not apply to multiplatform where a much more planned and iterative economy is in place.[41] This difference had significant implications for the ability of multiplatform and television production teams to work together. For example, the emphasis on television ratings over and above any multiplatform components made both the scheduling and branding of a program liable to be subject to late changes made by channel controllers or TV commissioners. Unmindful of the lead times required for the digital teams involved in making multiplatform content, such decisions could undermine months of planning when a program TX date was brought forward months ahead of an agreed schedule or a last minute change in program name was requested—decisions the multiplatform producers were rarely, if ever, consulted on.

This long established TX culture in television production has further ramifications for multiplatform production, particularly as broadcasters have begun to embrace social media as part of their digital strategies. For the BBC, however, the ability to harness social media is complicated by the way in which a TX culture emphasizes the project-based nature of television work: aside from live programs, production teams are often disbanded and "have moved on to something else" by the time of transmission.[42] As a result, social media promotion and interaction often rely solely on the goodwill of producers, which, given one former multiplatform commissioner's assessment of *Creative Future* as failing to "bed down," was rare. As he put it, "multiplatform was seen as a distinct 'thing.'"[43]

Again, however, it would be erroneous to put the blame solely on the level of production cultures or strategy. Two further, interrelated, areas are worth exploring here: firstly, the wider economic and ideological mediascape; secondly, the organizational restructure of *Creative Future*, which split Vision creative content production from technology teams based in FM&T. In terms of the former, the BBC's bold vision of multiplatform expansions was almost immediately arrested by the freeze placed on online commissioning in 2007–2008 after the BBC Trust found that the Corporation's online education venture, BBC Jam, had breached its terms of service and skewed market impact. Separately, but coinciding with the Jam debacle, was an apparent £36 million overspend on the Corporation's online presence, bbc.co.uk. Taken together, the result was that the BBC found itself widely accused of colonizing digital space.[44] Whilst there isn't room here to detail the issues that surrounded these events, we can say that the resultant freeze on all online commissioning had a profound impact on the ability to develop multiplatform projects. Its effect was an impasse between development of multiplatform creative ideas and television producers and commissioners going about "business as usual" until the freeze was "sorted out."[45] As a senior multiplatform executive later reflected, the freeze caused a loss of

> momentum and confidence . . . and the trust from the linear producers again. . . . You didn't have the resources behind it to deliver what you promised . . . . We were never given enough [room for creative] risk to make one [platform] affect the other.[46]

In turn, where multiplatform ideas were developed during this period, there was a "bottleneck" in content ideas and the technology builds required to facilitate them when the freeze was lifted.

However, the cause of these bottlenecks was not merely technological. Rather, they resulted primarily from a further cultural clash that emerged from the strategic management structure envisaged by *Creative Future*, wherein technologists were separated from editorial. Here, much more entrenched divisions of production culture emerged between editorial—television and digital producers—and technologists, with the former often viewing the latter as someone you "had to work with,"[47] outsourcing to a disinterested party—or "chucking content over a wall."[48] To one senior executive, this split of editorial and technologists was "the biggest mistake" of *Creative Future*, causing tensions that would see editorial teams complain of long delays in building technology to support their content ideas.[49] According to one multiplatform producer, "'Television say, 'they just need to knock together a website don't they, that's easy.' And obviously it's not as easy as that. Conversely FM&T don't seem to understand what a deadline is," when butting up against the TX culture of the linear production schedules.[50] For multiplatform producers, charged as intermediaries between television and technology production cultures, these tensions were acutely felt, most frequently in the form of compromises to the ambition of multiplatform ideas. Such inability to meet deadlines, however, was not merely the result of a difference in production culture. Rather, it was largely caused by a disjunction in the respective departments' interpretation of the *Creative Future* strategy. Under the management of Eric Huggers, formerly of Microsoft, FM&T eschewed the vision imagined for it in *Creative Future* as a facilitator of 360-degree ideas, taking the BBC's in-house content teams into a brave new digital future. Instead, it would focus on innovating products, such as the iPlayer, with big market impact. Effectively, therefore, almost immediately after the *Creative Future* restructure, the BBC was pulling in different directions. As one multiplatform commissioner told us:

> You had a situation where you had a formal editorial strategy and a set of projects that you had to do. And then you present that to FM[&T]. And FM[&T] go "well, we've got a strategy and it's different . . . we'll support *these* things." (emphasis added)[51]

This was not simply a matter of different production cultures or top-down-management strategies. Rather, the approach to multiplatform taken in FM&T was arguably commensurate with the emphasis on creativity and innovation placed on the management of the Corporation by the successive director generalships of Birt, Dyke, and Thompson. Moreover, taking into account Hesmondhalgh and Baker's point about the more flexible nature of management in creative industries, such an approach allowed different notions of creativity to flourish in FM&T's development of the iPlayer from a download-only service, to online streaming, to recommendation algorithms, to building in levels of sociability, through to the roll-out across a range of digital platforms that have made it the ubiquitous signifier of the BBC's multiplatform strategy. The success of iPlayer, therefore, has not simply been about metrics or platforms, but also about the ability to align it with two prevailing discourses of cultural and creative management: on the one hand, tying it to an emerging strategy of "fewer, bigger, better" that would emphasize the need for BBC innovation at an enterprise level; on the other hand, aligning it with a vision of the Internet that a long established broadcast production culture was "comfortable with." Such a strategy was in synch with the linear legacies of television producers who, "when the iPlayer came along, [thought] 'oh that's good: the Internet's now finished.'"[52] Whilst it might not mean the Internet is "finished," the success of iPlayer certainly hurried the shift away from multiplatform.

Conclusion: Products, Markets, and
Multiplatform Management

Creative Future, and the success of the iPlayer within this, indicates how a top-down managerial strategy was incapable of evolving a *broadcast* organization into a truly multiplatform one. In a way that is far from the "culturally convergent" logic of media production described by Deuze, we have argued that these failures were as much a result of entrenched production cultures and wider ideological, technological, and economic considerations as managerial strategy. In turn, 360-degree productions have largely been deemed surplus; as creative solutions, they are no longer necessary in a wider mediascape of increasingly ubiquitous social media tools and an in-house adoption of templates that would enable an efficient allocation of resources within FM&T, given the emphasis on the iPlayer and innovation at an enterprise level. Thus, instead of creative solutions, the BBC now fulfills multiplatform via the creation of products, which program teams can choose to utilize or ignore as they wish, and an automated program support (APS) system that automatically generates a webpage for every BBC show. In-house producers have thus been encouraged to view multiplatform through the APS system as a simple check-box, completed via uploading "one clip per program."

Such a shift may serve as a straitjacket for those teams that had embraced multiplatform. Returning to the example of *Bang Goes the Theory* discussed above, figure 3.2 reveals the impact of the move away from multiplatform as 360-degree productions at the BBC. Here, the multiplatform production team has largely been retrenched, and the TV teams are now responsible for uploading primarily video content to the site, which "limits creative freedom and ambition." This felt, as the producer put it, "like you're having your balls cut off just when you're doing something right."[53]

Five years after the *Creative Future* initiative to reimagine the BBC as a 360-degree multiplatform commissioner and producer, very little cultural change in the creative thinking of the organization about digital platforms appears to have occurred. Asked if *Creative Future* and its management had changed the way she worked or thought about production, one television producer responded: "no." After a significant pause, she reflected, "but I think that's really sad. I want to say 'yes.' But

Figure 3.2. "New" *Bang Goes the Theory* site.

the truth is, I'm doing what I saw APs doing when I first joined the BBC [in 2003]."[54] As another producer lamented, "The sad truth . . . is that day-to-day the only change is that you have to make a clip for your program webpage."[55] The attempt to manage such a large-scale change as envisaged by *Creative Future* was perhaps always doomed to failure, given the "vested interests," "un-thought prejudices," and "world views" already operating within a strong broadcasting culture.

Deuze, following Richard Peterson and N. Anand, argues that structural ambiguity and uncertainty in media work get translated into two institutional logics that govern organizational decision making: an editorial logic and a market logic (2007: 98). He goes on to suggest that, with liquid life, there is an emergence of a trend to "to move beyond traditional (and dichotomous) market and editorial institutional logics of cultural production towards a more complex, culturally convergent logic" (235). Whilst he's careful to suggest that this convergence will not necessarily be "seamless," the attempt to bring them together in the BBC's multiplatform strategies suggests that the lived production experiences of trying to manage convergence culture are fraught with difficulties. These management strategies, moreover, are further complicated by changes in the wider mediascape. If *Creative Future* could be understood as an editorial strategy to boldly position the BBC at the heart of the United Kingdom's emerging digital public space, then *DQF* must equally be read in light of O'Connor's discussion of the way that neoliberal theories of management aligned creativity with innovation and the drive "to economic competitiveness" in creative industries. Accordingly, the shift to "products," including the iPlayer and APS system, can be seen as a response to the need to rationalize the costs of the BBC's digital operations. This is partly due to the pressure to tack to prevailing winds of political change which, in the United Kingdom, have changed in favor of a Conservative government ideologically driven to make cuts to the public sector. As Schlesinger points out, the BBC is "endemically highly sensitive to ideological change" (2010: 272). Under neoliberalism, as Hesmondhalgh and Baker argue, the "general erosion of . . . public service broadcasting means that managers are much less likely to take risks when it comes to supporting creative autonomy" (2011: 99). Thus, we have also tried to stress that it is not merely questions of management structures, policies, and approaches that have shaped the meaning of multiplatform in the BBC across this period.

Equally important has been the conjunctural nexus of changes in the economic, ideological, and technological mediascape. To understand management in the creative industries as a product of these wider factors, and of the ways in which they play out across a range of levels and sites within an institution's discursive management of the corporate self, remains an important challenge for the critical study of media industries.

Finally, we must make some critical assessment of the iPlayer, particularly its claims to success against the rhetorical panning of the costs associated with previous 360-degree commissions. Whilst it is clearly unsustainable for the BBC to spend license-fee money on innovation for the sake of experimentation alone, the contrasts between the success of the iPlayer's 150 million views per month with 360-degree productions isn't wholly convincing. As one interviewee explained, "'no one talks about the economics of iPlayer. Having an extra viewer costs 4p," due to bandwidth and server costs.[56] Thus while the more successful element of a 360-degree commission was that it would cost less per unique user, the iPlayer effectively inverts this cost per user model. Ultimately, to return to Mark Thompson's assessment, the success of the iPlayer demonstrates the BBC's "cultural limitations."

This has profound implications for the future of public service broadcasting in the United Kingdom and the role of the BBC as its cornerstone as we move into an age of public service media. The change in approach to multiplatform at the BBC has resulted in a massive "brain drain," as one interviewee put it, of talented digital producers who thought about public service in terms different from traditional linear content.[57] As Channel 4 has increasingly moved into this newly vacated space, there is still a sense that creative freedom aligned with public service in a digital space may by possible in the United Kingdom. Moreover, it is intriguing to consider that it was the feeling of despair at the BBC that they were beaten to the first truly innovative UK multiplatform production, Big Brother, which kick-started the BBC's period of experimentation and creativity in this space. As then Director of New Media, Ashley Highfield, was reported to have said in 2001, "The landmark marriage of broadcasting and the internet was exactly the kind of thing on which the Corporation should have led the way" (Teather 2001). Management, therefore, must be seen as an ongoing process, and so this is unlikely to be the end of the story. Moreover, if we take Ryan's (1992) suggestion that creative management should be understood as neither top-down nor inflexible, then we must take stock of the BBC's integration of multiplatform training into all its television production courses. As Simon Smith, Program Manager of Multiplatform Training at the BBC Academy, explained, the BBC "no longer ha[s] a distinct multiplatform unit. What we've done is integrate multiplatform training into all other aspects of training . . . because everyone is de facto a multiplatform content producer."[58] Whilst it may take many years for producers emerging from those courses to begin to affect the way the Corporation thinks about multiplatform, we must understand cultural change through creative management as a long-term process. That lessons may have been learned from the failures of *Creative Future* is, perhaps, best emphasized by returning to Thompson himself and his reflection on the limitations and possibilities of the BBC's future in a digital, multiplatform mediascape:

> When I talk about the BBC's cultural heritages, I think we were founded by engineers. . . . . Building out the transmitter chain was as important an achievement as programming. And we're rediscovering the centrality of engineers and how we can embrace the creativity of engineering, as well as in content. So what my view is that I would go back to our heritage and say: "we can find our future in our heritage."[59]

Getting these production cultures to understand one another to ensure the creative renewal of the BBC in a digital age remains a significant challenge at a strategic, cultural, and technical level. For now, they remain as poles apart as those early transmitters.

NOTES

This work was supported by the Arts and Humanities Research Council, AH-H018522-2. The authors would also like to acknowledge that this piece wouldn't have been possible without the hard work of our fellow research team members, Paul Kerr and Dr. Andrea Medrado. We're also grateful for the input of Andrew Chitty, Illumina Digital, for his thoughtful comments on a draft of this piece.

1. Anonymous, personal interview with authors (Interview 27), February 3, 2011.
2. Anonymous, personal interview with authors (Interview 64), September 30, 2011.
3. Anonymous, personal interview with authors (Interview 21), August 9, 2011.
4. Anonymous, personal interview with authors (Interview 69), November 11, 2011.
5. Anonymous, personal interview with authors (Interview 29), February 24, 2011.
6. The calling into question of achievement is perhaps best exemplified by a number of interviewees with whom we spoke two or more times across the course of the project: often being wildly enthusiastic and supportive of multiplatform on our first meeting, and distinctly underwhelmed by the strategic achievements on our second encounter (often at a point where they were leaving the Corporation).
7. Anonymous (Interview 69).
8. Dominic Bird, Senior Producer, personal interview with authors, September 14, 2005.
9. Anonymous (Interview 64).
10. Anonymous, personal interview with authors (Interview 42), May 18, 2011.
11. Richard Williams, MiPTV 2007.
12. Simon Nelson, personal interview with authors, September 19, 2010.
13. Anonymous, personal interview with authors (Interview 45), June 1, 2011.
14. Anonymous, personal interview with authors (Interview 52), August 9, 2011.
15. Anonymous (Interview 29).
16. Anonymous (Interview 45).
17. Anonymous (Interview 64).
18. Anonymous (Interview 52).
19. Anonymous, personal interview with authors (Interview 10), November 26, 2011.
20. Anonymous, personal interview with authors (Interview 33), August 11, 2011.
21. Anonymous, personal interview with authors (Interview 28), February 23, 2011.
22. Anonymous (Interview 29).
23. Anonymous (Interview 69).
24. Anonymous, personal interview with authors (Interview 43), May 27, 2011.
25. Nelson, personal interview.
26. Anonymous, personal interview with authors (Interview 36), April 11, 2011.
27. Mark Thompson, personal interview with authors, February 17, 2011.
28. On the day of launch, the BBC's iPad app became the number one free app download on the iTunes app store within four hours of going live (interview with Mark Thompson).
29. See *iPlayer Performance Packs*, http://www.bbc.co.uk/blogs/bbcinternet/iplayer/ (accessed December 11, 2011].
30. Anonymous (Interview 29).
31. Anonymous (Interview 45).

32. Anonymous, personal interview with authors (Interview 66), October 11, 2011.

33. Anonymous, personal interview with authors (Interview 56), August 22, 2011.

34. Anonymous, personal interview with authors (Interview 54), August 17, 2011.

35. Anonymous (Interview 52).

36. Anonymous (Interview 54).

37. Anonymous (Interview 28).

38. Anonymous (Interview 56).

39. Anonymous (Interview 29).

40. Anonymous, personal interview with authors (Interview 48), July 12, 2011.

41. Anonymous (Interview 29).

42. Anonymous, personal interview with authors (Interview 55), August 22, 2011.

43. Anonymous (Interview 21).

44. The "overspend" was largely a misallocation of £24.9 million in overheads and other budgetary costs that had been represented in what the bbc.co.uk spent in 2007–2009 due to what the BBC Trust found to be mismanagement.

45. Anonymous (Interview 29).

46. Anonymous (Interview 10).

47. Anonymous (Interview 66).

48. Anonymous, personal interview with authors (Interview 65), October 11, 2011.

49. Anonymous (Interview 10).

50. Anonymous (Interview 52).

51. Anonymous (Interview 33). At the time of this interview, FM&T had been re-organized into two departments: Future Media, responsible for iPlayer, and the separate division of Technology.

52. Anonymous (Interview 64).

53. Anonymous (Interview 66).

54. Anonymous (Interview 56).

55. Anonymous (Interview 65).

56. Anonymous, personal interview with authors (Interview 1), October 8, 2010.

57. Anonymous (Interview 33).

58. Simon Smith, personal interview with authors, September 30, 2011.

59. Thompson, personal interview.

4

Enterprising Selves

Reality Television and Human Capital

LAURIE OUELLETTE

What is involved is the generalization of forms of 'enterprise' by diffusing and multiplying them as much as possible . . . this multiplication of the 'enterprise' form within
the social body is what is at stake in neoliberal policy. It
is a matter of making the market, competition, and so the
enterprise, into what could be called the formative power of
society.
—Michel Foucault

In his 1978–1979 lectures at the College de France, Michel Foucault
traced the neoliberal turn in capitalist democracies to the reformation
of individuals as the subjects of human capital. Trends of deregulation,
privatization, public sector downsizing, and welfare reform, along with
the demise of collective bargaining and long-term employment security, characterize neoliberal societies, broadly defined (see Harvey 2007;
Duggan 2004; Rose 1996). But these developments coincide with, and
depend upon, a fundamental "shift in the way in which humans make
themselves and are made as subjects" (Reade 2009: 28). As Jason Reade
(2009) eloquently surmises, the new regime of subjectivity identified by
Foucault involves a "massive expansion of the field and scope of economics," as the free market becomes the grid for making sense of sociality. The discourse of the economy "becomes an entire way of life, a common sense in which every action—crime, marriage, higher education
and so on—can be charted according to a calculus of maximum output for minimum expenditure: it can be seen as an investment," Reade

explains (28, 31). Within this encroaching market rationality, the citizen is conceived less as a subject of rights and collective interests, and more as an "entrepreneur of self," incited to manage his or her own conduct and maximize his or her own capacities as the condition of expanding freedoms (Foucault 2008: 226). The waning social contract and the exploitation associated with forms of unpaid and precarious labor are offered as opportunities for creativity and strategic investment in the self. This is no ideological ruse. As Foucault suggested, the subject of human capital is a *constitutive* dimension of the neoliberal project. The business of making and remaking enterprising selves is integral to the production of the contemporary conjuncture.

This chapter considers U.S. television's contribution to the production of subjects of human capital. Looking beyond the operation of the media industries, I analyze the role of reality entertainment in the management of personhood. Here, management refers to the techniques of everyday self-management demonstrated by a range of reality programs and their investment in and endorsement of an enterprising mode of human subjectivity.

Reality television is an obvious site for such analysis, to the extent that its multiplying subgenres share a preoccupation with documenting, evaluating, and shaping the performance of real people in their capacities as workers, housemates, romantic partners, consumers, family members, homeowners, and contestants. What's more, this engagement with human subjects unfolds within a neoliberal market logic, in which capitalist business principles are applied to social situations and everyday behaviors. Individual actions and choices are frequently evaluated according to a schema of investment and return (in the game and in life), and while everyone is presumed to be malleable and self-maximizing, success is inherently competitive. The enterprise form is extended across an expanding array of social niches as cost/benefit ratios, audits, strategies, calculations, and outcomes are brought to bear on personal relationships, the body, health, familial arrangements, style, personal finances, home decorating, crime and security, child rearing, job hunting, social problems (such as poverty, environmental destruction, and mental illness), pet ownership, and matchmaking. Enterprising subjectivities are exemplified by the disproportionately large number of reality television participants who work for long hours (and often minimal or no pay) in the broadly defined creative industries in the hope of eventually becoming top chefs, pop idols, supermodels, fashion designers, wedding planners, magazine editors, movie producers, boutique managers, or celebrity hair stylists. But human capital in a more quotidian sense can also be cultivated with the assistance of a cadre of consultants and experts who help ordinary people to increase their worth through wardrobe upgrades, plastic surgery, fitness programs, boot camps, interventions, life coaching, tough love, lifestyle instruction, and other methods. Reality television is significant because, through these tendencies, it renders the ongoing manufacture of neoliberal subjectivities patently visible. The process may be contradictory and even unsuccessful much of the time, but the impetus to make and remake *homo economicus* continues all the same.

Reality television operates as a cultural technology, a cluster of everyday dos and don'ts for living and mastering the managerial dispositions, knowledge, and skills valued by the enterprise form.[1] It does not dupe passive TV viewers, as much as it presents resources (advice, demonstrations, examples, motivational strategies, product endorsements) for achieving a model of personhood that requires active investment and participation. In this sense, television is not only a subset of a cultural industry *to be managed*: it is also stitched into the dispersed management of selfhood and everyday life. Looking beyond the activities of television executives, brokers, and producers, this chapter emphasizes the latter process, calling attention to the neoliberal market rationalities, forms of expertise, and self-shaping strategies circulated by and through reality programs. In this account, intermediaries include not only professional media workers or industry managers, but also a proliferating array of coaches, stylists, talent scouts, judges, motivators, and lifestyle specialists who mediate between the rationalities and demands of the market and the quotidian micro management of the self, lending their knowledge and flair to the maximization of human capital. Their expertise authorizes reality television's subjective interventions—and achieves unprecedented visibility through its profitable programs and accompanying websites and sales platforms. The enterprising self is thus a collaborative fiction, crafted through a swatch of detailed instructions in the spaces where the neoliberal economy meets culture. Few of us are likely to actualize the selves on offer, and yet the regime of truth to which reality television contributes nonetheless animates the policies and economic structures in which we live.

Neoliberalism and the Enterprising Self

Before elaborating on reality television's relationship to *homo economicus,* it is useful to consider the broader multiplication and dispersion of the enterprise form across two sites: government and labor. As James Hay and I (2009) argue in our book *Better Living through Reality TV: Television and Post-Welfare Citizenship,* reality television gained cultural currency in the context of privatization and welfare reform. While reality programs date to the origins of television, it wasn't until the late 1990s that a burgeoning swath of "non-scripted" entertainment began to take over network as well as specialized cable channels during daytime and primetime hours. There are various explanations for the dramatic rise of such programming, notably cost—reality programs are comparatively flexible and cheap to produce—and global trade— many are based on internationally circulating, generic formats that further minimize economic investment and risk (see Raphael 2009; Keane and Moran 2008). In the United States particularly, the programmatic objectives and cultural legibility of new forms of reality television are also shaped by the "reinvention of government" in the 1990s and beyond. The bipartisan move to reform government in the image of the market was encapsulated within political discourse and policy recommendations such as *Reinventing Government: How the Entrepreneurial Spirit is Transforming the Public Sector,* a blueprint endorsed by former President Bill Clinton (Osborne and Gaebler 1993).[2] This discourse provided the rational for downsizing the public sector, forging partnerships with firms, outsourcing state services and responsibilities to the more "efficient" private sector, and minimizing dependency on public welfare programs by radically reducing or eliminating them. Crucially, the reinvention of government also required a new conception of the enterprising citizen. Earlier models of citizenship rooted in the Keynesian welfare state and the assumption of collective rights and responsibilities gave way to a heightened emphasis on individual choice, self-reliance, risk-management, and personal responsibility, argues Nikolas Rose (1996).[3] In policy and political discourse, and in the reforms of the

1990s and beyond, the good citizen was reconceived as an enterprising subject who invests in himself or herself, takes responsibility for his or her actions, and secures his or her own fate and fortune.

As Wendy Brown (2003) points out, the "withdrawal of the state" from social life and the privatization of public services do not amount to the dismantling of government (6). On the contrary, these are specific techniques of governing, in which "rational economic action suffused throughout society replaces express state rule or provision." [4] When governments shift the "regulatory competence of the state onto responsible, rational individuals," the aim is to encourage them to "give their lives a specific entrepreneurial form" (Thomas Lemke, qtd. in Brown 2005: 44). This process isn't automatic, however: citizens are not born but made. Here, media and popular culture are relevant. The explosion of reality television, with its ongoing experimentation with human subjects, market logic, and pedagogies of the self, was not orchestrated by government reformers, but it does help constitute and circulate new requirements of enterprising citizenship. Operating outside official government, reality television brings an economic grid into the personal choices, investments, and outcomes of everyday life. It presents one means by which "individuals may be made responsible through their choices . . . through the shaping of a lifestyle according to grammars of living that are widely disseminated, yet do not depend on . . . political calculations and strategies" (Rose 1996: 57). And, the capacity to manage the self, by making enterprising choices in health, security, consumption, family, romance, work, and household, takes on a sense of urgency at time when public support systems have been dismantled and individuals and families are expected to produce their own sustenance and well-being.

Reality television also gained cultural currency within the neoliberal economy and its precarious labor conditions. Just as the reinvention of government required a new conception of the actively responsible and enterprising citizen, the collapse of long-term employment security and the intensification of temporary and freelance labor necessitated recasting the subject of labor as an entrepreneur of the self. Flexible production cycles, short-term labor, outsourcing, endless corporate reinvention, the expansion of the service sector, and the transition from manufacturing to branding had to be translated as people's capacities to carry out the new demands of work being placed on them. As Valerie Walkerdine (2003) points out, a "flexible and autonomous subject" who embraces lifelong learning and is capable of constant self-invention is required to "cope with the constant change in work . . . and with constant insecurity" (240) The subjective shift from dependent worker to entrepreneur of the self is also related to what Angela McRobbie (2005) calls the replacement of the social with work. As the public sector and, with it, social services are cast to the margins of social life, they are replaced with "competition, the seeking of self-advancement in work, and, in commercialized leisure spheres, self-improvement techniques," she explains. Consequently, work comes to mean much more than earning a living: promoted as the sole means of ensuring personal security, it "incorporates and overtakes everyday life" and exacts "new resources of self-reliance on the part of the working population" (99–100).

Within this context, corporate management visionaries such as Peter Drucker (1999), who advised reformers during the reinvention of government and was awarded the 2002 Presidential Medal of Freedom by George W. Bush, began to speak of a "revolution in human affairs" (166). The time has come, he contended, for workers to actively develop and manage themselves. According to management consultant Tom Peters (1997), the author of *This Brand Called You*, the individual is no longer an employee, staffer, worker, or human resource but the CEO of her own company—"Me Inc." Peters sums up the logic of investment and return through which the subjectivity of the worker is increasingly understood when he insists:

> You don't "belong to" any company for life, and your chief affiliation isn't to any particular "function." You're not defined by your job title and you're not confined by your job description. Starting today you are a brand. . . . The good news . . . is that everyone has a chance to stand out. Everyone has a chance to learn, improve, and build up their skills. Everyone has a chance to be a brand worthy of the mark. (8)

Just as reality television circulates the grammars of self-sufficient and enterprising citizenship, so it can be seen as a cultural technology for constituting laborers in the new economy as entrepreneurs of the self. Much reality programming showcases individuals who struggle to master flexible labor conditions, reinvent themselves, or bolster their human capital in the hopes of winning the competition, achieving fame and fortune, or simply maximizing their worth in the competitive workplace as well as the social marketplace. Reality television thus tends to value the strategic and self-empowering individual over the collective with potentially common interests and bargaining power. Television is stitched into the production of "Me Inc." as reality programs devoted to analyzing, evaluating, shaping, and ranking the choices and behaviors of individuals according to economic values achieve visibility. Reality television also multiplies and extends the sites in which subjects are to conceive of themselves as entrepreneurs of the self. The issue is not that public and private spheres are blurred, but that more and more slices of experience, from employment to dating to health to work, are understood and modeled in enterprise form. As Foucault (2008) observed, the regime of *homo economicus* does not imply that all human behavior *is* economic behavior, or that the subject is *inherently* or *only* an entrepreneur of the self; rather, it means that we live in an era where the "grid of intelligibility" for behavior is dominantly economic, and where power works on individuals conceived less as deviants or victims than as the subjects of human capital (244). Reality television operates within, and helps to produce and normalize, this grid of intelligibility.

Reality Television and Subject of Human Capital

One of the most visible and enduring reality television formats is the life intervention, broadly defined as the observation, diagnosis, and makeover of human subjects while the camera rolls. Since the late 1990s, life interventions have proliferated across daytime and primetime television, taking real people (not actors) as the raw material for addressing a proliferating range of problems and domains. What unites this strand of reality television is a mission to help failed or "at risk" individuals adopt a new-and-improved relationship with themselves, in which their everyday choices, behaviors, and actions are increasingly calculated through the lens of investment and return. Life interventions enlist human subjects to enact the freedoms and burdens of enterprising citizenship, while utilizing coaches, experts, and motivators to transform those who are deemed dependent and/or under-actualized into successful self-managers. More than any other strand of television, these programs challenge a wide range of individuals, organized by age, income, race, class, and lifestyle clusters, to maximize "their capacities, work harder on themselves, and exploit the resources of self-care made available to them" (Ouellette and Hay 2008: 472).

Life interventions require intermediaries to initiate and accomplish transformations of the self. In his influential account of cultural intermediaries, the sociologist Pierre Bourdieu (1979/1984) argues that media and cultural workers help to reproduce capitalism by "mediating" taste and consumer preferences. As members of the professional middle class, intermediaries reproduce the interests of capitalists and the privileged classes primarily by reinforcing cultural distinctions rooted in class hierarchies through their symbolic work. Some critical analyses of reality television, particularly in Europe, have extended Bourdieu's insights to the present, arguing that the never-ending supply of lifestyle experts found on reality programs reinforces existing class hierarchies by attempting (usually without success) to impose the allegedly superior tastes, habits, and dispositions of the educated upper classes onto the less well educated (see Skeggs 2009). In this formulation, reality television is important because it is a visible site for differentiating between the subjects of "legitimate" cultural capital (good taste, the right style, manners, etc.) and those who will never enjoy class privilege of this sort.

While Bourdieu's analysis remains indispensable for understanding the reproduction of class in capitalist democracies, it doesn't entirely capture the neoliberal ethos of reality television, especially in the United States, where the discourse of self-actualization has always been especially strong, and where the dispersion of the enterprise form into social life happened early and with particular vigor. On U.S. reality shows, intermediaries often reinforce taste hierarchies, and self-fashioning resources do tend to filter down from the well-educated and privileged classes. However, intermediaries also play a pivotal role in demonstrating and instilling techniques of self-reliance and self-maximization in subjects who are assumed to need them most. However stratified along axes of race, class, and gender U.S. society continues to be, everyone is expected to envision him or herself as an accumulation of human capital, a "unit of one." Everyone, from the chronically unemployed to the celebrity jet-setter, is expected to empower him or herself using the dispersed private resources (including reality television) available to them. Everyone is expected to produce his or her own happiness, success, and security. And everyone is expected to think and act in terms of "investment, capital costs, and profit—both economic and psychological profit—on the capital invested" (Foucault 2008: 244).

Reality television's intermediaries may specialize in quotidian matters of fashion, sex, parenting, and other lifestyle topics, but their advice coordinates with these broader subjective currents. Not surprisingly, many draw inspiration and techniques from the corporate sector. Many experts are modeled on the "life coach," a term that emerged from the world of business and made its way to the helping professions, where it currently refers to personal motivators who are less concerned with the "talking cure" than with helping customers achieve tailored behavioral goals and outcomes. Life coaches suit the regime of enterprising subjectivity in their claim to "get results" with short-term, practical self-empowerment strategies. Frequently self-made experts, without formal qualifications (life coaches are not regulated), many specialize in specific clientele and problem zones (weight, dating, work). While not all of reality television's intermediaries call themselves life coaches, they typically belie similar tendencies. Across formats, the experts on hand to help subjects help themselves often have no other claim to expertise than their own entrepreneurialism and embodiment of the lifestyle in which they trade.

On daytime television, the enormously successful personal advisor and motivator Dr. Phillip McGraw exemplifies the role of the life coach, as a new type of intermediary, in the production of the citizen subject demanded by neoliberal discourses and reforms. (With his profitable line of self-help books, merchandise, DVDs, and speaking gigs, McGraw also illustrates another dictate of good government—that it be entrepreneurial and profitable). Eschewing "psychobabble," Dr. Phil helps mainly lower-income women to "maximize themselves" and achieve the "results they want" in an increasingly competitive world through personal audits, cost/ratio analyses of behavior, and other managerial techniques of the self adapted from the corporate sector (Ouellette and Wilson 2011). Exemplifying how intermediaries translate the new demands of citizenship—particularly the imperative to take responsibility for and empower the self in the absence of social pro-grams—into a daily regime for living, Dr. Phil tells his customers: "As your [own] life manager, it is your job to 'keep you safe and secure from foolish risks, create opportunities for you to get what you really want in this life, take care of your health and well being' . . . It is up to you to 'require more of yourself in your grooming, self-control, emotional management, interaction with others . . . and in every other category you can think of'" (qtd. in McGraw 1999: 169–70).

This way of mediating between the market and the self understands that producing the self as a subject of human capital entails work that is never done. The rewards are in the accumulation of the human capital deemed integral to individualized conceptions of happiness, security, and success. Dr. Phil's remarks also point to the intensification of micro self-managerialism as a dispersed strategy of governing in which inter-mediaries play an important role. As Colin Gordon (1991) observes, the rejection of big government does not free us from government, as reformers and politicians often claim. Rather, it subjects us to the fur-ther dispersion and fine-tuning of governmentality, conceived as the conduct of conduct. "Economic government joins hands with behav-iorism" in the presumption that the citizen will be "perpetually respon-sive to modifications in his environment" (43). Certainly, the idea that even the most troubled individuals can learn to make more rational and strategic (economic) choices with the help of intermediaries animates the life intervention in all its forms.

On Lifetime's *The Fairy Job Mother*, a British-accented, self-pro-claimed employment specialist claims to help solve the recession by instructing and motivating unemployed individuals, many of whom have lost their jobs as a result of downsizing and layoffs. The primetime intervention follows many of the conventions adopted by Dr. Phil. The intermediary sets up shop in the homes of the unemployed, dissemi-nates practical advice on resume construction and dressing for success, and also coaches the subjects to overcome personal problems such as low self-esteem, poor hygiene, undeveloped work ethic, dependence on welfare, and other barriers to the achievement of employment. The structural causes of the soar in unemployment rates and related finan-cial difficulties are concealed, as are inequalities of gender, race, and class and their impact on vocational options and earning power. This is compounded in the case of lower-income female subjects, many of whom have small children, as the cost of daycare is never figured into the Fairy Job Mother's mission to help the women find any job, however low-paying and regardless of whether benefits (such as health care) or flexible work hours are offered. The onus is placed on the enterprising individual to exploit the resources (advice, skills, tough love) provided by the intermediary and produce "results" in their own lives. By the end of the episode, some of the participants have responded to the stimulus and advising of the intermediary, but some have not. To be sure, many TV viewers may have a difficult time seeing the securing of a minimum wage or part-time job (especially when the subject has lost a full-time, perhaps unionized position) as a satisfying return on investment. The point is not that television programs such as *The Fairy Job Mother* indoctrinate or dupe passive subjects, but rather that they collaborate in the constitution of the self-enterprising citizen as required by the governing rationalities of neoliberal societies. We may see through the programs, but the grid of intelligibility for understanding unemployment as an individual problem, to be solved through private life coaching and self-enterprise rather than public resources or interventions, operates nonetheless.

On VH1-1's *Tough Love*, the son of the owner of an elite matchmaking service coaches a range of women who have failed to find romantic partners while the cameras roll. In the debut episode, the women are introduced as failed subjects; each of them embodies specific shortcomings that prevent her from capturing a mate (for example, "Miss Bridezilla" scares mates away by pushing marriage too early, while "Miss Ball Buster" is too pushy). Like Dr. Phil and the Fairy Job Mother, the intermediary makes liberal use of shaming, ridicule, humiliation, and scorn in his "tough love" mission to help the women empower themselves. Likewise, he trades less in formal knowledge and credentialed expertise (he is not a licensed therapist) than in concrete skills, interpersonal advice, problem-solving techniques, intimate feedback, and motivational strategies drawn loosely from corporate management manuals. Through a series of tests, lessons, and experiments, the women are taught how to see themselves through the eyes of potential male partners (shoppers) and to make themselves more marketable in a competitive dating milieu. What's interesting about *Tough Love* is that love and romance are quite deliberately stripped of any romantic illusion; the quest for a partner is treated as a strategic challenge. Addressing so-called barriers from attitude to body language to wardrobe, the show instructs participants in the boot camp to reflect on, monitor, and change their behavior and attitudes, and in that sense to become managers of themselves, capable of overseeing and regulating themselves in particular ways so as to maximize particular outcomes. The quest for human capital takes an explicitly feminized form in *Tough Love* as the perpetual management of the self intersects with gendered assumptions about the body, beauty, personality, sexuality, and social power. While heterosexuality and marriage are enforced as norms, the "problem" addressed by the TV intervention—namely, being unmarried—is individualized as the failure/lack of a feminized self-enterprise. The grid of interpretation for understanding and changing the female subject is market-oriented here as well.

An economic grid also orients interventions in the domain of criminality, and similarities between the problematization and management of dating and crime speak to the breadth of the subjective changes Foucault describes. As many critics point out, the rising importance of compulsory personal responsibility and self-enterprise as post-welfare strategies of "governing at a distance" have coincided with intensified profiling and incarceration of individuals and populations who are deemed unable or willing to govern themselves properly. In the United States, such failures correlate closely with inequalities of class and race, and "risk management" approaches to crime target the poor and people of color disproportionately. Reality television partners with a burgeoning swatch of enforcement agencies, prisons, and specialized task units in such endeavors, and in this sense does not only endorse but actually participates in neoliberal practices of crime management.[5]

At the same time, a cluster of productions applies techniques circulating on makeover programs and interventions to potential or convicted criminals, as determined by current policies. These productions do not question the definition of criminality, or the racial and class politics of profiling and incarceration. However, they do claim to help rehabilitate those who are associated with, or considered at risk of, criminal behavior. One example is the OWN series *Breaking Down the Bars*, a reality series focusing on the rehabilitation of women who are incarcerated in the United States and deploying an individualized process that requires intermediaries to facilitate self-esteem building, cultivation of personal responsibility, and life coaching. Other programs similarly eschew any discussion of social conditions and policies and instead seek to help criminals or potential criminals (who are often cast as men of color, particularly as young African American males) become enterprising subjects. MTV's *T.I.'s Road to Redemption* follows rap star (and convicted felon) T.I.'s attempts to discourage criminal behavior among young male Latino and African Americans. The venture arose from a bargain that T.I. struck with an Atlanta Superior Court judge following his arrest for weapons charges. In exchange for a reduced sentence, the rap star was placed under house arrest and subjected to electronic monitoring. He also agreed to perform one thousand hours of community service in which he was to discourage "at risk" youth from following in his footsteps. This service was woven into the advertising-sponsored MTV series, which also conveniently provided a forum for bolstering his musical career. In episodes such as "You Are Responsible for Your Own Actions" and "Own Your Mistake," T.I. is shown speaking to schools and community groups about personal responsibility. He also searches out and works closely with "at risk" teenagers such as Peewee, a self-described hustler from New Jersey who is African American. As part of Peewee's redemption, T.I. requires him to spend several hours in a jail cell and takes him to a city morgue to "learn about the consequences of crime," claiming these frightening interventions will impact Peewee's "future decision making." What's interesting is that crime is not presented as a moral issue, nor are so-called potential criminals redeemed as moral subjects. The goal is to instill better choice-making capacities in subjects such as Peewee, so that they will more carefully evaluate the risks and cost/benefit ratios of their actions and in so doing stop crime before it happens.

In MTV's *From G's to Gents*, hip hop stylist Fonzworth Bentley, author of *Advance Your Swagger: How to Use Manners, Confidence, and Style to Get Ahead*, teaches young unemployed men of color (some of whom have served jail time) how to dress, eat, speak, and succeed as "gentlemen" as they compete for a cash prize. Like Bourdieu's cultural intermediaries, Fonzworth mediates the taste preferences of the well-heeled elite, ordering the contestants to wear blue blazers, master fine dining etiquette, play croquet, and thus awkwardly simulate the habitus of the genteel aristocracy. Intermediaries are also on hand to teach the young men proper grammar, manners, and self-esteem. Fonzworth himself functions mainly as a life coach, drawing on his knowledge and experience as a self-made hip hop celebrity to instill an enterprising ethic that sometimes exceeds the premise of the game. Fonzworth embodies the logic of self-enterprise in his rise from personal assistant to P. Diddy to reality television mogul, and in some ways his guide to mastering stylistic markers of confidence and success undercuts the naturalized superiority of the largely white aristocratic taste culture. Fonzworth has produced his own human capital, a feat that is not limited to learning the culture and habits of the privileged elite, but also requires the capacity to regulate and manage his own makeover persona toward strategic ends, not least of all commanding a lucrative reality show.

Intermediaries and/as Entrepreneurs of the Self

The talent competition is another important subgenre for tracing the crucial work of intermediaries on reality television. *From G's to Gents* is in some respects a talent competition, in that the young men compete to master the art of being a gentleman, or at least to perform that persona strategically so as to win the game and take home the cash prize. Needless to say, such a performance requires a total immersion in the labor of self-fashioning, so that any difference between labor, self-enterprise, and subjectivity is blurred. Most talent competitions similarly immerse contestants in competitive situations that require them to work long hours of unpaid creative labor, all the while being monitored, evaluated, coached, judged, and eliminated. Bravo's *Top Chef* and *Project Runway*, NBC's *The Apprentice*, and specialized programs such as VH-1's *I Want to Work for P. Diddy* are examples of talent competitions. On these programs, intermediaries adopt the roles of judges and mentors who design tests, administer challenges, and evaluate their outcomes. Contestants are in turn expected to develop winning attitudes, dispositions, and skills. These lessons are often less overt than the explicit pedagogies of the self circulated by life interventions. Often, what is involved is reflection on one's success or failure in the competition. Contestants re-examine their choices and behaviors through the eyes of the intermediaries who coach and evaluate them, enabling the sort of "feedback analysis" called for by management gurus. Self-management becomes a reality because the contestant, as a stand-in for the worker, is especially open to the dictate "adapt and improve."

Talent competitions are also sites for constituting subjects of human capital, conceived as a regime of subjectivity. Many ritualistically enact the dramatic reworking of the labor contract associated with *homo economicus*. Instead of merely exchanging his or her labor for wages, the entrepreneur of self labors to maximize his or her own human capital, in the hopes that it can be traded for income, status, happiness, and other rewards. Even if a wage is received, the laboring subject is encouraged to see her or himself as a self-manager, a CEO of the self who oversees an individualized process of investment and return. In this neoliberal model, labor is not limited to what happens in the office or the factory, because work is reconceived as an investment in the self as a personal enterprise that involves education, training, social networking, skill acquisition, and so on. This self-work is performed voluntarily and usually for free, in the anticipation of future payoffs. With their ongoing cycles of aspiring chefs, models, designers, business executives, creative workers, and many others willing to immerse themselves in the unpaid "all the time" labor of the competition (and not to mention the free labor of the television production), talent competitions enact and normalize a neoliberal conception of labor and the enterprising subjectivities upon which it depends.

It is significant that so many talent competitions are set in glamorous and creative fields such as fashion, art, media, cuisine, and design. As Angela McRobbie (2002) demonstrates in her study of fashion designers, the "talent-led economy" of self-expressive work demands "capacities for inexhaustible resourcefulness, resilience and entrepreneurialism" that (as with the art world) set the stage for the future of labor (102). However, such capacities still do not guarantee success in a "lottery economy," where opportunities for success are limited. McRobbie argues that the classic rags-to-riches fantasy has mutated into a less predictable mediation of success and failure, in which seemingly random factors such as "bad timing" loom large. This uncertainty is tolerated, she contends, because, as in the arts, creative cultural work is presented as a reward onto itself—a self-fulfilling enterprise. Building on this analysis, we might see creative media and cultural industries as "shock absorbers" of the neoliberal economy, similar to the new media professions astutely analyzed by Gina Neff, Sharon Zukin, and Elizabeth Wissinger (2005). In creative industries, as with new media fields, employment is often short-term and contract based; the allure of autonomy and creative expression is what enjoins workers to accept the precariousness of their situations. Workers in creative industries are also expected to work long hours, devote extensive off hours to honing their craft and developing a portfolio, and "accept risks previously mediated by firms (such as business cycle fluctuations and market failures)" (Neff, Zukin, and Wissinger 2005: 331). These risks and requirements are enacted across reality television's talent competitions, as contestants invest many hours of uncompensated labor in competitions that will only ever produce one winner. While the reward system is hierarchical and competitive, the subjective experience of the competition—not unlike the unpaid internship in a "dream" profession—is rationalized in terms of future payoffs, from skill-building, experience, and social connections to commercial endorsements and career success down the road. When one of the beleaguered designers from *Project Runway* emerges from weeks of toil and wins a contract with major retailers, or an eliminated contestant on *America's Next Top Models* scores a magazine advertisement or a new reality show, reality television's claim to nurture the production of enterprising selves is valorized. And it is this same grid of intelligibility that has come to prevail across the much less glamorous retail and service industries, in which salespeople are required to perform "on a stage" and baristas are "auditioned" on the basis of their talent and artistic skills (Couldry 2008).

It is significant how many reality programs follow rather minor creative entrepreneurs, from celebrity stylists to hair salon and boutique owners to wedding planners. These individuals, it should be emphasized, work in specialized fields that are increasingly integral to the current regime of investment in the self. The proliferation of programs such as *Split Ends, Shear Genius, Tabitha's Salon Takeover, The Rachel Zoe Project, Say Yes to the Dress,* and *Platinum Weddings* surely speaks in part to the heightened emphasis on self-fashioning, as a dimension of self-management, in the current juncture. These shows model makeover programs and interventions to the extent that they highlight intermediaries engaging in a mission to help people become better selves. Yet, similar to talent competitions, they also model the subjective shift from worker to entrepreneur. Here, intermediaries themselves are the subjects of our voyeurism and inquiry as we watch them mediate between the self and the market across increasingly specialized consumer domains, such as hip hop clothing and designer hair styling. To be sure, the micro melodramas of everyday life as experienced by these "ordinary people" can be intriguing. However, the subjects also embody the creativity, energy, disposition, and enterprising skills valued by the regime of enterprising subjectivity. They, like the contestants on talent competitions and life coaches who monetize their wares, circulate as living, breathing models of *homo economicus*, not because their entire personhood is reducible to the cold logic of enterprise, but because the framework for understanding their visibility on television is governed by economic rationality. Bethany Frankel, the *Real Housewives of New York* star who launched a multi-million dollar line of Skinny Girl merchandise, graduated to her own series of reality shows, hit the commercial talk show circuit, and now offers lucrative self-help seminars to women in addition to being a celebrity, is a good example of how getting on television has become part of the formula for reality television's intermediaries. In addition to mediating between the market and human subjectivity, celebrity intermediaries like Frankel embody the precise dispositions and skills ascribed to *homo economicus*.

America's Next Top Model is a talent competition set in the glamorous but notoriously competitive and precarious commercial modeling industry. On this reality show, young women competing for a professional modeling contract are immersed in a boot-camp training program/elimination process from which emerges a single winner. *Top Model* brings together many of the techniques, strategies, and rationalities of subjectivity discussed so far. The women work for free, performing as talent for the reality television production and as pitchwomen for corporate sponsors such as Cover Girl in the hopes of future payoffs. Each week, they participate in tests and challenges overseen by intermediaries that have as much to do with the cultivation of the enterprising self as they do with beauty. Professional stylists, designers, agents, and former supermodels serve as coaches to the aspiring models, and evaluate the results. *America's Next Top Model* was conceptualized by

Tyra Banks, who claims a biography of overcoming poverty to achieve supermodel fame and in this capacity acts as a subjective template for emulation by the female contestants, the majority of whom are lower income and women of color. Banks, who also has a successful talk show and a line of merchandise and has been profiled by *Fortune* magazine as an up-and-coming media mogul, attributes her stardom less to her appearance than to her entrepreneurialism: "I see women in the mall or on the streets who look 10 times better than I do," she claims, "but can they sell a product?" (qtd. in Margena Christian 2003).

The product manufactured and sold on *America's Next Top Model* is saleable female subjectivity. Within the context of the reinvention of government and the flexible neoliberal economy, the competition demonstrates through its pedagogical techniques and examinations that no woman can rely on "to be looked at-ness." It is no longer enough to be a passive object of patriarchal desire. The never-ending labor of producing enterprising forms of femininity, as ritualistically demonstrated on *America's Next Top Model*, is not hidden from view in the current conjuncture. The aspiring fashion model must continually work on her body, social skills, personality, and attitude—her human capital—and she must work even harder to produce the "right" (i.e., white, middle-class) capital if she is working class, Latina, or African American (Hasinoff 2008). This labor is characterized as a strategic investment in the self, overseen by intermediaries at first, but eventually monitored by the internal manager that resides inside each enterprising subject. Adopting a "tough love" philosophy similar to other intermediaries discussed so far, Banks claims to provide inside knowledge of the modeling industry but in fact operates much like a life coach. She is known to humiliate and scold those who disappoint—not to punish them, she claims, but to motivate them to improve or face elimination and, more importantly, to help them empower themselves (Blakeley 2006). Banks encourages the women to envision themselves as "CEOs of Me" in the sense advocated by contemporary managerial gurus, which means seeing oneself as a commercial asset or brand that requires perpetual reinvention: "Your product just happens to be your physical self and a little bit of your personality too," she explains. "When they don't want it anymore, don't feel discarded. Just know that your product is just not hot anymore. Know that you'll have to revamp that product or go into another field" (qtd. in Christian 2003).

Conclusion

Management involves more than behind-the-scenes activities of media and cultural professionals. The quotidian management of the self, as a technique of enterprising subjectivity, is an integral dimension of the reinvention of government and the contemporary neoliberal economy. How are enterprising subjects fashioned and called into being? Reality television, as we have seen, is an especially visible cultural site where techniques of self-management are demonstrated as a component of self-reliance and entrepreneurialism. What unites the various programming formats examined here is the application of market principles (cost/benefit ratios, risk-management strategies, marketing logic) to the cultivation of human capital. This application demands an intensification of everyday managerialism as individuals are detached from earlier notions of collectivity and public support and reconstituted as "entrepreneurs of the self" or CEOS of Me Inc.

Intermediaries are crucial to the heightened demands of self-managerialism in the current era. On reality television as in life, the scope of intermediaries has expanded, as lifestyle experts of all kinds now provide consultation, skills, resources, and motivational strategies, drawn from market principles, for maximizing one's own health, success, income, relationships, and well-being. The paradox is that as intermediaries are stitched into more and more domains of social life, the imperative to monitor, incentivize, and manage one's self accelerates. On reality television, virtually everyone is expected to be an entrepreneur of the self, incited to envision his or her humanity as the building blocks of a marketable personal enterprise. Everyone is expected to be strategic, to evaluate risks and benefits, to perform as a corporation of one. The rewards are alluring: beyond the financial and social security ascribed to strategic self-improvement, glamorous and creative work looms large in reality productions of all stripes. The technologies of the self currently circulated on reality television are deeply bound to established norms and hierarchies of race, gender, and class, but they are also posited as solutions to the fixity of inequality and the uneven distribution of resources. On reality television, everyone can be an enterprising subject, if this entails coordinating one's actions and choices with the free market rationalities of our times.

NOTES

1. The term "cultural technology" can be traced to Tony Bennett's (1999) application of Foucault's analysis of modern institutions to media and popular culture. See *Accounting for Tastes: Australian Everyday Cultures*.

2. For a more detailed analysis of the relationship between television and the reinvention of government, see Ouellette and Hay (2009), *Better Living through Reality TV*.

3. See Rose's (1996) "Governing 'Advanced' Liberal Democracies" for a detailed account of these changing regimes of citizenship.

4. Brown draws from early translations of Foucault's 1978–1979 lectures.

5. For a more detailed discussion of reality television's partnerships with law enforcement agencies see Ouellette (2011), "Real Justice: Law and Order on Reality Television."

II

Dispositions

5

Record Men

Talent Scouts in the U.S. Recording Industry, 1920–1935

KYLE BARNETT

In a 1971 interview, recording industry talent scout "Uncle" Art Satherley recounted his deep involvement in recording songs by key figures in country and blues music. Decades after he had left the recording industry, Satherley still felt it necessary to defend the people and the music he had recorded, from Ma Rainey to Gene Autry, from Patsy Montana to Blind Lemon Jefferson. Again and again, Satherley voiced an affinity for the "country people" whose music he recorded—music that, despite its popularity, had been regularly dismissed for decades as having little cultural or aesthetic value. Though this had started to change, Satherley warned his interviewers to take his life's work seriously, particularly as it related to "hillbilly music": "There's one thing I will command at all times, gentlemen, and that is respect for the subject. . . . I have been through the humiliation of this thing, for many years" (1971).

What was "the humiliation of this thing"? The defensiveness in Satherley's voice remained years after his retirement from the recording industry, despite recognitions that led to his induction into the Country Music Hall of Fame as one of the genre's patriarchs. His reverence for the music and the people he recorded reflects attitudes deeply informed by personal experience. But there was something else in Satherley's defense of the music he recorded and the people who played for him. Years after his pivotal role in recording those on society's margins, Satherley defended them out of a sense of what was right, but also as an assertion of his own worth, his own contribution to the recording industry, answering those who for decades had found him guilty by association.

This chapter examines how recording industry talent scouts negotiated a series of social and cultural divides in their everyday work during the industry's expansion and transformation between the World Wars. For many of these scouts, their work came to redefine an expanded mid-level managerial role at emerging and established recording companies, through managing talent, audience, and genre. Recording industry talent scouts moved through wildly divergent segments of society, working with ignored, ridiculed, or vilified people as a matter of course. Between the end of World War I and the rise of the Great Depression, the three foundational strands of American music—what we now call jazz, blues, and country—became viable genres in the U.S. recording industry. Talent scouts—not yet called "A&R men," or artists and repertoire agents—were key figures in this generic expansion, recording huge swaths of the American musical vernacular to find niches within which their record labels could compete. As talent scout Harry Charles remembered this speculative era, "You had to grab what you could get" (1968).

The descriptions of how they did this serve as early examples of what are now long-held beliefs within the industry. In *Music Genres and Corporate Cultures*, Keith Negus discusses how contemporary recording industry executives explain and attempt to lessen risk in the anxiety-ridden recording industry. He writes: "Corporate strategy aims to control and order the unpredictable social processes and diversity of human behaviors which are condensed into notions of production and consumption and which riddle the music business with uncertainties" (1999: 31). While Negus highlights attempts to explain the uncertainties of the 1990s industry, the desire to account for shifting tastes and attitudes of artists and audiences has long been at the heart of the business. Similar concerns are evident in the scouts' recollections of their own roles in the 1920s and 1930s, when the industry seemed all the more volatile and ephemeral. What is different in the scouts' accounts discussed here is that they spoke decades later, with the uncertainties they revisited safely in the past. Their role in assessing and responding to such risks was then placed in a larger biographical context, often in relation to their own industry legacies. The ways in which the scouts framed their roles tells us a great deal about how they managed the risk, as well as what they valued about their contributions after the fact.

Most talent scouts were white men, but there were exceptions. J. Mayo Williams, an African American talent scout for Paramount Records' race series, was key in locating talent in Chicago's burgeoning South Side music scene. In historical documents, passing comments about the role of female secretaries and assistants to these "record men" suggest that women may have played larger roles in terms of scouting talent than has been recognized to date. For example, Aletha Dickerson, Williams's secretary (and later wife), was a songwriter for the likes of Ma Rainey (Lieb 1983: 52). Further research will be needed to show the extent of the involvement of Dickerson and others in the recording industry's formative years. Decisions made decades ago regarding who was or was not important in the recording industry have no doubt influenced current archival resources.

To do their jobs, scouts were constantly working in at least three general registers: 1) managing the production, distribution, and sale of recordings for both their own profit and those companies for which they worked; 2) managing audiences, via gauging tastes and participating in the construction of genre categories; and 3) managing a range of socio-cultural differences in a variety of changing contexts. Tracing how the scouts understood their work helps to illuminate how such occupations emerged, while revealing the highly malleable nature of the talent scouts' managerial roles, particularly in the cultural authority the scouts asserted and the occupational tendencies of their everyday work. Studying these talent scouts in an era before such intermediate roles were defined allows a glimpse into how their day-to-day tasks blurred managerial and creative functions at a time when the recording industry was undergoing great change and nascent record companies were relying heavily on their expertise.

Talent Scouts, Industry Expansion, and the Phonograph Boom

In the first decades of the twentieth century, three companies dominated the sound recording business: Victor, Edison, and Columbia, known collectively as "The Big Three." Each of these labels was headquartered in the Northeast. Victor was based in Camden, New Jersey, while Edison's offices and labs were in West Orange. Columbia originated in Washington, D.C., but later moved offices to New York City with manufacturing facilities in nearby Bridgeport, Connecticut. These labels recorded a diverse array of material, often culled from talent they were able to locate nearby: military marches, Tin Pan Alley standards, Broadway tunes, light opera, sentimental pop ballads, and "foreign" releases geared to immigrant communities and the international export market.

Usually, the recording industry's first decades are told in terms of inventors, engineers, and technological innovation. In these narratives, Thomas Edison and Emile Berliner figure most heavily. Since Edison was closely linked to his Edison Talking Machine Company and Berliner had licensed his gramophone to the Victor Talking Machine Company, early histories tended to link inventor to technology to industry. But by the 1910s, the recording industry's dramatic transformation made such narratives untenable. This transformation was fueled by an influx of companies that had little or no previous involvement in the recording industry, which took advantage of expiring patents, and fought legal battles over playback formats in order to ensure their place in a growing business.

In the years during and following World War I, many of the patents that dated back to the phonograph's origins had expired, while others were being challenged in court. In just a few years, hundreds of new companies entered the recording industry, in many cases with little previous experience or knowledge. Initially, while new labels such as Paramount, Okeh, and Gennett pursued those musical genres that the majors were already recording, they quickly found that they could not challenge the majors by competing for talent working in well-established musical territory. Through trial and error, scouts at these companies soon realized that they would need to find market niches for audiences then emerging or long ignored and so turned to styles that the bigger labels had not yet fully explored. Rather than simply recording music already well defined by the industry, these scouts' roles expanded to encompass a broader managerial mission.

The recording industry's commercial and cultural expansion led scouts to music made by those derided by society in general. Several decades passed between the record industry's development and its commercial discovery of rural American music. While the U.S. recording industry's Northeastern locale may have kept it somewhat remote from rural musical sources, some generic experiments paid off, as happened with Mamie Smith's "Crazy Blues" (Okeh, 1920) or Vernon Dalhart's "Wreck of the Old '97" (Victor, 1924). In the aftermath of strong sales, industry insiders took notice, and scouts at most companies began to investigate.

Paramount, Gennett, and other labels took shape in the industrial Midwest, coinciding with the arrival of Southerners migrating there for work. This put such upstart labels in an excellent position to take risks with new genres. The migration was an uneven experience to be sure, with strictures often defined by race, class, and regional differences. While Jim Crow laws did not have the hold they had in Southern cities, black mobility in the industrial North was strictly limited. In a 1971 interview, Art Satherley mentions in passing black migration to Northern cities that had "opened up." White Southerners did not face the same difficulties, but nonetheless faced formidable socio-economic impediments. Chicago was a center for label activity, but significant amounts of recording and manufacturing also took place in smaller cities and towns. Gennett Records was launched by the Starr Piano Company in Richmond, Indiana, and is now known for its jazz recordings from King Oliver, Bix Beiderbecke, and Jelly Roll Morton. Paramount Records was launched by the Wisconsin Chair Company of Port Washington, Wisconsin, and is now recognized for blues recordings from Charley Patton, Blind Lemon Jefferson, and others. Companies like Paramount and Gennett learned how to manufacture their own records, after having gotten involved in the record business via making phonograph cabinets and phonographs (Barnett 2006). The foray that such companies made into an industry of which they knew little coincided with the arrival of Southerners, leading to subsequent musical collaborations with Midwesterners, and an expanding industry looking for new material.

The managerial roles of scouts required that they explain their work to their bosses, who relied heavily on the scouts' newfound expertise. To sell specific kinds of music by marginalized people to marginalized people, scouts needed a working understanding of that music's cultural importance—even if it was only to sell records. When interviewed about their involvement decades later, these men varied with regard to how they understood their roles and how important they considered the work they had done, as well as in the cultural distinctions they made between themselves and the musicians, genres, and audiences they helped to define.

Listening to the Old Cultural Intermediaries

Research on cultural intermediaries in the last decade has emerged mainly from developments in cultural studies, media studies, and the sociology of culture. This emphasis is not surprising, given sociology's emphasis on contemporary societal trends and the discipline's largely positive influence on both cultural studies and media studies. This chapter aims to follow Liz McFall's as-yet-unfulfilled call for greater attention to the predecessors of contemporary ("new") cultural intermediaries via media historiography. In "What about the Old Cultural Intermediaries? An Historical Review of Advertising Producers," McFall rightly argues that while roles for cultural intermediaries proliferated in the second half of the twentieth century, the roots of these "symbolic occupations" go back into the second half of the nineteenth (2002: 539). Yet little historiographic research has sought to account for the rise of cultural intermediaries with this long view in mind. Such a view may only be available in glimpses. Yet through analysis of archival interviews and other supporting materials, it is possible to better understand the crucial historical roles of talent scouts whose work challenges current distinctions between managerial and creative work.

In recent years, cultural intermediaries research has followed what has for some been an alarmingly broad agenda. Pierre Bourdieu's original definition of cultural intermediaries extended to workers "in all the occupations involving presentation and representation . . . in all the institutions providing symbolic goods and services . . . and in cultural production and organization" (qtd. in Hesmondhalgh 2006: 226). While the term was popularized via Bourdieu, most who write about cultural intermediaries at present agree that the work has reached far beyond his intended scope. In discussing the uses and misuses of Bourdieu's work, David Hesmondhalgh suggests that Bourdieu "seems to have intended the term 'new cultural intermediaries' to refer to a particular type of *petit bourgeois* profession, associated with cultural commentary in the mass media" and the specific emergence of new kinds of cultural workers in France during the 1960s—most notably, those in the advertising, public relations, and journalistic fields (2006: 226). Others, such as Keith Negus, argue for a more flexible use of the term, in that "it can be found used in a precise way, but in a quite casual manner" (Negus 2002b: 502). My fundamental concern is not how well the occupations I describe here map onto Bourdieu's specific formation. I instead am interested in the representational work of an earlier era when such occupations were less defined and gaining in importance. I want to emphasize the evolutionary nature of these occupations and the historical context in which they emerged.

Changes in the recording industry between the phonograph boom at the end of World War I and its consolidation with the radio industry through the early 1930s were so great as to suggest a shift in the field of cultural production. A shift in a series of social contexts (*field*) led to a corresponding shift in subjective responses (*habitus*) (Özbilgin and Tatli 2005). For Bourdieu, fields and sub-fields are created and recreated in what Hesmondhalgh characterizes as a "battle between established producers, institutions and styles, and heretical newcomers" (2006: 215–16). "Heretical newcomers" accurately describes those working at insurgent 1920s labels who created new niches in the recording industry through reshaping it. "These *position takings* by newcomers," Hesmondhalgh adds, "restructure and recreate the relevant sub-field and field" (2006: 216). At stake in the recording industry was the value of the content being recorded, in an aesthetic as well as economic sense. "The artistic field is a *universe of belief*," Bourdieu wrote. "Cultural production distinguishes itself from the production of the most common objects in that it must produce not only the object of its materiality, but also the value of this object . . . the recognition of artistic legitimacy" (1993: 164). This expansion of the field within the recording industry effected changes in industry *habitus*, and led to a "strategy-generating principle" allowing agents to act upon subjective dispositions based on experience, which the strategy itself represents (Bourdieu 1977: 72).

Much of the evidence here is culled from archival interviews with scouts from the era, recorded by folklorists, journalists, record collectors, and fans. This research would not be possible without their work. Interviewed scouts discussed here at length include Ralph Peer, who worked for Okeh and Victor Records, recording Jimmie Rodgers and the Carter Family at the famous "Bristol Sessions"; Art Satherley, who worked for Paramount, American Record Company, and Columbia, recording classic blues singers such as Ma Rainey, Blind Lemon Jefferson, and others, before turning his attention to the hillbilly market with Gene Autry and later, Bill Monroe. Unlike Satherley and Peer, Frank Walker spent his career with Columbia, where he was key in Bessie Smith's career. Walker was also involved early on in recording hillbilly artists such as Riley Puckett and Charlie Poole.

The interviews were all recorded in specific contexts and for specific purposes, which are not my own. While my contemporary interest is in the managerial and intermediating work of the scouts themselves, two different eras with several different agendas are represented here: 1) the 1920s and 1930s, or the era in which these scouts worked and early interviewers were most interested; and 2) the 1950s, 1960s, and 1970s, when later interviews were framed both by the interviewers' questions and methodological approaches and by the scouts' remembrances about the business with which they were involved.

Historiographic work in the recording industry faces various obstacles. Archives have not always recognized something as ephemeral as popular music and recorded sound to be of lasting significance. Many archives collecting recordings have not used their collections of print materials to place recordings within specific industrial contexts. Nor has recorded sound research had any clear home in existing academic disciplines; this has sometimes encouraged useful interdisciplinary approaches, but has also contributed to a lack of research treating the recording business as a media industry (Barnett 2009). And while we shape historical narratives around what evidence exists, it is also important to consider what is missing. When those involved discuss their scouting and recording practices, they do not indicate how these practices may be directly understood as management. Finally, the rise of interest in recording industry talent scouts did not always coincide with their life spans. Paramount's Mayo Williams died while plans were being finalized for an in-depth interview. Gennett's Fred Wiggins and Ezra Wickemeyer died before renewed interest led researchers to their doorsteps.[1]

Origin Stories: Getting into the Business

Most recording industry talent scouts of this era came from *petit bourgeois* backgrounds. Their fathers were shopkeepers, ministers, and farmers. Most were born and raised east of the Mississippi River. Not all of them identified themselves as "musical" before their involvement in the industry.[2] Many of them served in World War I and returned to the United States during an economic expansion that would lead to a bust in the early 1920s, followed by a boom for much of the rest of the decade and ending with the Great Depression.

The country within which talent scouts did their work was undergoing tremendous changes amidst great social volatility. The 1920s was an era of economic expansion, social change, and cultural creativity. If the "roaring twenties" replaced Victorianism with modernity, some Americans were energized while others felt threatened by shifting societal attitudes toward race, class, gender, and immigration. Jim Crow laws continued to enforce racial segregation in the post-Reconstruction South, while institutional racism existed in much of the rest of the country. Racial violence in the post–World War I years reached every corner of the country, with lynching being one means of enforcing racial subjugation along with race riots led by white mobs in Chicago, Tulsa, and elsewhere. In its mid-1920s resurgence, which included a national march in Washington, D.C., the Ku Klux Klan presented a more wholesome public face, while speaking in favor of "100% Americanism." Condemning African Americans, Catholics, Jews, and newly arrived immigrants, the Klan attempted to undermine these groups by seeking political control and continuing decades-old terrorist tactics (Kyvig 2004: 167). New economic opportunities available in urban areas did not appear in rural America, and the cultural gap between the cities and the countryside widened. Meanwhile, women continued to assert their cultural power in the decade after the passage of women's suffrage, as reflected in the temperance movement that led to prohibition, as well as the "flapper" culture that challenged traditional notions of femininity. In short, as a dizzying mix of changes shaped the decade, differing groups thought societal transformations had either come too fast or not fast enough (Down and Huber 2004: xv).

Amidst this societal churn and economic growth, some scouts got into the recording business in an opportunistic manner, with the sense that the music they recorded might prove to be ephemeral at best. Others considered it their life's work. All but a few of the most successful scouts stopped their work as record companies folded with the rise of the Great Depression, and many labels were purchased by radio companies. This effectively ended the era in which the recording business existed as an autonomous industry. The scouts understood themselves primarily as businessmen, whose work in the recording industry was a kind of happenstance. They often prided themselves on their ability to manage and organize in an industry known for being volatile. Most of them learned the record business on the job, figuring out their place in an industry in flux. In hindsight, scouts evaluated their work for the recording industry in a variety of ways, in terms of their managerial prowess, their industry successes, or the larger societal impact of the recordings they helped make. For some, looking back decades later, their involvement had little importance, while others sought to claim their roles in shaping American popular music. Despite differing attitudes regarding their roles, the shared commonality between these men was a sense of pride in the work they did, whether they understood it as a means to a financial end or part of larger societal transformation.

The scouts' differing backgrounds may have played into how they understood their part in the record business. Art Satherley, who worked for Paramount and Columbia, among others, came to the United States from Bristol, England, in 1913. He settled in Wisconsin, due in part to his interest in Native American culture.[3] Satherley's career in the recording industry had an anthropological component, perhaps tied to his role as first-generation immigrant, which led him to view his adopted country as an enthusiastic participant-observer. He soon had a job working for the Wisconsin Chair Company of Port Washington, Wisconsin. In 1918, the company launched Paramount Records, as part of The Wisconsin Chair Company's New York Recording Laboratories division (though the company's New York ties were tenuous at best). His employers asked him to learn the record business from the ground up (Bastin and Cowley 1974).

Frank Walker, unlike many scouts in this era, spent his entire career with a major label, Columbia Records. Walker grew up in a farm family in Fly Summit, New York. After his father's early death, Walker went to live and work on a nearby farm to support his family. He also played harmonica and "Jew's harp" in groups at local dances. After stints in business school, banking, and then military service in World War I, Walker relocated to New York City to work on Wall Street. Francis Whitten, an officer under whom Walker had served in World War I, had been appointed president of Columbia Records and asked Walker to work for him.[4] Walker remembered: "I said, 'I don't know anything about a phonograph record,' and he said, 'Neither do I, so you can be my assistant'" (1962). This relationship was emblematic of a larger industry dynamic, in which those who controlled company hires hired those they believed could learn the industry for them. Walker was able to learn how phonograph records were made at Columbia's Bridgeport plant.[5]

Ralph Peer is perhaps the best-known scout from this era, through his work for Okeh and Victor. Peer's father was a Columbia dealer and ran an appliance store in Independence, Missouri. While working with his father, Peer took the inter-urban trolley line to Kansas City where he picked up records and repair parts from Columbia's offices; this led to his being hired there to replace workers on summer holiday (Peer 1958). After a military stint during World War I, Peer returned to Kansas City, but soon left for New York, following one of his employers to Okeh. More than Satherley and Walker, Peer was born into an entrepreneurial family and sought to profit from the recording industry in ways that many other scouts did not envision. He helped to create mythic narratives about his artists which became key parts of his sales pitch, although decades later, he was dismissive of those he recorded. To some extent, scouts' backgrounds and sensibilities informed their approaches to their work as well as their understanding of its lasting relevance.

Getting the Job Done: Occupational Strategies, Cultural Attitudes, and the Rise of Hillbilly

Once established in the business, their reputations grew. Scouts' exploits sometimes appeared in the pages of *Talking Machine World*, the U.S. recording industry's trade magazine of note. A typical story of this kind, "Ralph S. Peer Visits Important Points South," appeared on May 15, 1925, and recounted a Florida trip Peer took with Okeh "jobber" (wholesaler) P. C. Brockman. "Both he and Mr. Brockman were highly gratified to find that Okeh records had achieved considerable popularity throughout this State, and they offered important sales suggestions to Okeh dealers that will undoubtedly be reflected in the retailers' activities in the next few months" (85). To an audience of retailers, scouts like Peer were represented as role models and depicted as self-made men whose triumphs and failures were their own. And if a retailer had faced difficulties, it was due to not following the advice of *Talking Machine World* or scouts like Peer. While articles offered advice as assistance, often the implicit message was that if a retailer faced difficulties, it was the retailer's fault. Scouts and their bosses were held up as examples on which retailers should base their own working lives, in a language borrowed from the emerging self-help business culture and popular psychology of the era. If *Talking Machine World* was filled with the latest industry accomplishments and occasional reports on scouts' efforts, the day-to-day reality of the work demanded a knowledge of shifting public tastes and a flexible approach to getting records to market and into the hands of listeners.

The scouts' everyday work responsibilities collapse any simple distinctions between management and creative labor. The recording industry's historically low barrier to entry has long set it apart from other traditional media industries, and newly formed labels of the era had small staffs who performed numerous tasks that we might now understand as managerial (organizing recording or sales trips) or creative (writing or choosing material for artists, determining the best take from a given recording session). It is clear from what historical evidence remains that recording industry scouts had a high degree of autonomy from their employers, many of whom knew little about the music they were recording or the social milieus from which it came. Those scouts who worked within record companies regularly performed tasks that bridged managerial and creative roles. In many of the new record companies that launched in the years during and after World War I, their staff was too small for them not to be called upon to function in a variety of managerial roles.

Art Satherley's work for the fledgling Paramount label confirms this approach: "Well, at that time, I was doing three things: I was selling, I had the eastern seaboard from Boston to the Florida Keys, on the race and country, and I had the studio in New York, recording. So therefore, I was looking for talent at the same time, you see" (Satherley 1969). Satherley began developing the Paramount label by perfecting the chemical formulas for record-making, focused on using as little shellac as possible due to its expense. Once he helped get the record manufacturing plant in place, he turned his attention to selling records, which then led to a larger scouting role. As he visited stores in larger Northern cities, he found that those dealers who were selling phonographs and records had already signed exclusive franchise agreements with Victor or Columbia. For Paramount and other such labels to try to compete with Victor, Columbia, and Edison by recording similar material was not a viable strategy.

By the early to mid-1920s, scouts were experimenting with recording music from a variety of sources. Following Paramount scout Art Laibly's experiments with recording what we would now call the blues, Satherley attempted to convert shopkeepers under exclusive franchise contracts with Victor and Columbia by offering Paramount's so-called "race records" (recordings of and for African Americans):

> I was then put on the road to sell these records. I was informed in Harlem, I was informed all through New York, and I was informed in Chicago that "we have a franchise with Columbia," and the next store would say "we have a franchise with Victor, and therefore we're not allowed to

take on any strange things. By the way, what stuff is this? I've never heard such funny stuff." And I said, 'Well, I say, you may hear of it later on in years." (Satherley 1969).

For scouts to convince stores to carry their records, they also had to explain the value of the largely unrecognized music they had begun to record. This need to convince prospective customers to consider these "strange things," recordings for which shopkeepers had sometimes little or no social, cultural, or aesthetic understanding, carried over to the scout's managerial tasks: to produce, distribute, and sell recordings, one also had to manage how these recordings were understood across a variety of contexts. Scouts like Satherley had to make the pitch that customers would want this music even if retailers didn't always understand the music they were hearing or the people making it.

What a lack of understanding meant in these historical accounts is difficult to interpret. Satherley suggests that retailers did not even have a frame of reference for understanding the music he had brought them. Enough scouts' accounts generally corroborate this, but lurking in this description is the possibility that scouts also encountered retailers' existing biases attached to the music and the culture from which it rose. Such biases are more easily seen in scouts' conversations with their employers at established recording companies, where bosses usually had to be convinced before recordings were brought to market. If scouts at smaller labels had an easier time convincing their employers amidst the search for a market niche, it was more difficult for those working at established labels with successful reputations to protect.

Concerns over how to manage emerging genres show up in specific ways. Marketing race and hillbilly recordings also presented a problem for record company cataloging. By the 1920s, recordings had been routinely given matrix numbers, identifying them as part of a discrete series. As they had previously done with records for the international and immigrant market, labels also launched separate series for both hillbilly and race records. As often happens when new genres or sub-genres emerge, future approaches were based in existing models with proven viability. Thus, domestic music from the rural United States was understood and managed in terms of protocols created for international and immigrant listeners. In an interview he gave decades later, Ralph Peer remembered the connection he had made: "I saw that this was really a business, like our foreign record business" (Peer 1958).

In his early work recording hillbilly groups, Columbia's Frank Walker found it was unwillingness more than a lack of familiarity that led to an inability to fully embrace the music. Walker recounted that it "was not understood [by] my own people. And they said under no circumstances would they put anything of that sort on the market. But after due pleading, pleading on my part, they agreed to let me do it providing we not make any mention of it in any way" (1962). Walker created a special matrix series, which effectively separated these recordings from the rest of the Columbia catalog. While this might have been to highlight the new series, Walker's recollection suggests that Columbia was concerned that the music of rural whites might somehow damage the company's reputation. As Walker remembered, his approach reflected his employers' reticence: "We would make a record and we would manufacture and release it and offer it quietly by a little letter to our various distributors throughout the South. And slowly, it caught on" (1962). In Satherley's recollection, he emphasized how Paramount executives had similar trouble with seeing the value of hillbilly as well as race records despite a need to differentiate itself from larger labels: "That's the country . . . folklore. They used to call them 'extreme illiterate.' . . . But they had no idea how big this thing would grow, in the years to come, and they did not recognize it for a quarter century, to be frank with you" (1969).

After initial sales warranted further releases, then came the matter of naming genres. The difficulty in creating a name that would work for musicians, audiences, and the companies themselves led to often telling periods of experimentation. This is nicely illustrated through the series of names used for what we now call "country." Initially, the recordings were labeled "old time music," or "old familiar tunes." The paradox of this music's commercial emergence is this: as a new marketing category for the 1920s recording industry, it arose looking back at an idealized past. In advertising copy, rural white musicians were sometimes represented as cultural missing links, sometimes earnest and often humorous remnants of a past era. The mixed feelings of company executives were imprinted in their depictions of those who made the music. As Karl Hagstrom Miller suggests, "Companies pitched the music as an ambiguous combination of folklore and hillbilly stereotypes that ultimately denied much difference between the two." (2010: 210–11). The effect was to offer up these performers as exasperating figures, whose behavior also engendered a strange kind of respect in their link to real or imagined tradition—who were packaged as a musical take on local color literature. This is evident in a 1925 article published in *Talking Machine World* entitled, "Henry Whitter, Okeh Artist, Real Hill Country Type," where we also find a useful reminder of just how long the recording industry has been selling authenticity to its listeners:

> Mr. Whitter is a real specimen of the Hill country, coming from Galax, Va., and on his first few trips to New York could not be induced to stay over night, coming in to the city in the morning, making what recordings were necessary and leaving before midnight arrived. Although he has overcome his shyness to some extent, he is still averse to what might be called 'seeing the town.' He insists that his trips from the railway station to the hotel and then in the recording laboratories are sights enough for him. (35)[6]

It would follow that talent scouts would play a key role in naming these new genres, after their work in locating, recording, describing, and packaging the music for both listeners and for executives at their own companies. Their work in this regard was part of a larger cultural circuit in which they operated. In the same year that *Talking Machine World*'s Henry Whitter article appeared, Ralph Peer asked another group of musicians from Galax, Virginia, what they called their band. When musician Al Hopkins responded, "Well, we're only a bunch of hillbillies from Virginia and North Carolina. Call us anything," Peer had found his name (Green 1965: 213). Yet the group was so nervous about their new moniker's effect that they stayed on the road longer out of fear of their hometown's reaction. When they returned home, Hopkins suggested that their own improving fortunes and the music's increasing popularity were part of a larger change in attitude. "Things happened so fast that by the time I did get home the name was real dignified" (qtd. in Hagstrom Miller 2010: 211). As "hillbilly" replaced "old time tunes" and other provisional terms for a wide swath of musical styles and approaches, many recording artists began to understand the term's power when used for their own purposes. Others would never make peace with it. Years later, it would be Peer who would take credit for popularizing "hillbilly" along with "race" as marketing categories for emerging genres. By transforming a variety of loosely organized styles under an evocative and malleable term with a long U.S. history, Peer had found a way to use a managerial approach to language—a careful, myth-infused framing of the artists he recorded—to attract listeners and increase sales.

The recording industry's initial approach to selling hillbilly and race records seems to suggest that companies were not sure whether these new categories would have much impact, and if they did, for how long. While a few of the most successful artists were supposedly signed to "exclusive contracts," it was common practice for artists to record for a variety of labels simultaneously, sometimes using one or more pseudonyms in the process.[7] But the major labels did not usually bother with such contracts. As Peer remembered from his Okeh scouting days, "Victor was so overpowering and Columbia so overpowering, they didn't see any reason to tie up the artists. They just let them do whatever they could" (1958). Art Satherley suggested that the lack of exclusive contracts at labels was due to a sense that these genres were likely to be ephemeral. In the common parlance of the time, Satherley and other scouts referred to exclusive contracts with artists as "tying them up": "This thing was so migratory, in those days, that no one thought of tying anyone up 'cause they didn't know, you see" (Satherley 1969).

As tentative and provisional as this sounds, the rise of new genres represents a significant turning point for the industry, one closely linked with scouts' experiences developing and managing new audiences. The genre categories were designed to target specific groups of listeners based on discrete differences in race, class, and geography, as well as musical taste. As Hagstrom Miller writes, "The decision to separate race and old-time music from the general catalogues marked a pivotal change in approach, the implications of which spiraled through the music industry in the 1920s. Separate catalogues suggested a correspondence between consumer identity and musical taste . . . they implied that unique segments of the population were satisfied by particular kinds of records yet uninterested in others" (2010: 188). This connection between consumer identity and musical taste would not have been as easily articulated without the speculative work of scouts in this era, whose work with a variety of constituencies allowed for this connection and subsequent transformations.

From the beginning, dividing race and hillbilly from the larger catalog and from one another involved an artificial separation of tastes and cultures. Just as folklorists had discouraged musicians from playing music outside of their perceived genre, the scouts attempted to neatly divide music for their own purposes, affecting people and music already connected in deep and complicated ways. The management of these artists, as well as the marketing and cataloging of these recordings did not so much recreate the eclecticism of existing tastes as they reflected what the scouts understood their prospective audiences would want, how they scouted music, and how they sold it within genre categories in regular transition.

Managing Genre, Managing Audiences

The history of the "race records" genre is long and complicated. Like hillbilly after it, the recording industry was generally reluctant to record it. This is not to say that African American artists went unrecorded. As Tim Brooks has convincingly argued, performers such as George W. Johnson, Bert Williams, and others recorded in the industry's earliest years. But in the 1920s, such recordings increased dramatically. The first race records focused on Vaudeville blues, which commonly featured a female vocalist backed by a small jazz band. Okeh Records was the first label to successfully experiment with what would soon be loosely known as "race records."

The Okeh recording responsible for race records' emergence was Mamie Smith's "Crazy Blues." Smith was a thirty-seven year old veteran of the Theater Owners Booking Association (T.O.B.A) circuit, which essentially functioned as an analog to mainstream Vaudeville for largely African American audiences. It was not a scout but a songwriter and musician, Perry Bradford, who convinced Okeh's Fred

Hager to record Smith after several appeals. Previous to race records, the *Chicago Defender* had long pleaded for more African American artists to appear on records. Even before the first Mamie Smith record was released, the newspaper celebrated the recording: "Now we have the pleasure of being able to say that [the record companies] have realized the fact that we are here for their service" (qtd. in Sutton 2008: 47). Once it was clear that Smith's "Crazy Blues" was a smash, competing labels all signed female blues singers, including Ethel Waters, Ma Rainey, Lucille Hegamin, Sara Martin, Bessie Smith, and others. While the labels first looked for a similar formula to Okeh's success with Mamie Smith, they soon started recording a wider variety of musical styles, including church choirs, vocal quartets, dance jazz, and African American string bands, as well as the country blues, which for some has now become synonymous with race records in general.

Based on conversations in the African American press, it is clear that audiences were anxious to have quality recordings that represented the breadth of their own creativity and experience. But how to find a market for such recordings outside traditional spirituals, Vaudeville numbers, or minstrel "coon songs" was far from evident. Even after artists were found and recordings were made, it was still an open question as to how they would be sold through retail stores. Not surprisingly, it was those working at a smaller label who were willing to take a chance. At Paramount, Art Satherley and other scouts had encountered difficulties getting race records into retail stores. His innovative response was to make a direct appeal via the African American press: "I went back to Port Washington, and we had a meeting there, and we decided that we would go to the *Chicago Defender*. Now, this is going away from what you might call country music, but this is still country music! . . . This was music made by the country colored people, you called them. Or called 'race records'" (Satherley 1969). The appeal made in the *Chicago Defender* ads had immediate impact, as Satherley described decades later, in language that inadvertently emphasized his own sense of the long-standing U.S. racial divide: "And we advertised for hundreds of agents, direct . . . uh, to sell records by the people . . . by *you* people and for *you* people. These records will cost you 45 cents a piece, be your own jobber, and you'll sell them for 75. That is how we got into the market to sell all stores, especially in the towns like Philadelphia, Newark, and New York, or anywhere that they had colored people that knew their own language" (1969). After their success with the *Defender*, Paramount started advertising in African American papers across the country.

As Paramount's scouting trips increasingly focused on what became known as "country blues," Satherley credited his own boyhood summers in the English countryside for his somewhat romantic understanding of the rural music of the United States: "I knew their qualities and I knew what would please them most" (1969). In framing his relationship with the music he recorded, he bragged about his managerial ability to win over prospective rural performers of different races, which he also indirectly linked to his father's role as clergyman and Satherley's own familiarity with sacred music. Thus, when being interviewed decades later, Satherley actively participated in the mythology surrounding the people and music he recorded. He had posited an intersection between his own history in the recording industry and his embrace of egalitarian Americanism, which he also linked with his Christian faith. In a 1969 interview, Satherley added: "My point is this. . . . That however lowly you are . . . is as great as you are. Because the heart of the average man *is* good." Beyond his management of what we now call blues for Paramount in the early years of the genre, Satherley also worked to contextualize what he did within a larger social agenda regarding race in ways that show up most clearly in interviews he gave in the last years of his life.

While "race" music was generally understood as an uplifting term and used in the pages of the *Chicago Defender* before the industry had settled on the name, the term "hillbilly" was somewhat derisive at the start. For Frank Walker, a sting from his own rural upbringing may have remained long after he had left the farm:

> It's sort of a billy goat who climbs up and down the side of a mountain, and for that reason he's called a hillbilly, and that's true of the people that lived down in that area. I mean they were people who climbed up and down the sides of mountains, and they were hill-country folks, so they became "hill billies," but it wasn't a favorable term, it's not a complimentary term at all. (1962)

Despite the record industry's expansion into race records, and increasing competition between record labels, rural white music remained largely unrecorded in the first half of the 1920s. "It was a matter of ignorance," Satherley recounted (1969). Another scout, Ralph Peer played the decisive role in establishing hillbilly as a marketing category. However, his attitude regarding the people he recorded lies at the ambivalent heart of American popular music in the 1920s. It may be that Peer's use of "hillbilly" suggests that he understood the possibility for the music's appeal far beyond its regional roots, and that the humorous aspects of the hillbilly persona might have a larger cultural appeal. It would be hard to imagine the U.S. recording industry without Peer's contributions, and yet he saw his involvement in these genres as a means to an end, managing and making visibly smart decisions about the recording business. In his own recollections, he focused on asserting himself as a skillful businessman who understood how to make money in the music industry more than anyone else.

Above all, Peer understood the power of exaggeration and of mythologizing the people and the events surrounding the music he recorded. As someone largely unromantic about the music he helped bring to market and the industry in which he worked, Peer nevertheless understood the use of sentimentality in selling records. More so than Satherley, Peer's mythologizing seems rooted *in the era in which he recorded* rather than in hindsight. He understood that myth might help sell records, and it was Peer who steered views of his legendary "Bristol Sessions" recording expedition along the Tennessee/Virginia border. "Almost from the start," Charles Wolfe writes, "the Bristol sessions were viewed through stereotyped and romantic lenses" (2005: 18). To manage the emerging genre and cultivate audiences, Peer steered the narratives towards those that he sensed audiences wanted. Wolfe recounts comments that Peer gave regarding Jimmie Rodgers, already a seasoned musician by the time of the sessions, as if he were a hapless wanderer, "running around in the mountains" before Peer recorded him, and was "laughed at" when he came in to record (2005: 18). From his recollections of recording the Carter Family years later, it's hard to tell whether Peer himself could separate what he had lived and what he had said. Peer recalled, "Well, remember that they were the very poorest farmers in a country where farming isn't much. And they didn't even have the clothes on their backs. They came in to record and brought the children dressed in rags, and we made these records" (1958). Despite evidence to the contrary, presented in subsequent biographical accounts, Peer's framing the Carter Family as stereotypical hillbillies had a lasting effect.[8] "Local tales in Bristol depicted the Carters as never having worn shoes and as never having been in town before," Wolfe observes; "such tales even characterized the Carters as having climbed into the studio via the fire escape because they were too embarrassed to be seen in public" (2005: 19). Peer recalled helping to further their career as their reputation grew, intimating that he might have preferred them to record something other than their rural repertoire and that he was disappointed in what he saw as the family's refusal to capitalize on their crossover potential: "So three years after that they were very prosperous people indeed and I kept, uh, building them up as much as I could. . . . What they recorded then, what they record now, is really low-down hillbilly" (1958).

Scouts' managerial decisions were often based on first-hand experience: encounters through traveling and meeting with storeowners, musicians, and consumers indicated what people liked and what they didn't. Scouts also often developed their own approaches to making sales or garnering talent, as well as to learning a bit more about prospective audiences. Frank Walker remembered a promotional event he planned while scouting and selling for the hillbilly market. While on a scouting trip, he tried an in-store experiment in Corbin, Kentucky:

[The shopkeeper] had a machine in there, an old-type machine and he used to sell some phonograph records. I said, "We'll make some signs and we'll put 'em on the window and we'll invite the folks in on Saturday afternoon, to listen to new phonograph records." I think we had a hundred and sixty that showed up. . . . Then I put on this new record and played it, all the way through. . . . One that nobody ever heard before, a new release that I had, but I just wanted to try it out. So I played it, and then I said, "How many of you people would like to own this record, have it for yourself?" Everybody held their hands up. Now I said, "How many of you would like to buy this record? Seventy-five cents, you know. How many of you would like to buy it?" And I would say out of the maybe one hundred twenty-five or thirty people there that maybe twenty or twenty-five held their hand up. And I said, "What's the matter with the rest of you, don't you like it?" And they said, "Yes, we've got no money." . . . They all wanted it, they all liked it, you see . . . but they didn't have the money. (Walker 1962)

The audience kept listening as Walker played more records, but when the storeowner wanted to go home in the late afternoon, Walker played a recording from operatic Italian tenor Enrico Caruso, which cleared the room (Walker 1962). In towns across the country, Walker would replicate this experiment, inviting people to a local store to hear the latest records, as both a way of selling records and garnering information about what consumers would buy and how much they could spend, as well as getting more detailed information about shifting consumer tastes. In town after town, Walker gathered information that would inform his decisions about the music he recorded and how the records might be distributed. Like many scouts, he developed a strong sense of how a given type of music might sell in one area as opposed to another.

Scouts also developed ways to garner talent and to further their own name recognition by word of mouth. Recognizing the advantage of having as many musicians come to them as possible, they could glean the best from what had been offered. Art Satherley developed a simple but effective method to create interest in recording with him among musicians, which he bragged about in later interviews: it consisted of a photograph used as calling card, autographed and featuring his name and address on the back side. He handed out thousands of photographs to potential artists, including those he had no intention of recording, in order to spread the word:

I used to have my picture taken every year. . . . So, I would go around first, then I would go and see our boys and girls playing, performing. . . . I would give out to all the boys . . . pretenders, rather, with their guitars and what have you, a picture, autographed to you. . . . I must have 20,000 pictures of myself out over the years, which understand are still in the houses, still in the guitar cases, today. (Satherley 1969)

Whether he recorded those specific musicians or not, the pictures served to spread the word of Satherley's recording activities and led to artists contacting him, which in turn allowed for a greater swath of musicians from which to choose.

When Ralph Peer left for Victor Records, after years of relative autonomy at Okeh, he recounted his difficulties in adjusting to work within the world's most powerful record company. Peer had planned to pay $25, his going rate at Okeh, for each recording. Victor had been interested in Peer's expertise in the hillbilly market, and as Peer prepared for his first scouting trip on behalf of Victor, he had a conversation with the company's director of classical music, Nathaniel Shilkret. Shilkret was a legendary figure at Victor Records, a composer and musician in his own right, heading up its light classical and international recording departments. In many ways, Shilkret acted as guardian of the Victor brand, which had become one of the most recognizable global brands by the 1920s, with tremendous financial reach and cultural capital. When Shilkret heard Peer's intentions, he felt such a price would reflect poorly on Victor. Why would a company at the top of the world's recording industry pay so little for a recording? As Shilkret told Peer, "You can't make any recording for $25 a piece. . . . this might get out, and we couldn't stand that kind of publicity" (Peer 1958). The interaction puzzled Peer, whose plans would be less and less tied to Victor or any other label in time. They would instead be focused on amassing a lucrative publishing company, Southern Music, which would become his primary business by the 1940s, with popular songs like "You Are My Sunshine," "You're Nobody 'Til Somebody Loves You," and others becoming radio staples at the time. Songs published by Southern Music were made famous by celebrities in both music and film, including Bing Crosby, Frank Sinatra, and Deanna Durbin. By the time Peer was interviewed in the 1950s regarding work he had done before his publishing business, his comments suggest that he considered it a means to an end, more important for what it allowed him to accomplish than what it was. If there was any value to his work with those jazz, blues, and country artists of the 1920s and 1930s, it was in developing his business acumen—and that was considerable. For him, that was the lasting importance of the recording work he had done.

Conclusion: What the Work Meant

In the oral histories recorded decades after the scouts' participation in an increasingly distant musical era, their range of responses concerning their work is striking. Those being interviewed attempted in a variety of ways to construct or reconstruct narratives about the work they did. For some, the memories were just too distant, and they were unable to recall enough to contribute. Nonetheless, talent scouts' archival comments do coalesce in a series of common explanations of their roles in the recording industry and how that industry worked.

Earlier in this chapter, I referred to Keith Negus's discussion of managing risk in the modern recording industry. Negus lays out two primary if incomplete means of explaining the industry's volatility, through what he called "cynical" and "mystical" approaches. Cynical approaches embrace overproduction in hopes that one or two recordings will connect with listeners, or alternately wait for entrepreneurs at other labels to establish new and viable paths (Negus 1999: 33–35). While Negus suggests that these descriptions are lacking in terms of explaining larger dynamics in the much more complex industry of the past few decades, they are more accurate when considering the somewhat simpler industry of the 1920s (1999: 33–34).

But what is more important in terms of the scouts' descriptions of their work lies in what Negus calls "mystical" accounts of industry change. In such mystical accounts of the recording industry, great music is discovered in good time, due to "inspirational, idiosyncratic 'music men,' despite the odds stacked against them by the obstructive 'suits' and mean-spirited accountants" (Negus 1999: 34). While present-day demarcations between "creatives" and "suits" were not as pronounced in the 1920s, the scouts who managed the expansion of the recording industry probably understood their own largely autonomous managerial roles as being fundamentally different from their employers'. In nearly every case, their ability to function autonomously, moving through society and working with many different constituencies, makes this clear. While there were differing views in later years on the people with whom they worked, ranging from admiration to disparagement, some scouts expressed as much or more comfort with the artists they recorded than with their bosses back home. But no matter their personal differences, recording industry scouts of the era clearly saw themselves as the kind of rugged individualists and "music men" whom Negus describes. (1999: 34).

How scouts' general identifications played out decades later depended on the importance each figure placed on his involvement. In recalling his pivotal scouting activities with Okeh, Ralph Peer blithely remembered the music in which he played a key role: "That's where I heard of the hillbilly and the nigger stuff" (1958). Given Peer's all-important role in the recording of American vernacular music, his comments about those who recorded for him are troubling in relation to other scouts, even given the virulent racism of the era. As Mark Zwonitzer and Charles Hirshberg note, Peer had little complimentary to say about hillbilly performers and was even worse regarding race records artists, despite professional friendships with Perry Bradford, Louis Armstrong, and others (2004: 84). For Peer, the hillbilly and race recordings in which he was involved were noteworthy mainly in relation to his business, as a stop on his way to creating a lucrative song publishing career. In his recollections with interviewer Lillian Borgeson, Peer was also particularly interested in settling scores, as when he discussed his tense financial negotiations with Jimmie Rodgers' widow, Carrie. When Borgeson asked Peer if he would admit whether the music he recorded was more important than he suggested, that in a hundred years the music "will be something that will have a lot of meaning to a lot of people," Peer responded: "Oh, it's just somebody had to discover it. And I did discover it and I figured these things out. But I did think that if I hadn't, somebody else would've figured it out" (1958). For Peer, race and hillbilly music was something to escape, though he was at the center of their emergence as marketing categories: "What I was doing unconsciously [sic] was to take the profits out of the hillbilly and the race business and spend that money trying to get established as a pop publisher" (1958). In his comments, it is evident that Peer wanted to emphasize his success as a businessman, though he often ended up undermining that accomplishment, along with the cultural capital he so desired, by downplaying his association with the people and the music that made him a key figure in recording industry history.

Art Satherley had scores to settle as well. Decades after he had left the record business, he was still defending the people he recorded and the music they made. All of these scouts were businessmen. It's how they defined themselves, above all: "This is my love, so therefore, wherever there was something going on, I was there. Saturdays and Sundays, to me my life. . . . I gave my life to this industry, to be frank with you" (Satherley 1969). In Satherley's recollection, his work, his Christian religion, and his adopted country were all connected. He referred to the U.S. as a "present-day Garden of Eden," while talking about how he recorded "the folklore" of the "country people" of varying races, ethnicities, and backgrounds. He wanted to celebrate the artists and the business people with whom he worked: "And I simply told them, 'you have not traveled far enough, or you don't know where you're living'" (Satherley 1971). In such comments, Satherley could sound more like a folklorist than a record executive. At the same time, he also wanted credit for his ability to manage artists, genres, and societal milieus in his long career in the recording industry. He called himself an "ear man," someone with an intuitive sense of what was or wasn't a good artist, song, or take (Satherley 1969).

Peer's dismissal and Satherley's glorification of the music they recorded and the people with whom they worked were both reactions to what Satherley called "the humiliation of the thing"; they were both responding to decades of derision. Despite his own dismissiveness, Peer lived long enough to see the folk reclamation of the music he'd recorded as interest in his earlier involvement grew. When the accolades grew in Satherley's later years, he clearly saw them as a vindication for himself as well as "the country people" he championed. Each mythologized his experiences through the explanations of the work they did and what it meant to them.

The layers of myth that obscure this era of the recording industry have been and will continue to be difficult to sort out. An additional difficulty lies in the recording industry's reputation as one of the least-beloved media industries, which predisposes us to champion artists and either denigrate or ignore those who worked behind the scenes. This is an especially sensitive issue, since many of these artists have not received their due. But the attention paid here to scouts has been an effort to offer a more nuanced and complex view of the recording industry and of their motivations and attitudes towards the work they did—particularly since so little detailed research of the industry exists, compared to other media industries. The recording industry's low barrier to entry and numerous eras of dramatic change mean that we are still figuring out some of the players involved in the business in which these scouts participated significantly. The sheer amount of recordings made further complicate attempts to sort it. As John Fahey writes, "We should now like to note that the largest repository so far of recordings American Folk Music (AFM) has been established not by academic institutions or folk music associations, but by the combined efforts of the American recording industry" (1997). The scouts had tremendous input in the shape that the industry took, via their management of the industry's sometimes dizzying transformation. The remaining curiosity lies in how they understood and expressed what their roles meant to them over time, in terms of the lasting importance of what they did.

NOTES

My thanks to the archivists at the Southern Folklife Collection at the University of North Carolina-Chapel Hill's Wilson Library and the Center for Popular Music at Middle Tennessee State University, who provided the archival audio interviews I use here. Thanks also to Moira O'Keeffe and the editors of this anthology for insightful and generous comments on earlier drafts.

1. Gennett researcher John McKenzie conducted a short phone interview with Mayo Williams, perhaps because of Gennett's involvement in the short-lived Black Patti label. See the John McKenzie Collection, Indiana Historical Society, Indianapolis. George Kay's 1950s research on Gennett mentions Wiggins's role as Gennett's recording director, though more recent research has emphasized recording engineer Ezra Wickemeyer's role. See Kay 1953.

2. Frank Walker noted his involvement in rural dance bands in New York, Art Satherley mentioned singing hymns in his father's church, and Harry Charles wrote songs that many of the artists he scouted would record.

3. "For some reason or other," Satherley remembered, "I chose Milwaukee because I'd read that up in the northern part of Wisconsin . . . there were quite a few Indian reservations." See Satherley 1969.

4. Whitten was a nephew of the duPont family, who had purchased a controlling interest in Columbia. See Walker 1962.

5. Once in the recording industry, not all continued to work in it. Walker left Columbia to start a concert business, promoting shows by Enrico Caruso and other popular classical performers in the upper Midwest and Canada, before returning to Columbia to scout talent. Between working for Okeh and Victor

records, Peer briefly considered work selling Norma automobiles, as well as thinking about opportunities in the pie business. For more information, see Walker 1962 and Peer 1958.

6. In the same issue, in an article touting Okeh's latest "Blue Book of Blues" catalog, a new "old time music" catalog is mentioned.

7. Identifying which artists used pseudonyms in which instances is an inexact process, seductive and maddening in turn. See Sutton 2005.

8. See Wolfe and Olson 2005, Zwonitzer and Hirschberg 2004.

6

Re-Casting the Casting Director

Managed Change, Gendered Labor

ERIN HILL

Though any commercial industry's mass-produced merchandise finds its ways to shelves in complex ways, this is especially true of the American media industry, which has developed complex work systems to manage a production process that is simultaneously factory-like and individuated in order to produce goods that are simultaneously commercial and artistic. Texts are created through an interlocking series of soft systems, developed over a century of massive technological and social change, and are held together by multiple, contradictory industrial mythologies, resulting in production processes that are often as messy, disconnected, and chaotic as their most successful products are clean, harmonious, and balanced.

The production sub-sector of film and television casting and, in particular, its gendered practices exemplify this messiness. Press and trade profiles of casting directors and their work tend to focus on casting's female domination,[1] in part because such focus provides a sense of historical symmetry, evincing shifts away from the old Hollywood values symbolized by "the casting couch," a euphemism for the exploitative practices for which casting was best known in the past. However, the profession's gendered state goes beyond a simple female majority in a way that is perhaps more indicative of regressive than of progressive industrial and socio-cultural values. In interviews, casting directors often make mention the of their job's gender-neutral requirements—the kinds of things that might be listed in a casting instruction manual. But far more often, they attribute their success in the field to their ability to regularly enact gendered performances and their aptitude for playing the feminine roles of wife, mother, hostess, and girl Friday. For both female and male casting directors, such gender binaries represent an important means by which to understand the field and their place within it, especially since many believe, per professional lore, that the job has been gendered in this way since the early days of film production.

For these reasons, at first glance, casting seems like a perfect example of the feminized fields whose work processes, conditions, and continued existence, I argue, are products of the sex segregation and feminization of certain types of low-status, extra-creative work in film history. However, closer examination of casting's history reveals significant complications to this theory as well. Unlike other, related feminized sectors, casting carries relatively high creative and managerial status in contemporary, below-the-line production hierarchies. And unlike those other feminized fields, the role of casting director was filled almost exclusively by men until the 1950s, and the profession continued to be male dominated until the 1970s. This male-dominated version of casting was an executive role, more closely linked with masculinized forms of management that emerged under Taylorism and requiring a largely different set of skills than those cited by contemporary casting directors as important to their work. Moreover, the kinds of creativity and leadership that are cited as modern casting's "best practices" defy simple categorization as originating in either historically feminized labor sectors or the studio-era casting director's practices and their 1900s Taylorist management roots. Indeed, rather than fitting neatly into one historical explanation or the other, casting is a mixture of the two, with some feminized aspects and some managerial aspects that descend from the scientific management tradition, along with many others which seem like unlikely hybridizations of both.

Here, casting will serve as a boundary case. Its contemporary practices, outlined in the words of casting directors themselves, will be traced from their origins in early twentieth-century systems of production, through the height of the Hollywood studio system's development in the 1940s, when executive-managerial casting decisions were made by male casting directors, but much of the other labor associated with casting was carried out by women in related, feminized production sectors. I will argue that these sex-segregated aspects of casting converged in the 1960s and 1970s, when the freelance, post-studio role of casting director shed its executive status and, as women entered the profession from related fields, acquired many of the same gendered expectations that had been imposed on female workers elsewhere in industry. I will further argue that in negotiating these expectations—performing gender in a manner acceptable to production culture, while also casting gender itself as a creative strength—female casting directors necessarily reformulated post-studio casting into the women's creative field it is today. Viewed in this light, modern casting can be understood as the product of a complex collision of economic and technological change, longstanding cultural scripts, and gendered expectations. The case of casting's feminization reveals the multiple, oftentimes fractured identities embodied by media practitioners through their roles in creative industries' complex work systems and the industrial logic underlying the continued existence of this and other gendered sectors of media production.

Scientific Management, Clerical Labor, and Women's Work

Contemporary casting directors frequently attribute their field's female domination to its considerable clerical/organizational component. Daily work in casting offices includes heavy helpings of such clerical-secretarial basics as "opening envelopes and answering telephone calls and Xeroxing sides and calling and setting up appointments, . . . scheduling the call-back sessions,"[2] as well as those organizational tasks involved in narrowing the field of actors for various roles, such as filing materials on different performers, checking their availability to work, typing lists of top candidates, etc. In professional history passed from casting director to casting director, the profession has "always been a women's field" (Meg Liberman, C.S.A., qtd. in Berman 2002: A8) precisely because so much of the work is clerical "drone work" of the type traditionally associated with women (Wallis Nicita, C.S.A., in Scott 1987). It is held that "it used to be the secretaries who took care of [this work] in the old studio system" (Deb Manwiller, C.S.A., qtd. in Seipp 2003) and that secretaries "were cheaper replacements when the men went on to more lucrative things like producing," because "we can type up our own lists and make a deal at the same time" (Jane Jenkins, C.S.A., qtd. in "Casting Directors" 1991). Though this oral history isn't completely accurate, the link it makes between casting's present female domination and feminized clerical labor is an important one. Its examination must begin with the oppositional relationship of the women's clerical sector and the new management tradition that emerged alongside one another in American industries at the turn of the twentieth century.

In the late 1800s, as the first motion pictures were being made in labs, the dramatic rise to importance of clerical labor in more established American industries was nearing its climax. To cope with rapid expansion, businesses in which divisions between clerical and managerial workers had previously been less clear devised more formalized hierarchies to allow functioning across multiple offices and factories. The introduction of Frederick Winslow Taylor's principles of scientific management, which promised maximum industrial efficiency through new systems of production, record keeping, and cost accounting, accelerated these shifts. Taylorism sought increased managerial control over employee work practice by re-appropriating special knowledge, supervisory responsibilities, and planning duties from previously self-governed production workers, and relocating these to managers in physically separate planning departments (Strom 1992: 41–60).

This efficient re-engineering of production resulted in vast increases in the number of non-verbal messages circulated at companies between increasingly deskilled and disempowered workers on factory floors and the increasingly powerful managers from whom they were now isolated both spatially and hierarchically. It also caused an important shift in the relationship of both message and messenger to the production process. Through their "clerical output" (Fine 1990: 12), clerical workers were increasingly responsible for linking all of an organization's employees through written marching orders without which "efficient" production lines could not function. To make the increase in clerical labor cost efficient, the clerical laborer's work process was similarly "subdivided into specialized tasks, mechanized, standardized and measured" so that it could be carried out more quickly and cheaply (Fine 1990: 95–99). Many men who had previously viewed clerical positions as apprenticeships exited the clerical sector and looked elsewhere for the level of pay, training, and advancement opportunity that sector had once promised.

Women were increasingly available to work at this time as whole families moved to cities to join the urban labor force. They were hired for tedious clerical jobs under the essentialist logic that women were neater, nimbler, and would "take more kindly than men or boys do to sedentary employment" (Martindale 1988: 18). The economic rationale that they could be paid less than their male counterparts was also crucial. Women's lower wages were culturally sanctioned by the widespread belief that their natural and preferred sphere was the domestic one, so much so that many companies instituted a "marriage bar" forcing female workers to retire once they wed (Strom 1992: 135). The minimal costs of training new female workers were offset by their disposability before they could demand the advancement or pay raises that had become economically unsustainable due to the proliferation of clerical positions (Harris 2003: 233). With few other options, female workers streamed into offices and factories as clerks, secretaries, stenographers, and an array of other clerical positions, so that by the 1930s, the percentage of female workers in some clerical fields had risen to as high as 95 percent(Davies 1982: 52). But though they tended to be more educated than male contemporaries who left school for farms or factories, few women advanced beyond clerical positions to managerial jobs, including even those management positions that oversaw female workforces in clerical departments. If men's production labor was devalued under Taylorism, women's clerical labor was rendered virtually valueless and invisible, producing no goods other than intermediate, paper products. Yet, through their labor, female workers absorbed the costs created by scientific management, and thus made possible the apotheosis of the figure of manager in industrial production and his endowment with the very power, knowledge, and agency that had previously belonged to clerical and production workers.

Though it was feared that women's work outside of the home would threaten the balance of perceived innate qualities that differentiated the genders—with woman being defined as moral, religious, emotional, aesthetic, intuitive, in complement to rational, logical, ambitious, strong, practical man (Davies 1982: 52)—these fears proved largely unfounded. Instead, when women took over clerical roles, the positions almost immediately expanded to include aspects of feminine performance and emotional labor and thus "sustained women's roles by extending their home functions to the job" (Harris 2003: 233–34). Business journals and women's magazines alike reconceived the new, feminine office as a home, and the new, female clerical worker as its mother, mistress, wife, caretaker, hostess, and moral center (Fleissner 2005: 70), brightening the office with feminine order and refinement (Fine 1990: 60-64), while gaining practice caring for male co-workers before they were required to do so for a husband (Harris 2003: 234). Like a housewife, the female clerical worker was expected to disguise her work through her "pleasing and delicate appearance" and manners (McHugh 1999:76). Qualities of a "good" female clerical worker were circulated by means of popular culture, as characters such as the true-hearted secretary quickly became staples in dime novels, plays, and the newest popular entertainment: motion pictures.

Though early filmmaking technology emerged from the masculinized realm of the laboratory, the businesses that sprang up around moviemaking were not unfriendly to women. Informal work systems that developed under cameramen and directors in the 1900s were more artisanal than industrial, with a few skilled craftsmen working in a loose hierarchy and observing few planning or cost accounting procedures (Bordwell et al. 1985: 116). Far from being segregated from male counterparts, female workers in early productions were encouraged to "double in brass," or pitch in wherever production called for them to do so (Mahar 2006: 38); in the process, many women rose to positions of creative importance (Francke 1994: 6; Beauchamp 1997: 37, 39). However, by the 1910s, increased demand for product prompted the building of studios with greater production capacity, and the implementation of Taylorist principles in their organization. Film labor was standardized, and production was divided into departments in units headed by directors (and later producers), reporting to central managers (Bordwell et al. 1985: 124, 135). Multiple, large-scale productions were planned and organized through distributed continuity scripts and thorough record keeping. Thus, by the mid- to late 1910s, film productions once under the steam of the cameraman or director alone now fell under the direction of managerial figures and ran on paperwork—all of which was typed and distributed by stenographers and secretaries.

Where clerical workers might previously have been ancillary employees in film companies, they were now indispensable primary elements of the filmmaking process (Bordwell et al. 1985: 135). And studios, eager to shuck off the entrepreneurial, outsider status of earlier days and demonstrate that they were players in a big business, reverted to the more traditional gender norms of other industries. High-status creative fields such as directing and producing became increasingly closed to women, while clerical labor, along with jobs rooted in feminized domestic and retail manufacturing labor sectors became associated with women almost exclusively. Entire clerical departments sprang up to connect increasingly distinct jobs and departments.[3] Film production jobs that were created through the process of standardization and separation of tasks, and that took place largely on paper, were soon feminized and segregated by sex.[4] Women's jobs at studios also acquired their share of feminized duties. Secretaries to moguls such as David O. Selznick and Louis B. Mayer not only typed, but organized, managed, femininely disguised, and performed their own labor in ways that fit the needs of their employers.[5] Their work included caretaking, nurturing, managing emotional content of messages, and filtering meetings, phone calls, and memos away from employers by standing in as their proxy. Similarly, on film sets, script supervisors like Peggy Robertson and Arlene Thompson served as timekeepers, ruleminders, and emotional managers for the creative process (Robertson 1995, Young 1977).

Emotional Work and Feminine
Performance as Creative Support

Contemporary casting directors also attribute the field's female domination to emotional aspects of the work that, much like the feminized duties women's studio jobs acquired, are tied to notions of gender and require acts of feminine performance.[6] Casting directors, like female studio workers, seem both to be aware of gender as a construct and to have internalized many of the very gender binaries that are a product of that construction. Instinct and intuition are often cited as keys to women's casting success since they "frequently have good instincts for casting" (Juliet Taylor, C.S.A., qtd. in Shewey 1982) for which actors have "the right chemistry" and for which is "the most interesting story to tell" (Janet Gilmore, C.S.A., qtd. in Seipp 2003). These statements echo traditional notions of women's intuition, which tied women to nature and emotion over logic and characterized their decision-making as more instinctual.

Communication skills are cited as important for casting, which, with its multiple sessions involving hundreds of potential hires and creative players, requires much back-and-forth relay of information. Though communication skills may be seen as gender-neutral in many contexts, here they are framed as qualities and talents in which women have a natural or socialized tendency to excel, because they "tend to be a little more natural communicators," are "better able to do more than one thing at the same time" (Janet Gilmore, C.S.A., in Seipp 2003), are better suited for a job which "requires great care for details" (Juliet Taylor, C.S.A., in Shewey 1982), and are predisposed to cooperative work. There is a conception of women as better suited to the social aspects of what is "a more people-oriented profession" (Juliet Taylor, C.S.A., qtd. in Shewey 1982) in which "you have to be enormously interested in people, to the extent that you put your own ego aside. Women are trained to do that, to listen and to be very interested in all kinds of people" (Juliet Taylor, C.S.A., qtd. in Shewey 1982).

Descriptions of casting's feminized aspects call to mind the concept of "emotional labor" advanced by sociologist Arlie Hochschild, in which workers in service professions are required to coordinate their feelings with their labor so that "the emotional style of offering the service is part of the service itself" (2003: 5–9). Hochschild describes emotional labor as any that requires the suppression of feeling in the worker "in order to sustain that outward countenance that produces the proper state of mind in others" (2003: 7). She further states that traditionally, the management of emotion "has been better understood and more often used by women as one of the offerings they trade for economic support," often through "creating the emotional tone of social encounters" (2003: 20). And thus, while men may do emotional labor for wages, they are more likely to be seen as individuals who happen to do so, whereas female workers are more likely to be seen as members of a group (women) whose members specialize in "the 'womanly' art of living up to *private* emotional conventions." (Hochschild 2003: 20).

The emotional labor required of casting is especially apparent in casting directors' descriptions of casting sessions, in which expectations and emotions of actors, directors, producers, and executives come into play. Casting directors carefully manage tensions by setting the emotional tone in sessions. They make sure "that actors feel very comfortable, that directors feel very comfortable, that you tear down as many barriers between them as possible" (Juliet Taylor, C.S.A., qtd. in Shewey 1982), while also ensuring "that everybody feels they are part of it" (Justine Baddeley, C.S.A., qtd. in "Roundtable" 2006). Indeed, "keeping everybody happy at the same time" (Kim Davis-Wagner, C.S.A., qtd. in "Roundtable" 2006) is regarded as one of the most difficult aspects of the work, requiring that casting directors "figure out how to please all of those people," when "you might have one, five, seven, twelve people who will all participate in the choice about who this actor is going to be."[7] Casting directors make frequent comparisons between their roles in these meetings and women's traditional roles in the domestic sphere. Since "it's almost like women have a genetic hostess gene," sessions are likened to home entertaining: "Sometimes you do feel like a hostess at a great party" (Juliet Taylor, C.S.A., qtd. in Shewey 1982), "introducing the directors, . . . making the actor comfortable in your home,"[8] "keeping the room alive, getting everyone excited about the next actor, lifting the spirits of the director if 20 people pass on the part. You're like a good wife in that respect. You make sure everyone gets what they want for dinner."[9] Casting directors cite other ways in which the job is "like being a wife"[10] or mother, such as the caretaking involved: "The better casting directors will nurture actors so that they're comfortable in the room,"[11] they say, while "casting directors who do not make people feel that they're well taken care of don't tend to work with those people ever again."[12]

As important as it is in casting sessions, emotional labor is equally important afterward, when delivering good and bad news. Both internal and external emotional management is necessary when "you have to tell people they did or didn't get parts,"[13] or that actors passed on parts, and while "it can get you down having to say 'no' to so many people so often" (Wallis Nicita, C.S.A., in Scott 1987), good casting directors can limit the emotional impact on others through understanding that "there's a politic way to deliver news without offending sensitive people. You have to learn who has a thin skin."[14]

Vicki Mayer has observed a tendency among reality "casters"[15] to "internalize a binary logic around gender and sexuality, emphasizing organic or natural bases for their talent," rather than training or job skills that are more associated with commerce. The effect is a devaluing of their labor, "undermining its skill set in comparison with jobs that required certification or the registration of formal education on a resume" (2011: 134–35). Though casting directors similarly cite "natural" talents, unlike Mayer's subjects, they also make much of those skills required by their jobs that are more in line with masculinized business traditions such as dealmaking, negotiation, budgeting, and pitching services to new clients. So while discourse around their work often begins with or focuses on female domination and women's skills, casting directors are also quick to point out that their work entails many more "hard" skills for the economic and political juggling act required to "make the budget work by delivering actors who satisfy the requirements of the roles while bringing a certain panache to the project" (Mike Fenton, C.S.A., qtd. in Scott 1988). They frequently emphasize the complexity of the dealmaking process, which starts with budgeting, for which casting directors must have a nuanced understanding of the inner workings of the production process, and know "a tremendous amount about deals. . . . How do I work it out with an actor who I want but has got another movie to figure out how they can do both jobs? How do I not have enough money for everybody I want

and manipulate my budget so I can get this actor?"[16] Casting directors must also be on familiar terms with the legalities involved in "putting together a deal memo,"[17] or contract, for which "you need to be
political on both sides."[18] Casting's other "hard" skills include pitching
casting services to prospective clients,[19] managing workflow to casting associates, assistants, and interns, as well as managing newly hired
actors before their first work calls and relaying scheduling and wardrobe instructions.[20]

These managerial duties (financial and organizational planning,
instrumental leadership) fall in line with more traditional, masculinized notions of management than the emotional management required
in casting sessions, and are a characteristic that contemporary casting
directors have in common with those in the studio era. However, the
similarities end there, since studio-era casting was more consistent with
Taylorist traditions of management than with contemporary casting's
methods.

Early casting practice was largely a modified version of theatrical
casting, in which actors were known and hired for "lines of business"
they'd been trained to play. Since their faces and body types were what
film audiences responded to, film actors were categorized by physical
rather than character type. "Typage" dovetailed nicely with developing
efficiency practices, under which casting quickly moved from something done by a cameraman or director, selecting actors from those on
hand, to a more standardized system (Bordwell et al. 1985: 149). Under
"casting efficiency," actors became simply another asset to be tracked,
as theatrical agents and, later, casting directors "divided humanity in
sections" (qtd. in Pickford et al. 1919: 29). Classifications were assigned,
recorded, and cross-indexed by early casting workers, essentially lock-
ing each actor into a specific type that was noted in their records for
ease in distributing them to various productions (Bordwell et al. 1985:
149). Studios developed the contract system by which they acquired
and retained actors as studio properties.

By the 1930s, the casting director was fully established as the lead or
primary manager of a studio's actor assets. Though studio bosses, various executives, producers, and directors might all participate, casting
directors guided the process of decision-making around the allocation
of studios' most important resources (Davis 1993: 41). In this sense, they

were much closer to mid-to upper-level decisional managers of operations or production than their contemporary counterparts. The casting
director's studio-era managerial/executive distinction was reflected in
casting's typical separation from production, both geographically and
in terms of studio workflow and hierarchy (typically grouped with the
studio's legal and executive branches, which served as the center of studio planning and management).[21] Moreover, casting was often housed
in offices near those of other planning departments such as publicity
and advertising, all of which were headed up by male executives and
supported by a largely female clerical staff (Davis 1993: 42). In keeping with sex segregation, the female workforce typed and maintained
the clerical output—casting lists, meeting notes, memos, etc.—that was
casting's physical product. As was the case in other scientifically managed firms, men occupied the managerial role of casting director almost
exclusively, and heavily dominated the related positions of casting associate and assistant.

In an early production study, James S. Ettema (1982) used the concept of "players-in-position" to describe media workers whose roles
place them in position "to participate in the decision-making of the
organization," based on hierarchy, expertise, control of information,
and access to channels of agency such as negotiation (94). However,
though contemporary casting directors do negotiate on behalf of
the players-in-position in their productions, they do not see themselves as such players. Instead, they frequently mention their position's lack of direct agency in statements such as "actors think we have
that power, . . . [b]ut we aren't the ones who make the decisions on
who gets hired" (Mike Fenton, C.S.A., qtd. in Maslin 1977), and "it's
all really the director's choice. . . . In the end, we're invisible" (Billy
Hopkins, C.S.A., qtd. in Collins 1990). They characterize their power
as limited to the indirect agency of subtly influencing and persuad-
ing decision-makers. In the words of one casting director, "there is a
LOT of psychology involved in handling the large groups of the creative team. . . . You want them to hire 'your guy' and you have to get
them to feel that it was their idea in the first place!"[22] Others describe
delimiting the solution to the casting equation, rather than deciding on it themselves, saying, "I'll try to read 30 or 40 people for any
decent sized role and whittle it down to 5 to 10 for the director" (Ellen

Lewis, C.S.A., qtd. in Kane 2010). Or they say that "The only power we have . . . is to tell an actor, 'No, you can't go in to see the director'" (Mike Fenton, C.S.A., qtd. in Maslin 1977). Still others imprinted their tastes by suppressing their own egos when "you see what you think is right in fact, but you can't go in and tell people. . . . I think it's easier for women to kind of throw back their own vision and sort of nurture people into [a decision]," than "be heavy-handed about my ego needing to say 'This is it.'"[23]

In fact, modern network and studio executives in charge of casting are much more closely aligned with studio-era casting directors, overseeing casting directors, other executives, and decision-making at the level of a "player-in-position."[24] Casting executives do not work on individual projects under the aegis of the studio or network as casting directors do; they also function similarly to the other executives that contemporary casting directors describe as having to please through performing emotional labor. However, as shall be seen, these executive casting positions are also a site of early gender integration, and thus do not fully explain the departure of men from the profession of casting director or the arrival of larger numbers of women in the field.

There is evidence that female clerical workers began to make limited inroads into casting, as well as other paper-based planning departments, in the late studio era.[25] However, with few notable exceptions, these workers never rose to the level of manager or head of their departments. Other than Ruth Burch, who claims to have been promoted to casting director by Hal Roach sometime in the 1930s or 1940s (Steen 1974: 354), there is little evidence to suggest that any women ascended to the level of casting director until the post-studio 1950s, when Marion Dougherty and others report promotion to casting director, often in new TV divisions. Still, this lineage does little to clarify how it was that between the 1950s and the late 1970s, casting became not only gender-integrated but heavily female-dominated, or how feminized duties became not just an added value provided by female casting directors, but their primary value and a means through which they operated creatively.

In truth, many of these feminized, emotional labor duties did exist in the studio era, not in casting but in nearby talent departments (Davis

1993: 80). While the traveling talent scouts tended to be male, most other jobs under the banner of "talent" went to women, presumably because of the "feminine" skills associated with them (Davis 1993: 85). After the executive decision was made to sign talent, it fell to the drama coach and other female studio caretakers to nurture and develop them, both personally and professionally. To prepare for stardom, young contract players underwent an extensive training program, from acting, dance, movement, diction, riding, fencing lessons, right down to the selection of their clothes and, if they were successful enough, the setting up of households in keeping with their image (Davis 1993: 132). Drama coaches read studio projects with new hires in mind and brought the hires to the attention of producers and executives who could place them once they were ready (Davis 1993: 86). Unlike studio casting directors, talent workers made daily use of the female-associated skills that today's casting directors describe, such as intuiting actors' "rightness" for roles, nurturing actors, performing emotionally as acting teachers, and participating in the decision-making process through influence and solution delimitation, rather than direct commands. Here again, the studio can be seen making use of women's labor in specific, targeted ways. And here again, women can be seen adding value to their labor through feminized duties.

Though producers and executives controlled studio casting, today's casting directors emphasize that the director is the leader of the process and the person whose vision they follow: although "our job might be to keep everybody happy, it really is to direct the casting process for the director" (Debra Zane, C.S.A., qtd. in "Roundtable" 2006). The ideal work experience is "when you really are in sync with the director. It is almost like you are trying to crawl into their brain, and it is about fulfilling their vision" (Ellen Lewis, C.S.A., qtd. in "Roundtable" 2006). This form of mindreading-as-service seems linked both to emotion work and to the new creativity identity of contemporary casting directors, who see themselves as artists and craftspeople rather than executives. In the years of studio decline, contemporary casting's trailblazers began to distinguish between themselves and casting directors in the old Hollywood style, whom Marion Dougherty described as "a grocery-list maker [who] believed casting meant that if you make a list of everybody from Shirley Temple to Tallulah Bankhead, somewhere in between you had to have somebody who was right for the part" (qtd. in Georgakas and Rabalais 2000: 26). This negative assessment of "grocery list" casting hints at a shift away from scientific management practices such as typage. Where previously it had been standard practice at Warner Bros. "for the producer and director to sit down with the casting director and cast a film in 20 minutes" (Shewey 1982: 19), studios' economies of scale were changing.

In the economic downturn that followed the Paramount consent decree and forced divestiture of 1948, downsizing studios gradually ended the contract system for most talent and craft workers and outsourced much production labor on a freelance, per-project basis (Cook 2002: 21–22). Smaller firms sprang up around various aspects of production (from craft service to sound mixing) and ensured their survival through the strategy of "flexible specialization," under which work processes were customized to fit the individual needs of clients (Scott 2005: 39). Though there were casting directors on staff and talent departments in operation at studios throughout the 1950s and 1960s, as the number of contract players dwindled, casting was increasingly outsourced to independent casting directors who had begun their own firms for the purpose.[26]

In its freelance incarnation, casting struggled to reconcile studio-era practices with a new economic model. Casting directors now drew from a pool of actors that reached into the tens of thousands and that included freelance stars who had to be courted and hired rather than simply assigned as they were in studio days ("C.S.A. Searches" 1989). The process initially veered toward tried and true efficiency techniques to narrow the field and cast dependable, understood "types" in roles quickly (Turow 1978). However, new Hollywood soon sought a less generic, more organic version of casting.[27] A new generation of film directors came to the fore, emphasizing location shooting and grittier, more "authentic" stories, aesthetics, and actors. Freelance casting directors, in line with the trend toward flexible specialization, adjusted their process to fit different directors and producers. They were increasingly expected to "read a script with the insight required to understand how it would translate to the screen and with the knowledge of acting talent needed to cast every role" (Georgakas and Rabalais 2000: 26). It was no longer useful "to bring in 20 people who are similar"; rather, it became important to consider different ways roles could be played and bring the producer or director "five different but very good actors for consideration for a single role, not 100 clones" (Wallis Nicita, C.S.A., qtd. in Scott 1987). The process of reading actors for roles became more intense, and multi-staged. Freelance casting also involved more negotiation between more players on all sides, and was more fraught, dramatic, and emotional as a result.

Divorced from studio hierarchy, casting shed its executive identity and took on one more in line with production crew positions that had also gone freelance. In the process, it absorbed many feminized duties previously carried out by female talent workers, and saw an increase in its clerical and administrative workload. Women flocked to and flourished in the role of freelance casting assistant, associate, and director. In fact, so many women had become casting directors by the late 1970s that when studios and networks began gender integration of their executive ranks in order to head off public pressure for equal rights, they hired female VP's of casting, rather than production, since "casting was one area of the industry where companies thought it was safe to put women, and where they thrived" (Gregory 2002: 11). By 1980, women dominated the field,[28] and by 2001, this female domination had reached new levels in areas such as major industry awards, such that "of the 24 casting directors nominated for feature film work in [that] year, 23 were female; and of the 54 nominated for primetime TV, 43 were women" (Bergman 2002: A8).

Given this history, traits of contemporary casting that do not fit neatly with traditional notions of management or feminization may be viewed as a hybrid of the two and, in their efficacy, be seen to represent innovation. One of these hybrids is evident in the form of leadership that characterizes most freelance casting companies, wherein most casting directors work in partnerships. The arrangement allows for more work to be taken in, since, "if you have two partners, you can have eight jobs, whereas, if you just work alone, it's very hard to split yourself up, and you only can do one, maybe two jobs."[29] Because of these partnerships, leadership tends to be more collaborative as well. In order to keep up with the complexity of multiple projects at multiple phases, each requiring a heavy volume of clerical, informational, and

communication work duties are shared out amongst staffers in something closer to a lateral network, rather than a single, linear chain of
command running from casting director to intern. At casting offices
in the midst of casting several roles, it is common to see casting staffers shouting bits of information about actors and availability across the
room to casting directors—some of whom work so closely that they
share offices with their partners—pooling knowledge in a form of collective intelligence that sidesteps formalities often imposed in more traditional, top-down businesses through rank and hierarchy.

This level of cooperation is unusual even for traditional business
partnerships. It resembles the organizational model of the democratic
workplace, in which management is shared more evenly among workers. This model, which predates the twentieth-century system of com-
mand-and-control, has begun to be re-popularized by organizational
theorists in keeping with their field's new focuses on group cohesion
rather than corporate strategy.[30] It is also an organizational mode that
has been identified with groups of women, who are socialized from
childhood to form and maintain lateral same-sex interpersonal networks of peers by seeking consensus, connection, and rapport with others. Meanwhile, men, driven toward contest by biology and socialization, seek status in a hierarchy among opponents and even peers (see
Tannen 1994). It seems possible that a more democratic organizational
mode has found greater functionality in the largely female world of
casting because such collaborative practices have already had space to
take shape there.

Casting directors' continued adaptability, forged through their
unusual path to the field, may also be seen as useful in helping them
adjust to constant change on managerial, creative, informational, and
emotional levels. Flexibility of this kind is a sign of a skilled casting
director, who "helps from the moment that you do the list or pre-read
that actor, pick that actor and navigate the whole process with them"
in a process that's constantly evolving: "You're always dealing with new
people and new situations. So you have to become adaptable. And it's
psychological in some ways in terms of how to manage different people
and different situations to get the best possible cast."[31] In the current
global economy, in which technological and economic complexities
demand increasingly responsive workers, casting directors, as adaptive

feminized-managerial hybrids, may represent the ultimate flexibly spe-cialized service professional.

However, this incarnation of casting can't be seen in an entirely positive, progressive light, since, in fitting themselves to the needs and expectations of their clients, industry, and larger culture, female workers always have necessarily engaged in an act of contortion. Like the traditional wife to whom several interviewees compared them-selves, the casting director's ability to impact a film or television text rests primarily on her ability to perceive and respond to the thoughts and feelings of others, rather than her own. Meanwhile, like a tradi-tional husband, the producer or director of a project is able to directly control the experience of the casting director. Said one interviewee, "when you feel like you're just a waitress serving up actors where they don't care about your opinion, you oftentimes don't have a connection to it."[32]

For these reasons, though casting directors want and deserve to be seen as artists, their work falls in line on a number of levels with what I characterize as "creative support" in professions requiring various com-binations of emotional work and feminized duties to facilitate the cre-ative vision of a superior. One casting director's statement that casting was "more support art, it's more of a craft in some ways, . . . and it's a craft that supports the art of other people,"[33] reflects this creative sup-port function directly. Others indicated this more indirectly in state-ments about getting inside the heads of directors to help with their cre-ative vision. Still others compared casting to another kind of creative facilitation that, while not feminized, has traditionally been more open to women: editing. Again, this form of creativity comes through delim-itation as "you're not bringing in the whole world, you're editing the process" by cutting out "90% of what is sent to you and showing the 10% that they need to see."[34]

The indirectness of casting directors' agency magnifies their sense of lowered creative status amongst peers in production, such as cinema-tographers or art directors. Many casting directors feel a lack of respect toward their profession in "an industry that sees us as technicians rather than artists," and where "casting isn't seen as an autonomous creative process" (Risa Bramon-Garcia, qtd. in Collins 1990). And as in other feminized fields which are often undervalued, casting directors are often erased from the creative product in terms of credit. They believe in their own creative importance to the process, but however essential they are to movies and series' success, casting directors only recently became eligible for the Emmy, and are not eligible for Academy Awards at all.

This lack of professional respect and creative credit seems to be reflected in casting directors' pay, which, though it averages in the mid five figures for studio films, is considered low given the twelve to fourteen weeks that a staff of two to upwards of ten people will spend to cast a film. Marion Dougherty was reportedly fond of saying that only women could afford to do casting (Juliet Taylor, C.S.A., in Shewey 1982), and this statement takes on additional weight in light of the fact that, until 2005, the field had no union to collectively bargain for the salary guarantees, health benefits, and pensions enjoyed by nearly every member of film production crews above the level of PA (Dyan 2005). In 2001, Tracy Lillienfield explained the lack of unionization by saying that after casting became freelance, "we were fighting for jobs and struggling to get people to recognize that there was even a job called 'casting director.' We just worked so hard to do what we do that we forgot to take care of ourselves. I've worked for 23 years and I have no pension" (qtd. in Bergman 2002: A8).

In truth, casting directors did not simply forget to take care of themselves, but rather chose to take care of potential employers first, as a strategy for making creative inroads. In the late 1970s, a small group of casting directors led by Mike Fenton attempted to unionize through IATSE (International Alliance of Theatrical Stage Employees) as the Casting Director's Guild Local 726 ("C.S.A. Searches" 1989). But this union was quickly scuttled by other casting directors who took out an ad in *Variety* stating that its signatories believed that such a union would have a detrimental effect on their casting functions, as well as on "the producers, directors and writers with whom we work."[35] The anti-union faction —of which fifty out of sixty-four members were women—was motivated by the fear that if they submitted to collective bargaining, they would be viewed as enemies of the creative elite whose recognition and acceptance they had been courting since they became independents. Though casting did later unionize, casting directors haven't

achieved the standards of pay and work regulations of nearby, unionized, male-dominated fields ("C.S.A. Searches" 1989). And, despite their
decision not to unionize in the early 1980s, they haven't been accepted
as peers by the ranks of the creative elite, either.

Conclusion

Miranda Banks writes that "in subtle ways, much of the work women
do in Hollywood is—both through language and through economics—
treated as 'women's work'" (2009: 95). The contemporary feminized
field of casting attests to the truth of this statement. In their efforts to
keep their heads down, focus on increasing their field's prestige, and
wait for their creative importance to be recognized, it has been difficult
for female casting directors to lay down the gendered baggage that has
followed them from the film industry's past. For, though casting didn't
truly emerge as a woman's profession until the late 1970s or early 1980s,
the conditions for the shift were put in place half a century earlier with
the demarcation of certain kinds of film labor as "women's work" and
the expectations and work culture that developed around feminized
labor at studios.

The logic that has underwritten gendered labor since the turn of the
twentieth century has ensured that during times of economic change in
the media industry, female workers could be counted on to do more for
less and to absorb costs through their freelance labor. Like workers in
several other film-specific "women's fields," casting directors were able
to acquire additional creative capital and to innovate in terms of leadership, management, and organizational style, but the price for these
gains has been invisibility in terms of creative agency, credit, and status, as well as a work experience that depends on the desires of others
and requires management of status, emotion, and gender as much as it
allows for management of other workers.

It remains to be seen whether female domination or feminization
will ever have the entirely positive effects for female film workers that
it seems to have for those who hire them or if, when women are attributed some skill, the implication won't follow that that it is one of lesser
importance or worth to creative products. Still, consolation can be

found in the fact that, contrary to many historical narratives about their total exclusion from film production after the 1910s, women have found ways to participate in media production at high creative levels and to make their mark on media history, often through the very non-threatening "women's skills" that were once used to relegate them to typewriters and sewing machines.

NOTES

1. Neither the 399 teamsters nor the Casting Society of America, of which most casting directors are members, collect gender data from members, but as of March 2012, the C.S.A. directory lists of 131 male members (15 casting associates and 116 casting directors) and 390 female members (42 casting associates and 348 casting directors), which translates to 74.8 percent female (ambiguous names were verified against IMDB.com listings and casting-company websites). This figure includes a small number of overseas casting directors, and excludes the reportedly small number of casting directors unaffiliated with the CSA, nor does it include commercial casting directors, reality casting producers, and casting agents, which function as completely separate, distinct professions from that of casting director. See Casting Society of America, "Find a Member Page," http://www.castingsociety.com/.

2. Marcia Ross, C.S.A., personal interview by author, Los Angeles, CA, December 8, 2004.

3. Female-led stenography and secretarial departments were established at studios in the mid- 1910s and on into the late 1920s, as were an increasing number of "overhead" departments such as tabulation, payroll, and personnel, which were also maintained largely by women. See "All This and Sadie, Too" 1940, "Interviewing Wynn Haslam" 1941, "Interviewing Helen Gregg" 1941.

4. A women's vocational guide from 1934 lists clerical or clerical-related professions such as researcher, continuity writer, dialog writer, continuity clerk/script "girl" or supervisor, and reader as being strictly women's work. See Filene 1934, 432–33.

5. Studio newsletter descriptions of female studio workers attest to this expectation through their singular focus on the workers' smiles, looks, pleasing manners, giggling, chatter and gossip.

6. As outlined by Judith Butler, under which gender is constructed by the individual in a tacit agreement with society to "sustain discrete and polar genders" by means of "a stylized repetition of acts, product of continuous reiterated acts of performance" (1999: 179).

7. Marcia Ross, personal interview.

8. Sharon Bialy, C.S.A., personal interview by author, Los Angeles, CA, December 3, 2004.

9. Debi Manwiller, C.S.A., phone interview by author, Los Angeles, CA, December 8, 2004.

10. Marcia Ross, personal interview.
11. Sherry Thomas, C.S.A., personal interview by author, Los Angeles, CA, December 3, 2004.
12. Marcia Ross, personal interview.
13. Marcia Ross, personal interview.
14. Debi Manwiller, phone interview.
15. Reality casters do not look for performance skills in actors, but for the actual real "personalities" or "types" around which shows' reality narratives will be built. Workers are thus part casting director, but also producer, salesperson, and psychologist.
16. Marcia Ross, personal interview.
17. This negotiation is sometimes carried out by lawyers, depending on the salary being negotiated. See Ross interview.
18. Sharon Bialy, personal interview.
19. See Bialy interview; Scott 1988.
20. Described in Marci Liroff, "Inside the World of Casting, Part 1," *Facebook Note,* http://www.facebook.com/note.php?note_id=10150158264996721, April 4, 2011, Last Accessed March 20, 2012.; See also Ross interview.
21. For example, see "RKO Studio Organization Chart from 1934," printed in Jewell 2007: 47.
22. Liroff, "Inside the World of Casting."
23. Marcia Ross, personal interview.
24. Marcia Ross, personal interview.
25. For one example of a woman receiving promotion from secretary to assistant in casting, see "Film Secretary" 1936. Publicity was the most integrated, and women's infiltration of positions there is discussed at length in Davis (1993: 137–58), as well as in the oral history of Robert Vogel, who served as vice president of publicity for MGM in the late studio era; see Vogel 1991.
26. Transition detailed in Bandler 1982; "C.S.A. Searches" 1989.
27. This newer, more organic form of casting did not, however, extend much further than the old form had to minorities, who, in most mainstream films and especially in TV, were at this time supposed to be limited to reflect studio and networks' conceptions of the racial makeup of the "real world." Detailed further in Turow 1978: 22–23.
28. In March 1980, when fifty-six of the "top" casting directors took out an ad in *Variety,* forty-two of them were women. See Untitled Full-Page Anti-Union Ad, 32.
29. Sharon Bialy, personal interview.
30. Mike Duffy explains that though much development has been seen in top-down, executive-mandated strategies, far less has been done to engineer consensus among the workers to whom those strategies trickle down, or to weigh those "best practices" often lauded by gurus from other businesses against a particular organization's "unique history and culture" (2001).

31. Marcia Ross, personal interview.
32. Sharon Bialy, personal interview.
33. Marcia Ross, personal interview.
34. Marcia Ross, personal interview.
35. Untitled Full-Page Anti-Union Ad.

7

Brazilian Film Management Culture and Partnering with *os majors*

A Midlevel Approach

COURTNEY BRANNON DONOGHUE

More than a picturesque coastal city immortalized in glossy telenovelas and the recent cycle of *favela* movies, Rio de Janeiro has emerged as a multi-faceted media capital with expanding transnational production opportunities and audiences for local films. Today, local production cultures and practices within Brazilian cinema intersect with their increased flow across globalized cultural economies. The Brazilian industry has attracted high profile international co-productions such as *The Twilight Saga: Breaking Dawn—Part 1* and *Fast Five*, as well as producing a steady line of commercially successful local films ranging from the *favela* (urban slum communities) franchise *Tropa de Elite 2* to the music-driven biopic *Dois Filhos de Francisco* (See Azenha 2010, Guerini 2010b). This chapter investigates the fluid and complex nature of local film co-productions in Brazil and the management cultures that produce them.

My analysis is part of an ongoing project examining local language co-productions between local producers and global film operators like

Sony, Fox, Warner Bros., Disney, and Paramount, also known in Brazil as *os majors* (Hazelton 2011). Based on extended trips to Brazil during the mid- to late 2000s, this chapter builds on previous research investigating the Brazilian film industry, its major institutions, key individual players, and stylistic and production practices since the 1990s.[1] Primarily, I am interested in situating the management cultures behind these films within the larger political, economic, and cultural context of contemporary Brazil. I focus on an elite group of commercial film executives (the general directors and presidents) who manage prominent production and distribution companies and are actively involved in the financial and creative decision-making for co-productions. How do these creative executives manage partnerships between local and transnational players as well as understand their own roles, motivations, and identities within the process?

I have three overall objectives for this essay. First, I offer a broad picture of the growing film market in Brazil and the variety of players involved, particularly through the prevalent model of the local co-production. Second, I foreground how issues of access, performance, and PR spin shaped my fieldwork and methods for investigating contemporary creative management beyond U.S. industries. Third, I explore the multi-faceted, culturally specific, and at times contradictory management culture and "trade stories" circulating around Brazilian cinema. How do local producers and distributors understand and navigate this industry culture? Many times scholars and industry professionals understand local co-productions between transnational media divisions and local players as a strategy by Sony or Fox to enter and cultivate local markets. Instead, independent Brazilian managers running Rio-based production and distribution companies interpret these film partnerships through their own notions of locality and control. Brazilian managers cultivate their own home market to be competitive with Hollywood and develop alternative partnerships for local production and distribution. These individuals imagine their roles less as being confined by early dependency debates and more in terms of Brazil's shifting position with the global cultural economy.

My analysis complements a recent wave of scholarly works including *Media Industries: History, Theory, and Methods* (2009), edited by Jennifer Holt and Alissa Perren, and *Production Studies: Cultural Studies of Media Industries* (2009), edited by Vicki Mayer, Miranda Banks, and John Caldwell. These two collections highlight the need to connect and ground larger forces of globalization, convergence, conglomeration, and digitization within closer industrial analyses of institutions, practices, and creative workers with Holt and Perren, in particular, arguing that unprecedented changes in regulation, policies, economic trade, geopolitical alliances, technological convergence, and audiences require media scholars to embrace cross-disciplinary methods and rethink earlier understandings of business models and practices (1–3). Furthermore, Timothy Havens, Amanda D. Lotz, and Serra Tinic's essay on "Critical Media Industry Studies: A Research Approach" (2009), which emphasizes midlevel processes for examining "the complex interactions among cultural and economic forces" playing out within the business culture of media industries (237), also influenced the scope and methods for this on-going project. A "helicopter" view reveals the complex and contradictory power dynamic of creative workers and management within large media institutions that is often missing from traditional top-down, "airplane"-level political economy approaches.

In order to explore the midlevel dynamics of a management culture in the booming Brazilian media industry, I ground my methods in international field research and interviews in ways that are similar to the work of Havens, Lotz, and Tinic, Michael Curtin (2007), Marwan Kraidy (2009), and Joseph Straubhaar (2007). Specifically, Havens, Lotz, and Tinic propose the adoption of

> institutional case studies that examine the relationships between *strategies* (here read as the larger economic goals and logics of large-scale cultural industries) and *tactics* (the ways in which cultural workers seek to negotiate, and at times perhaps subvert, the constraints imposed by institutional interests to their own purposes). (247).

This helicopter view offers a useful approach for understanding how midlevel media professionals (producers, distributors, etc.) act as managers and how they negotiate and internalize larger political economic forces alongside tensions surrounding how a particular industry culture/culture industry operates. Whether internalized or actively pursued by these managers, many of the different strategies and tactics

Brazilians undertake to produce local films with or without Hollywood partners are informed by varied discursive tensions across Brazilian identity, "localness," cultures of production, and a competitive, commercial cinema.

As illustrated by the language they each use and how they understand their work, strategic differentiations between *os majors* and local partners shape everything from personal identities to creative decision-making. John Caldwell's (2008) concept of "trade stories" helps to explain how a different set of stakes emerges in shifting ideas of national identity, creative motivations, and Hollywood's historical occupancy of Brazilian screens. These lines of discussion offered a clearer understanding of how industry information and narratives circulate, their own position in the industry as performance, and the larger stakes involved for Brazilian professionals working with Hollywood studios. Caldwell emphasizes the constructed nature of these types of conversations and the promotional stakes surrounding them. He identifies the "inverse credibility law" whereby the higher a researcher moves up the "industrial food chain," the more the stories emerge as "suspect and spin-driven" (3), because, as he argues, "insider knowledge is *always* managed; because spin and narrative define and couch any industrial disclosure; and because researcher-practitioner contacts are always marked by symbiotic tensions over authenticity and advantage" (2–3). In turn, these trade stories offer a dynamic look at particular management cultures as well as questions of promotion and spin within the Brazilian film industry.

This essay contributes to media industries conversations and methods by offering a close analysis of media managers and how promotional strategies and tactics circulate within a major market beyond the Anglophone region. As Brazilian managers invoke their control and authority though discourses of "localness" and legacies of Brazilian production cultures, they are beginning to ground their issues of agency within economic and cultural terms. Whereas cultural questions of influence frame earlier debates surrounding Hollywood's place in the global film market per *Global Hollywood* (Miller et al. 2005) and Toby Miller's (2005) discussion of the New International Division of Cultural Labor, today, many of these managers frame their concerns about economic policies and global competitiveness in terms of

Brazilian agency and identity. In turn, many Brazilian managers adopt a neoliberal, free-market logic that involves revising cultural policies to promote ideologies of foreign investment and expand consumer choice.

The Market: A Booming Brazilian Cinema and Its Key Players

Brazil is the fastest growing film market in Latin America. The market share for locally produced Portuguese-language films has more than doubled from 9 percent in 2001 to over 19 percent in 2010, while theater admissions increased from 10 million in 2006 to over 25 million in 2010 ("O Mercado" 2011). As theatrical infrastructure expands beyond urban centers, annual productions increase, and audiences grow, the decades of the 2000s and 2010s represent a pivotal moment within the transformation of a national media industry. In a country of 200 million, this industrial expansion parallels larger economic development, rising incomes, lower unemployment, an expanding middle class, and increasing foreign investment. This economic climate, which has been credited largely to President Luis Ignacio Lula da Silva's administration (2003–2009) (Guerini 2010a), has come to be a highly publicized "economic boom" and has made Brazil the sixth largest economy in the world. Media managers have adopted this boom rhetoric surrounding the country's growth as a promotional strategy for its national cinema (see Fick 2011; Inman 2011).

Current conditions reflect the Brazilian film industry's pivotal restructuring over the past two decades from a nationally focused, state-supported enterprise to a more globalized and commercialized incentive-driven system. Previously, the state-run Empresa Brasileira de Filmes (Embrafilme) served as the central enterprise financing, distributing, and supporting national film production from 1969 to 1990. During that time, "the government became an active agent and productive force in the industry" in order to develop and protect the national industry against Hollywood's widely believed imperialistic tendencies (Johnson 1987: 137–38). Embrafilme financed films such as the widely popular *Bye Bye Brasil* (1980, dir. Carlos Diegues) and produced some of Brazil's most commercially successful films within a period that reimagined and celebrated both the popular and artistic character of this national cinema (Johnson and Stam 1995: 368).

However, the Embrafilme period was not sustainable. The enterprise did not survive major global and national shifts in political and economic policies reshaping Brazilian cultural industries during the 1980s and 1990s. Due to neoliberal policies and pressures within Latin America, a number of government funded cultural agencies were closed (or later resurrected and privatized) to revive Brazil's faltering economy. Embrafilme's 1989 dismantling led to a collapse in film production and distribution. After a complete overhaul of audiovisual policies, institutions, and funding mechanisms in the mid-1990s, the Brazilian industry experienced a *retomada* (rebirth) and steadily recovered with the support of private and corporate financing. A number of privatized funding mechanisms and tax incentives, such as Article 3 (discussed below), were introduced to replace earlier state subsidies and attract local and international corporations to invest in the filmmaking process (Rêgo 2005). The government also established institutions such as the Agência Nacional do Cinema (ANCINE) to facilitate these investments through managing, creating, and awarding funds. In recent years, there have also been a number of awards created to reward box office and commercially successful projects. As a result, the Brazilian film industry has experienced a boom bringing local production totals to 135 in 2010 ("Informe de Acompanhamento" 2011).

Contemporary film financing and distribution are also grounded in financial and creative partnerships with transnational media conglomerates and their filmed entertainment divisions such as Fox, Sony Pictures, Warner Bros., Paramount, Disney, and Universal. These Brazil-based divisions, known locally as *os majors* (the majors), are central to co-production and theatrical distribution for the majority of commercial Portuguese-language projects today (Johnson 2005). *Os majors* distributed between 30 and 37 Brazilian films inside the national market during 2009 and 2010, respectively, which accounted for 21 to 22 percent of all local projects released those years ("Informe de Acompanhamento" 2011; "Informe de Acompanhamento" 2010).

It is important to situate these current practices within the legacy of *os majors*. By the late 1920s, Columbia, Universal, Paramount, Warner

Bros. and Fox had set up distribution outlets in Brazil, and American film occupied over 80 percent of the local market (Johnson 1987: 36). While the market share continued to fluctuate over the next century, the Motion Picture Association of America (MPAA, formerly the Motion Picture Export Association of America/MPEA) remains a constant presence in the Brazilian market. Earlier film scholars such as Thomas Guback (1969) and more recent books such as *Global Hollywood* (Miller et al. 2005) criticize the expansive presence and impact of MPAA as a powerful distribution monopoly controlling markets outside of the United States. As in debates regarding media imperialism, these works understand the role of major media conglomerates in international markets through an economically determinist lens.[2]

Due to tax incentives introduced during the 1990s, particularly Article 3, international companies are allowed to reinvest a portion of their taxed income back into local co-productions. In terms of structure, the typical commercial film co-production is intended for wide theatrical release on 200 to 400 screens and costs an average $US 2.9 to 5.8 million.[3] While *os majors* may develop a project in-house, a more common practice is for an established production company to approach Sony, Paramount, or Fox with a project already in development. For example, Sony may enter the partnership as a co-producer by allocating a portion of its Article 3 tax incentive funds for production costs, provide funding for theatrical and home entertainment distribution, or both.

In turn, *os majors* have emerged as important co-producers for commercial films during the 2000s. In order to understand the various political, economic, and cultural factors at play, it is necessary to consider general industrial analysis of *os majors'* position and activities beyond questions of why the MPAA are present in the Brazilian film industry. Older understandings of Hollywood's position within Brazilian media industries traditionally located co-production partnerships within an imperialism model. My field research traces the structure of these partnerships and how management culture impacts and conceptualizes these partnerships. These Portuguese-language films do not exemplify the one-way flow of culture of English-language content originating from the United States. Instead, these managerial relations and negotiations reveal a more complex situation.

The average commercial film intended for a national audience typically involves a mix of partners including: the local division of a transnational conglomerate (Sony, Warner Bros. Fox, etc.); a mix of local independent production companies including a majority producer (ranging from Conspiração Filmes to Lereby Produções); the division of a national media conglomerate (Globo Filmes); and possibly a local independent distributor (Downtown Films or RioFilme). This configuration is not always the case, but has emerged as the transnational partnership model representative of contemporary Brazilian cinema. While the size and position of a partnering independent production or distribution company varies, there are a few common categories of producers involved in these projects. Many of the most active players in these co-productions come from major companies that produce two to four films per year and are led by internationally recognized and long-established industry players. Conspiração Filmes, LC Barreto Filmes, and O2 Filmes consist of three to eight executive producers and more than a dozen in-house directors, including Fernando Meirelles, Bruno Barreto, and Andrucha Waddington.[4] In addition to being the most active groups, these are the filmmakers and production companies that receive both top billing at international film festivals and the widest theatrical releases locally. Other key partners include independent distributors such as Downtown Filmes and Globo Filmes, the filmed entertainment division of the Brazilian media conglomerate, Globo. Both partners may work with Sony to release and market Brazilian co-productions across the local theatrical and home entertainment market.[5]

Sony's participation with these industry players has been less about mandating their production strategy and more about developing a process of managerial negotiation. One independent producer I interviewed described the creative relationship with *os majors* and the challenges for Sony to adjust to the role of partner, and not employer, of Brazilian producers, particularly when it came screenplay, casting, and marketing decisions.[6] In the case of *Chico Xavier*, a 2010 biopic based on the life of the famed Brazilian medium, Sony Brazil was involved in creative and financial processes alongside Lereby Produções and Downtown Filmes. Sony entered as a co-producer and co-distributor after the president of Downtown Filmes leveraged and negotiated the studio to drop their participation in another film.

An understanding of the multi-layered nature of the typical commercial Brazilian film requires looking at the various local, national, and transnational players involved and how competing management styles and notions of national cinema emerge. One key observation drawn is how these Brazilian co-productions are categorized by a flexible notion of space, place, and ownership. Whether a film is labeled as a *filme nacional* (national film), a local language production, or an international co-production depends greatly on who is doing the categorizing. Namely, each local, national, and transnational stakeholder involved understands and locates these "co-productions" differently. Questions of geography, money, and intended audience determine co-production categorization, with important factors including where the professionals (both creative and management) are located, what language is spoken, the culturally specific content, and whether the final product is intended for local audiences or international film festival circulation. Many times professionals working at *os majors* classify these co-productions as a "local language production" and part of a larger corporate strategy managed by executives in U.S. headquarters. Thus, these Portuguese-language films are distinguished from their more "mobile" English-language films intended for global release. In contrast, Brazilian independent producers and distributors do not distinguish these co-productions from other mainstream national cinema. Instead, they categorize them as *filmes nacionais* or national/Brazilian films intended for Brazilian audiences. (However, local professionals also distinguish *filmes nacionais* from co-productions that utilize official treaties with other national industries, such as Spain's or Argentina's, or international financing from the South American MERCO-SUR common market or European Union initiatives). These differing organizational and management cultures shape the various competing categories for what constitutes Brazilian cinema. As illustrated in the following section, managers for independent companies and *os majors* utilize different discourses of Brazilian cinema as locally and globally grounded in promotional strategies.

The Management Culture: Trade Stories
and Competitive Strategies

Through the course of my interviews, the complex partnerships between *os majors* and independent Brazilian professionals revealed themselves through histories or "trade stories" of professional relationships, production practices, and motivations. In studying Hollywood production, John Caldwell explains how these stories illuminate "the ways production culture in Los Angeles makes sense of itself, to itself, through trade narratives and practitioner storytelling rituals" (2008: 37). After acknowledging the level of PR spin involved, I did see in this process a glimpse into the inner management structures and culture and how negotiations are made and personalities clash in creative and financial negotiations within the Brazilian context. Conversations with various producers, distributors, government officials, and policymakers revealed a variety of perspectives on the state of the industry, shaped in and by contradictory accounts, colorful personalities, and differing biographical details.

Questions of access, trade stories as promotional strategies, and how *os majors* and their partners negotiate their co-production relationships reveal how competing notions of quality, national identity, and global mobility circulate. How these managers understand their co-production work and the dynamics of their transnational partnerships within the shifting notions of a national audiovisual industry differ from their partners working at *os majors*. Yet, as suggested by Havens, Lotz, and Tinic, these trade stories should be understood within the larger *strategies* or economic logic driving Brazilian cinema as a cultural industry as well as in terms of the *tactics* these cultural workers utilize to manage or negotiate institutional constraints to their individual authority (Havens et al 2009: 247). In relation to this co-production strategy, national cinema is framed and reimagined through the promotion of a Brazilian boom and its competitive relationship with Hollywood. Although opinions about *os majors* vary depending on who is asked, alternative partnerships to challenge this dominant model also participate in a particular neoliberal, free market logic.

The greatest challenge in conducting industry interviews involved creating connections with and gaining access to key players in the

Brazilian film industry. Sherry B. Ortner's (2010) ethnography work within Hollywood addresses the issue of industry access for scholars, mainly the difficulty in arranging interviews and participant-observation inside the insular Los Angeles community. Yet, conducting industry studies outside of the United States comes with a range of challenges not addressed by Ortner and Caldwell—namely, understanding linguistic and cultural barriers, different processes of networking, and motivations for participation. In turn, Brazilian media professionals manage access and information about their practices and personas through specific myth-clichés of the creative process and discourses of Brazil as global and booming.

Access to executives and creative professionals is managed through official and unofficial circuits within the Brazilian media industries. An example of an official channel located in Rio de Janeiro, Globo's Globo Universidade program supports academic research and teaching initiatives. In a company known for its tightly managed PR and protection of internal workings, this program requires a formal proposal submission and initial screening for the possibility of accessing Globo's archives and/or creative staff and executives. Although I met with Globo representatives and submitted a proposal, the process of dealing with this bureaucratic system proved too slow and inefficient for my purposes.

Instead, I found success by gaining introductions and securing interviews through unofficial channels. Across all Brazilian classes and communities, introductions are socially and professionally vital for advancement and function as a form of social capital. While this may reflect common media industry tactics based on networking, Brazilians identify this culturally specific tradition as *"jeitinho,"* a method of sponsoring introductions and sidestepping formal channels of access (Barbosa 1995). My most lucrative contact, and process of *jeitinho*, came from a longtime industry insider and American expat Steve Solot—the former Vice President of the Motion Picture Association of Latin America.[7] While currently Solot's job at the Rio Film Commission (RFC) is to promote Rio as an international production center, his twenty-five years of cultivating relationships in the Brazilian industry led to invaluable introductions that facilitated my research. At one point during our meeting, he opened up his Blackberry and casually asked, "Who do you want to talk to?" This strategy represented a way to circumvent more formal methods of receiving industry access. After dozens of email introductions with leading producers, distributors, and directors of major studios, this insider "introduction" lifted the most important industrial barrier to access and provided me with contacts for 85 percent of the interviews during that research trip. Instead of traveling through official administrative or public relations staff, I was able to bypass these barriers with Solot's introductions, which allowed me entry as both an American and an academic.[8]

Whether speaking to someone in Los Angeles or Rio de Janeiro, one finds that the most obvious PR spin involves seeking to ground producers' motivations in purely artistic and creative desires. Each conversation with midlevel professionals typically unfolded in stages, moving from more generic public relations sound bites to larger interrogations of Brazilian culture and identity in relation to Hollywood. In interviews with independent producers and distributors, how Brazilian media professionals promote their industry and films both as locally grounded and globally relevant informs the construction and circulation of various national identities. When asked how language and cultural specificity factor into filmmaking and audience preference, many interviewees invariably relied on "myth-clichés" (Caldwell 2008: 368) surrounding the integrity of the creative process.[9] One major female producer at Conspiração responded that quality scripts or talent drive the business and are the key to "good" films. She suggested making quality films benefits the industry's development as a whole: "each time *filme nacional* is a success, whether Conspiração or not, then it is good for the whole market. [Brazilian audiences] begin to see the films have quality, good stories, [and] there is a public demand to see *filmes nacionais*."[10] There is a promotional angle for her production company but also for the collective nature of the Brazilian film community. By framing their decision-making around issues of the quality and integrity of the creative process, many Brazilian managers separate their own artistic motivations from economic forces driving the industry, including access to financing or barriers to theater distribution.

Many conversations situated notions of contemporary national identity against a booming Brazilian cinema within a growing global context. Brazilian media executives imagine their roles as media consumers and producers who are not exclusively bound within national borders.

For the most part, the level of English integrated into the everyday industry workings does reflect their internationalized nature. More and more younger executives and creative professionals speak some English and/or have been educated in the United States, and, on an individual level, many Brazilian professionals proudly demonstrate their knowledge of Hollywood practices, terminology, or productions. While one prominent independent producer quoted at length from an English-language screenwriting manual about the characteristics of a good story that he incorporates into his own filmmaking philosophy, others emphasized their love of American cinema or "quality" serial dramas such as *Mad Men*. There is a certain level of cultural capital associated with the consumption of American media among Brazil's upper classes, especially individuals working within the media industries (Straubhaar 2003: 75–105). It is apparent that these Brazilian professionals work to project an image of themselves as global and savvy.

On an industrial level, Brazilian management "speak" is sprinkled with English-language terminology primarily associated with Hollywood practices. Although I conducted interviews in Portuguese, the interviewees' code switching became a central way to express the integration of a national cinema operating within a larger global media market place. Whether they spoke fluent English or not, management often framed their projects or processes in Brazilian filmmaking within English-language industry categories such as *os majors*, soft money, blockbusters, and art cinema. One independent producer proudly showed his profile in the English-language trade journal *Variety* representing him as one of the top ten producers to watch.

A number of individuals strategically used these English-language terms to describe how their national film market *está crescendo* (is growing) and becoming more competitive with Hollywood films. Drawing on rhetoric similar to that of the myth-clichés mentioned previously, director of RioFilme Sérgio Sá Leitão explained: "In reality, we produce films here in Brazil with the same quality of Hollywood."[11] Where historically Hollywood's global presence was a controversial issue, today Hollywood knowledge and credibility are simultaneously sought after and criticized. The integration of English-language and commercial practices has become a strategy for independent Brazilian managers to promote the distinctive nature of this "booming" local industry.

In contrast, the directors running local operations for *os majors* understand their own position as managers from multiple perspectives. A description of the global company culture and brand would be followed by discussions of Sony Pictures do Brasil or Paramount Pictures Brasil as a local company and their personal identity. When asked about the dominant presence of his operation, Sony's general manager Rodrigo Saturnino Braga defended its position—"we are Brazilian just like [our partnering producers and distributors]."[12] Furthermore, the managers themselves asserted their nationality as Brazilians through identification with local culture as *cariocas* or *paulistas* (individuals born/living in the cities of Rio or São Paulo). This negotiation between corporate identities and cultural identities reworks Joseph Straubhaar's discussion of "layers of identity" or how race, gender, class, sexuality, nationality, and so on, shape Brazilian media audiences and their television consumption patterns in various ways (Straubhaar 2007). Instead, these same layers of identity tend to operate within Brazilian production cultures in significant ways. In the case of film management, neither the executives working for or with *os majors* understood that designation as totalizing. Instead, production and distribution managers described their own identities within the industry as something more fluid and involving multiple factors.

Significantly, all of the directors of *os majors* were recruited from the local industry. As part of a group known as *geração de ouro* (the golden generation), the directors of Sony and Paramount both worked at Embrafilme during its most productive period in the 1970s.[13] Although the national film enterprise was shuttered over two decades ago, the Embrafilme legacy still holds a prominent, albeit heavily criticized, position within the industry today, bringing long-term relationships and contacts with it. The directors of Fox and Warner Bros. came from other sectors of the Brazilian film industry with experiences in independent distribution and corporate exhibition.

The idea of home-grown or native industry workers emerges as an important element for navigating these relationships. Studio managers serve as cultural intermediaries between their international group bosses and their Brazilian partners. On a practical level, Sony or Paramount General managers can ease certain legal or cultural differences in negotiating deals for an individual project. Yet, on a symbolic level, connection between locality and national identity for these Brazilian managers embodies a particular value or cultural capital. *Os majors* work to negotiate their local co-production strategy and justify their participation in this national cinema as authentically home grown. Insofar as value is represented through their cultural investment in national cinema, *os majors* try to neutralize or legitimize their economic investment in the audiovisual industry.

Co-production and distribution managers also understand their working relationship with *os majors* through various levels of agency and decision-making. As Caldwell argues, "the world of film/video production involves the continuous negotiation of complex forms on *both* sides of the equation: *control* (space, boundaries, continuity) and *agency* (action, imaginative behavior, change)" (2008: 71). Whether discussions involve pitch sessions, screenings, or deal-making, the entire process of producing Brazilian cinema exists in historically contested spaces. It carries historical baggage of economic dependency, colonized screen space, and competition for local audiences. Not surprisingly, how independent managers understand these dynamics reflects a more complicated scenario of control and agency than anticipated.

Producer and director of the independent Rio-based distribution company Downtown Filmes, Bruno Wainer described his relationship with Sony do Brasil across multiple film projects as a "mutually beneficial."[14] Sony has resources to invest, produces marketing materials, and researches test audiences whereas its partners bring the scripts, talent, and industry experience. Sony supports a large portion of mainstream commercial filmmakers who mostly like the incentive support and the cachet of the studio's brand. One manager humorously characterized the relationship in this way: "I think many of the [Brazilian] players have a sexual fantasy to see their film with the majors' name at the beginning of the credits. It is the realism of a sexual fantasy."[15] This metaphor raises questions about the value the studio brand brings to Brazilian cinema in the eyes of local professionals and audience members.

Stories circulate of the almighty American studio executive's control over a final theatrical cut, particularly in demanding a different ending or in the heavy-handed editing done by the likes of Harvey Weinstein after a film's acquisition. In the Brazilian context, *os majors* managers will see various cuts of a film and provide their input, but, ultimately, as the co-producer and distributor, they have no final say on the final theatrical version. In the case of the earlier example of *Chico Xavier*, filmmaker Daniel Filho and his production company, Lereby, controlled the creative decision-making process. Yet, *os majors* still control the vast majority of theatrical distribution in Brazil. Even though the independent producers maintain creative control, they still need Sony, Paramount, Fox, Disney, Universal, or Warner Bros. to distribute the co-production.[16]

Many industry professionals see "the rest of the world" adopting a U.S. model wherein the major studios can control creative and financial decisions from pre-production to distribution. Brazilian film professionals differentiate themselves by maintaining their own industry practices that originate from a legacy of authorial cinema within the periods of *Cinema Novo* and Embrafilme. Whereas *os majors* utilize their local managers to legitimize their participation as co-producers, independent producers and distributors invoke their local position and cultures of production to manage their authority over the creative process and their partners. With a number of parties involved having competing motivations, this tactic by independents becomes a way to negotiate (and promote) their control over a contested space.

One partner working with *os majors* proudly argued for these Brazilian industry practices:

> A major [MPA] partner has the capacity of a parent to invest money in [Brazilian release] but this does not signify well-made work. Not everything is resolved by money. [Everyone involved] needs to understand each film, what is the best way to release this film, what would be correct for [the local market].[17]

In other words, the might of the major's dollars is not seen as the formula for success in the Brazilian film market. Familiarity with market conditions as well as audiences and local culture is key for many of the managers with whom I spoke. Local management imagines their identities within an artistic hierarchy in a manner consistent with discourses surrounding authorship and earlier auteur movements. The producer above values his participation in producing and releasing a local film in

relation to the perceived Hollywood model. The intimacy, craftsman-
ship, and personal attention he promotes are signatures that come to
stand in for the Brazilian management culture itself.

It is important again to acknowledge that my findings are based on
the opinions of an elite group working in the most inner-circle of Brazilian cinema and thus particularly subject to Caldwell's inverse credibility law. Speaking mainly with *os majors* and their partners results
in a limited and insular view of relationships between key management and production cultures. Apart from that, though, there is also
a growing faction in the industry which, not surprisingly, criticizes
the presence of *os majors*. Smaller independent company perspectives
may differ greatly, as when a São Paulo–based distributor described
the business practices of *os majors* as an "oligopoly" due to their hegemonic position as the key distributors of English-language and Brazilian films: "it is bad for the market, bad for the people, and bad for
the country." Yet, he clarified this criticism in a significant way: "I am
not against American cinema. It is not that American cinema domi-
nates the theaters but four companies have 95 percent of the market.
The fact of American films, Brazilian, or Chinese films is a secondary
question. It represents an oligopoly."[18] Interestingly, the most common
criticism I heard against the position of *os majors* was not the typical
cultural imperialism argument many would assume. As the São Paulo
distributor above argued, it is more about the company's control over
the market than the cultural impact of its content. In fact, independent
managers consistently criticized *os majors'* market share as an effect
of the government's history of protectionist measures and regulations
intended to develop local cinema, as exemplified by Article 3. While
the above response may imply another form of imperialism, the director of RioFilme, Sá Leitão, frames his perspective more in terms of free
market factors:

> I don't want to villainize the majors. . . . It is good for the country that
> they are here. It is good that American cinema is available because the
> public likes, people like it. I like it a lot. I want access to these films. Now
> we are doing our part, we are competitive. . . . It needs to be free demo-
> cratic and what people want to see. The control of the consumers.[19]

Interestingly, from Sá Leitão's perspective, Brazilian film professionals today are less concerned with vilifying the presence of *os majors* or
disavowing their own consumption of American cinema. Instead, he
is part of a younger generation of film executives who are rethinking
this older system of strategies driven by protectionist policies and reac-
tionary funding mechanisms. As Downtown Filmes' Wainer suggested:
"I am not struggling against the majors but am struggling against the
[incentived] system."[20] After decades of state-subsidized funding and,
more recently, tax incentives, many independent producers and distributors are arguing for the end of what they call financing regulations
that continue a state of dependency on *os majors*. Both of these types
of managers employ the discourse of Brazil's economic boom to justify this reasoning. The recent national economic growth has led to an
increase in available resources from Brazilian investors and corporations. Many independent managers see the boom as a way to compete
against Hollywood within a more "level" system. This argument signals
a move away from an earlier strategy battling Hollywood's cultural and
economic occupation with protectionist policies to an internalized narrative based on neoliberal logic emphasizing a free film market wherein
local companies can and should compete fairly with Hollywood for
Brazilian audiences.

So, how are Brazilian independent managers developing strategies
for a more "competitive" system outside of partnering with *os majors*?
During my field research, a local blockbuster emerged, providing a
turning point in this debate. Filmmaker Jose Padilha and his company,
Zazen, chose to independently release *Tropa de Elite 2: O Inimigo Agora
É Outro* (2010), the sequel to the 2007 hit film *Tropa de Elite*. For both
films, they did not partner with a major as co-producer nor utilize the
Article 3 tax incentive that funds the majority of these partnerships.[21]
Instead, Zazen independently distributed the film to more than six hundred screens without the help of an international studio. To put this in
perspective, the average Brazilian commercial co-production premieres
on 350 to 400 screens. While the strategy was risky, *Tropa de Elite 2* paid
off, becoming the most watched Brazilian theatrical release of all time
with over eleven million admissions (Guerini 2011a). Due to growing
market conditions and increased financing available from local investors such as the national petroleum company, Petrobras, and the Banco

do Brasil, producing and releasing a major commercial project without *os majors* is becoming more of an option for this group of established managers.[22]

Largely due to the theatrical success of *Tropa de Elite 2*, a group of the elite managers (many of whom are discussed in the first section of this essay) is developing new networks for independent distribution. One new company, Nossa Distribuidora, embraces "an alternative business model, where the producers will be able to distribute their own films, retaining the copyright and having a greater control over the box office sales" (Guerini 2011b; De La Fuente and Cajueiro 2011). Nossa Distribuidora involves prominent production companies and filmmakers such as Padilha, Andrucha Waddington, Fernando Meirelles, and Daniel Filho, all of whom have benefitted from relationships with *os majors*. Similarities to Serra Tinic's findings in *On Location: Canada's Television Industry in a Global Market* (2005) about Canadian producers can be drawn. Many Canadian producers claimed that they gained experience and resources by working with Hollywood studios, which, in turn, allowed them to develop their own projects that functioned as a form of resistance against state-subsidized funding. From this perspective, the experience, creative success, and financial gain that came from working with *os majors* could allow these producers and filmmakers to create alternative commercial models outside of these partnerships.

What Nossa Distribuidora represents is how different local professionals negotiate and leverage their relationship with *os majors* to reimagine local industry practices within these discourses of competitiveness. It is not a situation of complete submission or complete resistance. In the end, how many Brazilian professionals manage their relationship with *os majors* varies and reflects larger implications for their position of authority in the industry and multi-faceted local identities. In turn, many independent professionals are moving away from cultural policies reflecting older development and protectionist ideas and, instead, embracing a relaxed and booming marketplace.

Conclusion

Transnational co-production and distribution partnerships featuring *os majors* and prominent Brazilian professionals are a product of the post-2000 market. Due to key tax incentives and cultural policies promoting corporate investment in production, local divisions of Sony, Fox, Warner Bros., Disney, Universal, and Paramount have emerged as prominent (but not always dominant) partners in Brazilian commercial filmmaking. Brazil's booming market, history of state support, and strong filmmaking tradition largely shape this management culture. As my midlevel analysis suggests, these partnerships reflect a complex process of negotiating financial investment, creative decision-making, and notions of local cinema. One of the most revealing features of my research suggested that negotiations within these creative partnerships are less static and that the nature of Brazilian management identities are more fluid than earlier academic scholarship presumed.

These partnerships also reflect the shifting dynamics of an industry simultaneously aiming for both a strong local cinema culture and an increased international profile. The local film co-production is only one strategy within a larger audiovisual industry aspiring to become an internationally recognized media capital for production. Part of this drive involves attracting international co-productions that include such big commercial project as Disney's animated *Rio* and Summit's fourth *Twilight* installment. As international media attention and public relations efforts accompany these productions, many in the industry encourage the rising profile of Brazil, particularly Rio de Janeiro, as both a competitor and collaborator with industries such as Hollywood. As suggested by management interviews above, an either/or binary that may have distinguished Brazilian and Hollywood industries in the past is breaking down.

A recent campaign by two Rio-based audiovisual institutions represents the city's media capital ambitions.[23] RioFilme and Rio Film Commission released a publicity image of the iconic Corcovado Mountain with the Cristo Redentor. Adhered to the side of the mountain is the title "Rio de Janeiro" with lettering fashioned to emulate the famous Hollywood sign. The ad states: "Rio. A City of Cinema . . . Rio is now the Brazilian city that invests the most in cinema . . . . as the principal site in Latin America. Rio. This is the moment. This is the place."[24] Significantly, the imagery employs specific iconography from both Hollywood as an industry and Rio as a tourist destination to signify the city's media capital status. As illustrated by this advertisement, local officials and creative professionals are pitching Rio as the cultural/industrial cluster for Brazil and Latin America. Many managers I spoke with welcome this transformation as part of the "it benefits us all" discourse. The director of RioFilme argues that local industry professionals "make films that can compete in the international market *and* nationally like France, Korea, England . . . countries like India."[25]

Whether driven by cultural policies or developing infrastructures, these globalizing efforts are attracting financing, talent, and projects that will continue to challenge earlier understandings of Brazilian production practices and partnership models. One thing that is certain is that production partnerships with international players (whether Hollywood subsidiaries or not) are now being framed within discussions of competition and growth and not solely in terms of dependency. On the one hand, Brazilian managers utilize specific managerial and promotional tactics to highlight their own changing creative and financial agency in the local market. On the other hand, within this logic exists an implicit tension between earlier dependency debates and how current partnerships with Hollywood companies are continuously negotiated and renegotiated. The question remains how these efforts to grow the commercial production cluster will impact local co-production models and management cultures. What will be important to watch is how the management culture embraces these changes and negotiates the tensions that arise from the continued strategies and tactics aimed at growing a booming Brazilian cinema.

NOTES

1. For a more expansive look at this project in process, see Donoghue 2011b.

2. Earlier co-productions with MPAA member Columbia Pictures include *As Amorosas* (1968, dir. Walter Hugo Khoury), *O Homem Que Comprou O Mundo* (1969, dir. E. Coutinho), and *Pindorama* (1969, dir. Arnaldo Jabor); Randal Johnson's work on the Brazilian industry also examines this presence in relation to the evolving state institutions accommodating the MPAA's presence in Brazil through economic policies. For a further discussion of Brazilian cinema and state institutions prior to 1990, see Johnson 1987.

3. Figures compiled from interviews in Brazil during 2010.

4. Liane Fraccaroli, Publicity and Marketing, O2 Filmes, personal interview by author, September 17, 2010, São Paulo, Brazil; Eliana Soarez, Executive Producer, Conspiração, personal interview by author, August 25, 2010, Rio de Janeiro, Brazil.

5. Since 1998, Globo Filmes has co-produced many of the top grossing Brazilian films. Utilizing the parent company's holdings in television, broadcasting, print, and new media, Globo Filmes enters partnerships by contributing marketing and media relations such as television spots or print ad campaigns. Journalist Pedro Butcher suggests that the capital offered by Globo Filmes is not financial but "virtual capital" that materializes at the moment of distribution (see Autran 2010: 29). For a further discussion on Globo Filmes and co-productions, see Donoghue 2011a.

6. Bruno Wainer, General Director, Downtown Filmes, personal interview by author, September 9, 2010, Rio de Janeiro, Brazil.

7. I am incredibly grateful to Dr. Joseph Straubhaar and Dr. Randal Johnson, who gave me this introduction and opened the door to the majority of my contacts; Steve Solot, Rio Film Commission and former VP MPA Latin America, personal interview by author, August 22, 2010, Rio de Janeiro.

8. In addition, a number of my interview contacts came from informal encounters such as the cousin of the head of marketing for the major production company: Marketing Director, Luz Produções, personal interview by author, September 10, 2010, Rio de Janeiro, Brazil.

10. Soarez, personal interview.

11. Sérgio Sá Leitão, Director and President, RioFilme, personal interview by author, August 31, 2010, Rio de Janeiro, Brazil.

12. Rodrigo Saturnino Braga, General Manager, Sony do Brasil, personal interview by author, September 15, 2010, São Paulo, Brazil.

13. Senior VP Distribution for Latin America and Caribbean, Paramount Pictures, personal interview by author, August 25, 2010, Rio de Janeiro, Brazil; General Manager, Sony do Brasil, personal interview by author, September 15, 2010, São Paulo, Brazil.

14. Wainer, personal interview.

15. Independent producer, personal interview by author, September 2010, Rio de Janeiro, Brazil.

16. Wainer, personal interview.

17. Independent producer, personal interview.

18. Andre Sturm, Director, Pandora Filmes, personal interview by author, September 14, 2010, São Paulo, Brazil.

19. Sá Leitão, personal interview.

20. Wainer, personal interview.

21. At some point the producer and director Padilha had been in negotiation with one of the *os majors* to partner for the sequel but ultimately chose to produce and distribute it independently; Iona de Macedo, Former VP Production for Latin American and President of Columbia Films Producciones Espanolas, personal interview by author, January 17, 2011, Madrid, España.

22. Mario Diamante, Director, ANCINE, personal interview by author, September 11, 2010, Rio de Janeiro, Brazil.

23. Primarily, RioFilme is a mixed private-public film company overseen by the city government of Rio, which offers lines of investment for production and distribution of independent films. RioFilme, along with the Rio Film Commission, is promoting the city as an international destination for film productions.
24. This advertising campaign was featured on RioFilme's social media platform through Facebook and Twitter.
25. Sá Leitão, personal interview.

8

Constructing Social Media's Indie Auteurs

Management of the Celebrity Self in the Case of Felicia Day

ELIZABETH ELLCESSOR

In late November 2011, through her blog, Twitter, and YouTube channel, Felicia Day announced the availability of a video of her "playing with [her]self . . . as Tallis from @dragonage" (Day 2011b). *Dragon Age* is a videogame franchise published by BioWare, and Tallis is a character created by Day for a web series that extended the world of *Dragon Age* into a transmedia narrative, and which fed back into the game through the creation of downloadable content that extended the gameplay of *Dragon Age 2*. The video uploaded by Day is a kind of paratext to a transmedia text, offering additional information about her involvement in the web series based on the game series (Gray 2010; Jenkins 2006). The video, the web series, and the blog posts, Tweets, and other means of promoting this video are all also contributors to Day's transmedia star text, which relies heavily on social media content and connections to others. As I have explored elsewhere, though not a major Hollywood star, Day enjoys a subcultural stardom within science fiction, "geek," and gamer communities, and her use of social media to articulate her projects and build that star text of connection has enabled her to enjoy success on the margins of the traditional media industry (Ellcessor 2012).

The video itself is a kind of "let's play" video, a genre of user-generated online content in which individuals film their videogame play along with their own commentary (Rutherford 2010). The first several minutes are an edited collection of Day's attempts to say the "playing with myself" line, as she laughs in seeming embarrassment. Day is ultimately shown purchasing the downloadable content via XBox Live, waiting as it loads, and then playing through a scene in the game in which her in-game avatar engages with the character Tallis, whom Day originated in the web series, voiced, and performed motion capture for. As the scene goes on, Day talks to the camera, laughing as she chooses for her avatar to flirt with her in-game likeness, and discussing the game mechanics and fighting moves. This is not an entirely amateur production, as Day appears to be being filmed and speaking with camerapeople, rather than filming herself, but it does draw upon the cultural form of amateur "let's play" videos. Notably, it was released by Day, not Bio-Ware. It is a paratext of a paratext, a linking of her star persona to her creative works and the transmedia properties on which they draw. Such content reinforces the perception of Day as an authentic gamer, while promoting her creative work as a writer-producer. Its tongue-in-cheek sexualization further emphasizes Day's image as a "geek girl," a figure for identification for many female gamers, and an object of desire for many male and female players.

While "playing with [her]self" might have been hard to verbalize, this clip clearly articulates the ways in which Day is managing herself. Though she has a traditional cohort of support staff, including PR agents and a manager, as well as long relationships with creative collaborators, Day's use of social media creates a star text of connection that relies heavily on creative individualism, and on authenticity as geek and gamer. The strength of this star text overshadows the labor of others on Day's projects and minimizes the perceived influence of corporate relationships on the popular reception of her work, producing her as an indie auteur. Whether this outcome is intentional or not, it naturalizes the centrality of Day's persona to her various creative works, reinforcing an author-driven reading of her projects and managing the contentious relationship between creative producers and active audiences.

The type of management discussed in this chapter is not the management of employees or finances, but the manipulation of an image, or perception, that furthers success in the digital media entertainment industry while obfuscating the labor involved in that success. The management of a celebrity persona is similar to the work done by longstanding agents of stardom, including publicists, managers, agents, entertainment publications, and fashion and beauty professionals. However, as social media offers an individualism and immediacy that preexisting media outlets lacked, there is a greater perception of authenticity and individual control (Reed 2005; White 2006). The management of an online celebrity persona entails the production of an iterative, cohesive self, articulated to particular values. In this way, management of the celebrity self resembles management of the self as new media laborer. In the start-ups, freelance work, and contract labor that characterize new media work, workers become subject to a Foucauldian management of the self, in which technologies of selfhood call into being an always-active worker subjectivity (Gill 2010: 260). The management of the self as flexible creative worker is essential to the digital media entrepreneur as self-promoter, as well, blurring lines between workers and micro-celebrities (Marwick 2010). Particular forms of engagement, disclosures of the personal, and interactions with fans or customers become expected components of new media success, a blend of managing one's work and managing one's self (or, a constructed simulacrum of that "self").

Such "self" management, in the case of Day and others, has the effect of reinforcing perceptions of a new media indie auteurship. Auteurism, or the perception of individual creative personalities as the sole driving force behind their media productions, though partially challenged in film and media scholarship, continues to have currency, particularly in the reception of non-mainstream, indie, or cult texts. When articulated to stardom, as in the case of Day, who acts as writer, producer, and star of her own productions and continues to appear in various television projects, the individualist discourse of the auteur only gains strength. Day's (and her team's) management of her star text of connection minimizes audience disillusionment by performing this online indie auteurism even while participating in a larger industrial structure. Far from "selling out," Day's involvement with BioWare, in particular, can be understood as a kind of triumph, as her star text of connection high-lights her established persona and glosses over industrial relationships by emphasizing personal ones.

Projects and Projections

Felicia Day is perhaps best known as the star, writer, producer, and co-creator of the web series *The Guild* (2007–13), which follows the offline lives of a group of massively multiplayer online game players. Follow-ing a low-budget first season, *The Guild* attained a distribution deal with Microsoft and sponsorship from Sprint, releasing episodes first on MSN.com, Xbox Live, and Bing, as well as through their own website and on YouTube. Day participates in promotional events for Microsoft, and more recent seasons of *The Guild* have featured product place-ment of Microsoft's Bing Video. Several seasons have also been sold on DVD, and beginning in spring 2009, Day worked with illustrators and Dark Horse comics to produce a comic book based on the origin sto-ries of each *Guild* character. A *Guild* comic was part of Dark Horse's Free Comic Book Day release in spring 2012. As a whole, *The Guild* has been one of the most successful web series to date, with over 100 mil-lion viewers (BioWare 2011) in three years, and multiple Webby Awards, in addition to its financial success.

Day's involvement with BioWare's *Dragon Age* series was first announced in February 2011, as part of the launch of *Dragon Age 2*. The game, released in March 2011, would feature a later release of down-loadable content centered on the character and storyline developed by Day in *Dragon Age: Redemption* (2011); the six-episode series revolved around a new character, Tallis, an elven assassin within the same fan-tasy world as *Dragon Age: Origins* (2009) and *Dragon Age 2*. The web series, therefore, was conceived of less as a paratext that would enable ongoing engagement with the world of *Dragon Age* than as a compo-nent of a transmedia narrative. Watching Day's series could introduce new audiences to an extended *Dragon Age* universe, or enhance *Dragon Age* fans' understanding and experience of the downloadable content, *Dragon Age: Mark of the Assassin*, released in October 2011. BioWare, best known for its expansive role-playing games for console and PC systems, including *Mass Effect* (2007) and its sequels, as well as *Star*

Wars: Knights of the Old Republic (2003) and the massively multiplayer *Star Wars: The Old Republic* (2011), is a subsidiary of the major video game company Electronic Arts (EA). The emphasis on character development and narrative in role-playing games makes them especially well suited to narrative transmedia expansions such as *Redemption*. Furthermore, as a specialty division with its own brand identity within a major game studio, BioWare's own reputation is reinforced through its association with Day's indie persona.

BioWare's decision to work with Day on this project resulted in the formation of a text that is both an extension of the *Dragon Age* franchise and an extension of Day's star text and status among preexisting audiences (Ellcessor 2012). Day's work with Joss Whedon, in *Buffy the Vampire Slayer* (The WB/UPN, 1997–2003), *Dr. Horrible's Sing-Along Blog* (2008), and *Dollhouse* (Fox 2009–2010), as well as her regular Twitter exchanges with Whedon and his family, have cemented her as a cult star within the large, active fan community known as the "Whedonverse." Additionally, Day has cachet within self-described geek communities, particularly those related to science fiction, as seen in her work in the made-for television movie *Red* (SyFy 2010), the television series *Eureka* (SyFy 2006–2012), and her connection to Wil Wheaton, best known from *Star Trek: The Next Generation* (1987–1994), both through Twitter and his casting in seasons three and four of *The Guild*. By working within a fantasy role-playing game franchise, Day draws upon the existing investment of her star text in the fantastic and geeky.

Most important for BioWare, however, was Day's appeal to an audience of role-playing video game players. Day's star text has consistently presented her as a legitimate videogame player; through interviews, talk show appearances, Twitter exchanges, blog posts, and other venues, Day has displayed a deep familiarity with gaming jargon, gameplay experiences, and fan investment in particular games (Ellcessor 2012). Thus, when *Redemption* was released, Day's statement to *USA Today* was no surprise: "I am an organic gamer and I love games, and I particularly love this franchise. . . . I put every single effort into making this something that gamers will be proud of" (Snider 2011). Here, Day claims the identity of gamer and insinuates an accountability to a gaming community, positioning herself as much a fan as a producer. Day's investment in fantasy role-playing games, also seen in *The Guild's* focus on massively multiplayer gaming, makes this web series potentially legible as a fan production as well as (or instead of) an official production. This is only furthered by the limited budget of the series, which in parts appears to be produced at a relatively low level, as actors wander through a forest on a sunny day. The nearly amateur aesthetic of "Felicia plays with herself" described above, similarly aligns Day with fan audiences while emphasizing her status as a kind of superfan. This tension, fan-as-producer and producer-as-fan, is similar to that seen in the new *Doctor Who*, as authors of fan fiction and licensed original novels based on the original *Doctor Who* assumed creative control of the new series, regularly invoking their familiarity with existing texts and their authority to create new ones (Hills 2010).

Beyond the creation of the web series, Day's star text was extended and managed through the production of the in-game content for *Mark of the Assassin* as well as through the creation of paratexts surrounding *Redemption*. The character Tallis, in the downloadable content, can be approached and added to the player's four-person party for several missions. Day performed the voice acting and motion capture for this character, foregrounding her role as actress within the game, rather than her more writerly or producerly roles emphasized in paratexts surrounding *Redemption*. If *Redemption* contributes to a transmedia narrative of the *Dragon Age* universe, owned and managed by BioWare, many of the paratexts surrounding *Redemption* were produced by Day for her own audience, rather than BioWare's. In these texts, including the aforementioned video, a series of commentary videos on YouTube, and several Vokle streaming discussions with others involved in the production of *Redemption*, Day's authorial status is reinforced.

Taken as a whole, Felicia Day's career projects create a transmedia star text organized around creative individualism, authentic identity as gamer and geek, and a kind of underdog status. The commonalities in themes, characters played, and industrial roles filled allow for the formation of a projection of who Day "is," and what her work entails, and likely will entail in the future. Not merely typecasting, these are projections with value, which enable her to be hired for high-profile projects such as *Redemption*, and to be one of a handful of professionals making a career based on web video. The consistency of her transmedia star text, in its fidelity to gamer and geek culture, independent cultural production, and narrative of hard-earned success, additionally allows Day to act as a kind of uncomplicated canvas onto which viewers can project their identifications, desires, aspirations, and affective relationships to her creative works. Such unity of voice is made possible largely through the incorporation of online media into every facet of Day's work; with its associations of timeliness and directness, online media contributes to a sense of intimacy that heightens the perceived reality of star texts by allowing them to exist outside of traditional promotional venues (Ellcessor 2012; Marshall 2010). The display of connections, or relationships, to other social media users intensifies this reality by drawing attention to the personal, and the personal dimensions of the professional, and thus redirects attention from other industrial factors.

Management and New Media Labor

In the production and promotion of *Redemption*, Day can be seen to be engaging in self-management, or at least in the management of a constructed self. What is managed is the precise articulation of themes of individualism, creativity, identity, and success to the figure of Day. In tying these characteristics to her public persona, Day's image as an online indie auteur is heightened, as her role in creative processes overshadows those of her collaborators or crews, and her author-function serves to unify her projects and explain textual content.

The management of a public self has long been considered a kind of performance. Erving Goffman, in the influential work on *The Presentation of Self in Everyday Life* (1959), hypothesized that individuals adopt particular verbal and nonverbal behaviors in particular contexts, adopting "front stage" behaviors in formal contexts, and engaging in "backstage" behaviors in private or familiar settings. Importantly, neither performance is necessarily more truthful; both are merely aimed at different audiences. The feedback, or interpretation, of various audiences is central to the process of what Goffman called "impression management," in which all components of an individual's bearing and actions work together to form a desired impression.

Such impression management has been considered particularly crucial within the unstable context of new media labor, in which labor is increasingly casualized, individualized, and tied to projects rather than institutions. Rosalind Gill (2010) argues that in the absence of standard managerial structures, workers in this constellation of industries are called upon to "manag[e] the self in conditions of radical uncertainty" (249). One of the primary techniques through which they do so is the regular commodification of self and others, treating social exchanges as opportunities for entrepreneurial advancement. Alice Marwick (2010), in her ethnographic research on Silicon Valley venture capitalists, has argued that the creation of a "personal brand" through the strategic presentation of self and relationships via social media is increasingly necessary to success in technology start-ups. This instrumental use of social media is a form of self-management by which individuals may market themselves in response to labor uncertainties (Marwick and boyd 2011: 119). In cultivating online personas for professional purposes, these people may be described as engaging in the practices of "micro-celebrity" (Senft 2008), building a particular audience through engagement with others.

Public impression management through social media can be understood as a key component of new media labor, as applicable to those in new media entertainment fields as to those within technology fields. In the case of Felicia Day, looking to her uses of social media around the release of *Redemption* demonstrates several key features identified by Gill and Marwick as common to the new media industry.

First, Day demonstrates a consistent love of her work. Identified by Gill as crucial to new media labor (2010: 252), this enthusiasm allows new media workers to discuss their value in non-monetary terms, by framing their work as a labor of love to which they are entirely dedicated. This love of the work is seen in Day's aforementioned statement to *USA Today*, as well as her February 2011 appearance on *Late Night with Jimmy Fallon*. These venues, of course, are part of the standard promotional circuit for entertainment media; however, Day's appearances and statements in promotional media are almost uniformly about the work, and not her personal life, which further cements her centrality to these projects and suggests an auteurist read of them. In her interview with Fallon, Day says she was approached to do *Redemption* and replied, "Can I be an elf?" Fallon describes her as "geeking out about it," and the two joke about gaming and Twitter, both integral parts of Day's public persona ("Felicia Day interview" 2011). They do not, however, extend into the personal anecdotes or private disclosures common to late-night television. The performance of love of the work promotes Day and the web series *Redemption*, and upholds the ideas of creative independence and success of the underdog that have been tenets of her star image.

Secondly, Day performs entrepreneurialism and the willingness to engage in short-term, precarious work environments (Gill 2010: 253). *The Guild*, sponsored by Sprint and distributed by Microsoft, is a good example of the entrepreneurial commercialization of creative work. Rather than continue to labor on it as a speculation script for a television show, Day took the work to the web and divided a thirty-minute pilot script into a series of short episodes, building an audience and finding sponsorship through nontraditional means. However, despite the continued success of *The Guild*, Day was ostensibly "looking for a follow-up project" (BioWare 2011). The work cycles of new media labor are short, project-based endeavors, requiring workers to adjust to new situations and take on new challenges on a regular basis. By entering into an undisclosed financial arrangement with BioWare, Day essentially embarked on a contracted digital media project, at the conclusion of which she returned to *The Guild* and continued looking for similar projects on which to build her reputation as a successful writer, producer, and star of online entertainment media.

Finally, Day engages in strategic self-promotions, balancing the need of the entrepreneurial new media worker to draw attention to his or her projects with the need of the contemporary celebrity to offer strategic revelations of intimate details. The practices of micro-celebrity, both in new media industries and online celebrity practice, can seem inauthentic or too obvious (Marwick and boyd 2011: 127). Thus, while Day promoted each episode of *Redemption* on her blog, she did so by embedding the video and providing brief statements about which parts of this episode were her favorites to write or perform, or by discussing a small detail from production. These revelations provide an insider's perspective on the finished text, offering an ostensibly backstage view of production and personnel. Additionally, many of her attempts at strategic self-promotion work through the incorporation of sociality, making them legible as relational, rather than broadcast, messages. For instance, Day tweeted about game blog Kotaku's review of *Redemption*, externalizing praise of the series, and received a response from David Gaider, who oversees the writing of the *Dragon Age* story world for Bio-Ware. Gaider praised Day—"Yay! I can't wait to see what the fans think. You did such a great job, Felicia"—and in response, Day praised Gaider and the series' lore (Day 2011c). Through this exchange with an industry employee and perceived authorial source of *Dragon Age* information, those who followed both on Twitter were treated to what amounted to a promotion wrapped up in a friendly conversation, giving it an aura of intimacy. Such use of social media provides greater credibility to the promotion, hiding the work of promotion in a veneer of sociability.

The practices of impression management in new media labor may conflict with the central role of authenticity in the creation of celebrity or stardom, making negotiations such as those described above particularly important for those new media workers who also attract public attention. Joshua Gamson (1994) attempts to tease out the distinctions between an actor as a worker, on the one hand, and as a celebrity valued for his or her ability to command attention, on the other, and notes that the elements needed for success in the second capacity are not necessarily commensurate with those needed for success in the first (58). One of the crucial elements in managing celebrity is the creation of a perceived authenticity, which many performers achieve through strategic disclosure of personal information on personal websites or other online venues (Deuze and Steward 2010; Théberge 2005). Increasingly, authenticity is created through disclosures of backstage performances, which "creates a crisis for public performers, who must integrate the rehearsal into the performance, convert the backstage into an onstage performance, control their images by appearing not to control them" (Gamson 1994: 143).

Whether strategically promoting the "self" or offering strategic backstage revelations of that "self," the celebrity as new media worker is engaged in impression management on a grand scale. The construction of a star text, or persona, is therefore an amplified form of the regular impression management work done in daily life. The intended audience for this performance of self is larger and more diverse, and the constraints on front stage behavior are perhaps more stringent. Even subcultural celebrity can result in audience expectations that their idols constantly perform "onstage" demonstrations of public availability

(Wheaton 2011). Thus, the maintenance of control of all elements of the public image is crucial, and is closely related to managing audience expectations and perceptions. Missteps at any level may result in the failure of necessary performances as new media worker, (micro-)celebrity, or authentic star.

Social Media and Stardom

Given the importance of controlled impression management, the somewhat chaotic world of interactional social media may present a challenge. Stardom, in fact, has been altered by social media in as much as it has offered a new venue for the construction of star texts by stars themselves (Petersen 2009), while also offering an additional venue for the traditional labor of those who support celebrity formation. Unsurprisingly, perhaps, many social media accounts are managed by others on behalf of celebrities (Cohen 2009). Thus, just as critical work in star studies has analyzed the constructed star text, and not the individual, investigation of stardom in an age of social media must analyze the purported personal use of these venues, and be careful not to inadvertently attribute agency to an individual creator who may or may not be responsible for their social media activities. As I discuss Day's use of social media, I really discuss "Day's" use of social media—that is, the use of these tools by the constructed persona and agent that is represented as "Felicia Day."

The availability of social media, together with the proliferation of digital means of distribution, has challenged the traditional structures of the media industry. Historically, the film and television industries have been bottlenecks, funding, producing, and distributing only a small portion of proposed projects. To navigate this structure, writers, actors, and other creative personnel have relied upon cultural intermediaries such as managers or agents. The role of these intermediaries was to bring expertise to an individual's attempts to build and sustain a career in a highly competitive industry, while offering that industry a reliable way of finding and negotiating with its talent (Kemper 2009: 5). From the tight, centralized control of the studio system to the teams of "people" who now serve this role for individuals, the management of labor and popular perceptions has long been outsourced. In fact, Twitter may

be just the latest stage on which some of these management professionals produce material for public consumption on behalf of, and often in
the name of, those for whom they work. Looking to actors and similar
performers, the list of intermediaries only grows, encompassing representatives of the fashion and beauty industries whose job is entirely
focused on the management of public perception. This construction of
celebrity, through the decisions of legions of affiliated professionals, has
been understood to build a desired star text upon which the individual
may capitalize (Gamson 1994: 61).

While such managerial professionals have served a valuable role
for many stars, smoothing their contractual negotiations and public
appearances alike, their roles are frequently vilified. From their emergence in Hollywood, agents who work with both creative talent and
industrial representatives have been decried as two-faced, unnecessary,
and tricky operators (Kemper 2009: 1). Hired to be intermediaries, they
are regularly understood as barriers and decried as liars, opportunists,
sharks, or leeches who profit off of others' value and offer nothing in
return. The perceived opportunity to free stars and industries from the
tyranny of middle management via digital media is thus appealing; in
reality, however, these venues are also tightly (if differently) managed.

Use of social media by celebrities, or their teams, has begun to generate scholarly literature. Much early work in this area focused on the use
of personal blogs by entertainment industry professionals, including
television writers and famous athletes, among others (Chin and Hills
2008; Sanderson 2008). Paul Théberge (2005), using the example of
recording artist Moby's blog, argued that the small forms of interaction
made possible online nonetheless accumulated to create intense experiences for fans through their frequency and perceived directness. It also
appears that these online engagements can, for many fans, cement a
celebrity's importance in connection to their projects. This is equally the
case for performers and writer/producers. Actor James Marsters's use of
blogging appeared to grant him central legitimacy in the characterization of Spike on *Buffy the Vampire Slayer* and *Angel* (The WB, 1999–
2004) (Hills and Williams 2005). In the case of Javier Grillo-Marxauch,
a writer and producer for *Lost* (ABC, 2004–2010), blogging cemented
his authority over the text, despite the fact that many other writer/pro-
ducers contributed to the series. Bertha Chin and Matt Hills (2008)

state that personal blogs like his "attempt to share personal stories and anecdotes about fans' favourite media products, their daily lives, and their interactions with family and co-workers" (268). These disclosures are particularly important for what they call "subcultural celebrities," who exist outside the mainstream and balance performances as fans, media outsiders, and everyday people with performances of elevated status and authority over the text.

Turning to social networking, scholars have increasingly suggested the necessity of careful management and control of the intimate disclosures and interactive exchanges facilitated by these new media. Alice Marwick and danah boyd use Goffman's theories of impression management to unpack Twitter use and micro-celebrity, and Nick Muntean and Anne Helen Petersen (2009) use an ideological framework to examine the use of Twitter as a venue to share "real" celebrity selves that, conveniently, reinforce existing personae. P. David Marshall's (2010) work on "presentational media" suggests that the interpersonalization of the construction of identity in social media sets it apart from earlier, one-to-many forms of celebrity construction (42). This, in turn leads to the recursive creation of increasingly "private" public selves, as those in the public eye engage in disclosures that ostensibly go beyond the polished public image. The celebrity as presentational self, constructed and visible, may even become a model for a kind of late capitalist identity formation, Marshall argues, recalling arguments about the necessity of the entrepreneurial self in new media labor.

Social media, in its appearances of intimacy and practices of limited disclosure, allows for people within media industries to directly (or seemingly directly) manage their relationships to audiences, production, and distribution, bolstering and benefiting from the perception that traditional intermediaries are absent. In essence, the "talent" takes on the management of their own personas and relationships; where agents have cultivated reputation in order to engage with both talent and industry (Zafirau 2007), stars may now cultivate this managerial self in connection with their celebrity self. When this intimacy is well done, it can contribute directly to an emphasis on the individual that easily slides into an auteurist perspective on their work. Furthermore, insofar as social media use is experienced as not entirely within the constraints of the existing celebrity industry, it facilitates perceptions of individual celebrities as outside of the mainstream, as "cult" or "indie," a distinction that may carry over to their work. In the following sections, the role of social media in promoting discourses of auteurism and indie status is explored using Day's case.

Auteurs and Authenticity

Day's consistent display of a seemingly authentic identity as a gamer and fan generates a symbiosis with her projects, including *Redemption*. Through her perceived authenticity, she reaffirms the value of these identities and their centrality to her persona and, perhaps, her work. Day's status as both performer and creator of *The Guild* and *Redemption* builds a heightened association of her projects with her star text, facilitating the kind of authorial dominance seen in others' blogs. Finally, given that Day's major projects are a part of a larger gaming or geek culture, and that much of this culture has been described in terms of "cult" media, her performance of this identity facilitates a reading of Day as online auteur.

Day's acting work, and the unity of her on and off-screen appearances, facilitate a star text based on image and performed identity throughout her transmedia work and social media use. This authentic self—gamer, geek, and girl—is at least partially invoked in each of Day's major roles, and her use of Twitter, Goodreads, YouTube, and other social media sites maintains it over time and across media (Ellcessor 2012). As discussed already, celebrity use of social media is strongly tied to notions of authenticity, as stars can offer an "authenticating authenticity" (Dyer 1991: 133) through which their seemingly authentic embodiment of particular characteristics reaffirms the value of those traits in society at large. Additionally, however, the seemingly authentic celebrity individual opens the door to auteurist readings of their work by making their personality and biography available for consumption, analysis, and articulation to given projects. In the words of Andrew Sarris, "auteur theory is not so much a theory as an attitude, a table of values that converts film history into directorial autobiography. The auteur critic is obsessed with the wholeness of art and the artist" (1996: 30). The authentic star, as performer and particularly as creator, *is* his or her work, and vice versa.

Turning to Day's status as creator, we find that her use of social media amplifies her authorial voice, as the material she writes seems to harmonize completely with the authentic self displayed elsewhere. As an example, consider the brief YouTube videos released following each episode of *Redemption*, commenting on the behind-the-scenes process of writing, producing, or even acting in the episode. These videos serve a purpose similar to that of DVD commentary tracks, which produce additional content and knowledge about a central text (Klinger 2006). DVD commentary can also reinforce an auteurist reading of a text, making it "responsible for the inauguration of a new age of the cinematic author, returning like all repressed things do, with new vigor and omnipotence" (Orgeron 2007: 58). Day's videos are particularly prone to this reification, as they are shot from a neutral angle, framing Day, alone, from the waist up as she discusses the episode. Where actual footage from the set, for instance, would have included evidence of others' involvement, this setting reinforces her central position in relation to *Redemption*.

The claiming of authorship seen in these videos is crucial given the authentic identities associated with Day. Geekiness and videogames, particularly when articulated to femininity, are largely treated as niche interests within the larger structures of Hollywood and mass media. Thus, as only certain texts are granted authors, which function as a sign of their value (Foucault 1969/1979), the claim of authorship in niche or cult media is a move towards valorization. Though auteurism is most commonly associated with discourses about film, authorship has also become a growing concern within television reception, where the "showrunner," or writer-producer, of a distinctive program is granted the author-function (Kompare 2011: 98), and in relation to cult texts, which have been defined in part through their interest in production personnel. Such a move reclaims an ostensibly low culture artifact by using the tools of high culture (Hills 2002). For a niche web series, both televisual and cult media claims to auteurship have salience; web video remains a minor component of the global media landscape, and auteurship offers a means by which to elevate its cultural status.

Both creative producers and fans may use auteurist claims to legitimize such texts, but in doing so, they may also enter into peculiar conflicts of authority. Cult media, historically, has been built on active fan bases, many of which emerged "from literary science fiction fandom where issues of authorship are more clear-cut than in network television and where readers often have direct interactions with the writers of their favourite books and short stories" (Jenkins 1995: 187). This has required the consistent management of authorial dominance; the active, informed fan may claim an ownership of a canon that troubles relations of power surrounding the text. Given Day's claim to both fan and professional identities, her strong assertions of authorship function as a negotiation of these roles and her relationship to her audience.

In various social media, Day's promotions of her finished projects, discussions of her work processes, and exchanges with fellow fans regarding other media texts work together to manage her authorial identity. The thematic unities in her work manage audience expectations regarding content (Ellcessor 2012); however, they also manage power dynamics, setting Day apart from the average fan. Day has also engaged as a fan of Bethesda Game Studios' *Skyrim* (2011), exchanging tips and frustrations with others on Twitter; she similarly engaged as a fan of *Dragon Age* as she replayed the game in early 2011. Following the announcement of *Redemption*, however, such discussions of *Dragon Age* declined, replaced by tweets that related it to her project. Her transition from fan to producer was reflected in the ways she used social media, emphasizing her author function over her fan function. This was necessary because, although much contemporary media attempts to draw in audiences through multiplatformed content and opportunities for interaction, this strategy risks bringing fans and creators into conflict (Johnson 2007: 63). As in the case of the blog maintained by Grillo-Marxauch, Day's assertion of authorship serves to reinforce cultural hierarchies and differentiate fan/producer roles, managing audience expectations and behaviors. Claiming this authority enables Day to rally her fans around the release of new material, drawing upon her similarities to fans while using the power of authorship and celebrity to direct fan activity in desirable ways.

Most commonly, Day draws upon her similarities to fans while asserting her difference by requesting that her social media friends and followers aid in promoting her work. This call for amateur means of online distribution implies a personal relationship, and suggests that traditional marketing strategies are inaccessible for financial or ideological reasons, all while maintaining Day's authorial role as she manages her audience. For instance, in early November 2011, Day posted the following to her official Facebook page, along with the video in question: "Episode 5 of Dragon Age: Redemption is posted! It's my fave so far, blood and secrets :) If you like it PLEASE SHARE! We only have one ep to go, help us end with a BANG! I appreciate it!" (Day 2011a). In announcing her work so directly, with statements of ostensibly personal interest, Day creates an appearance of direct communication with fans. This is then used in the latter half of the status update, as she asks fans to share the video and help the series end well. Drawing upon the mechanics of viral or spreadable media (Jenkins, Li, and Krauskopf 2009), this request aligns Day and her work with amateur online content, and makes her fans a potential part of her success through their sharing, while maintaining her centrality to the project, its interpretation, and its success.

Insofar as Day can somewhat successfully balance a self-presentation as an authentic gamer and fan with a strong authorial voice, she creates a mutually reinforcing relationship between her creative work and her online identity. Her projects can be read through the auteurist lens of biography, drawing upon her public performances of self, and her online self can be seen as a naturalized source for her particular works. In this, the maintenance of a star text as a transmedia artifact is particularly clear, as a sudden departure in either her acting or producing choices might shake the foundation of authenticity on which much of her success has been based.

Indie Individualism

Day's persona is managed in such a way as to highlight characteristics of her work and aspects of her personality that accord with "indie" interpretations. Corporate connections are largely minimized, individualism and outsider status are highlighted, and a hybrid amateur-professional aesthetic is maintained in the work itself and her discussions of it. These negotiations augment her negotiation of authority and fan status, cementing her as an individual, independent creator.

Individualism is evident because, like many users of social media, Day produces significant content from a first-person point of view, using "I" and describing her daily activities, successes, and frustrations. For instance, prior to the announcement of *Redemption*, Day tweeted "Just ate half a bag of tortilla chips at 9am. This day of writing is not starting off with the self-discipline I would like, haha."(Day 2011d). This kind of self-deprecatory humor is common in quotidian uses of Twitter, and it performs a kind of authenticity in its relatability, humor, and its initial confession. It additionally performs the work of constructing Day as working individually, alone, on the writing that precedes all of her other web media production.

This individualism, characteristic of new media labor, and set apart from collaborative means of media production, allows for the possibility of reading Day as "indie." Variously defined, use of the term "indie" indicates that a person or text is in some way positioned in opposition to the mainstream and in alignment with "hip" or "cool" taste cultures (King 2009; Newman 2011). "Indie" can additionally be understood as not merely an adjective, but a culture, comprised of texts, institutions, individuals, and audiences that share particular expectations, as in the case of "indie" cinema (Newman 2011). Marks of distinction set "indie" media apart from mainstream texts, offering particular textual and paratextual indications of difference that appeal to a given taste culture.

Turning to Day's work, we can see how her success in online series production is tied in to markers of amateurism, even as she and her collaborators are now clearly professionals. Referring to productions or creative personnel as "independent" suggests that they are somehow "free, autonomous, and authentic" (Newman 2011: 3). Amateur web video, characterized by low budgets, online distribution, and a look that draws on web cam aesthetics as well as televisual or filmic tropes, is often understood in these very terms. This content exists in opposition to the polished professional content that also appears on social networking sites, and in its difference is made valuable. YouTube, for instance, features hosts of amateur videos, as well as professional music videos featuring major recording artists, clips of films and television shows, and official videos from various institutions (Burgess and Green 2009). *The Guild* incorporates many of these elements, particularly in its earliest seasons. The series, and Day as authorial creator, are positioned against a mainstream Hollywood media culture through interviews in which Day describes her decision to take her ideas to the Internet rather than a television network, and describes her intense work in creating the series on a shoestring budget (Brophy-Warren 2009). Such narratives emphasize the individualism of Day as a creative author. Though she often praises collaborators in these interviews, the singling out of Day as the voice of *The Guild* indicates the importance of "individuals in the process of cultural production, as well as the ideological importance to identify individual power in an era of democratic capitalism" (Marshall 2010: 46). As in new media labor, institutions and collective labor are overshadowed by the individual as the source of creativity and merit.

Alternately, the model of "Indiewood" is perhaps useful in analyzing Day's work on *Redemption*. Geoff King argues that Indiewood offers "a blend comprised of features associated with dominant, mainstream convention and markers of 'distinction' designed to appeal to more particular, niche-audience constituencies" (King 2009: 2). In the case of *Redemption*, the involvement of BioWare is doubly analogous to studio involvement in Indiewood film. BioWare itself is a specialty division of game publisher Electronic Arts, legitimating EA's annual crop of sports and shooter games through its emphasis on character and narrative. Through *Redemption*, BioWare reasserts its difference by aligning with Day and thus with an even more indie component of gaming culture, even as such involvement brings the web series further in line with major media industry logics.

The blend of indie and mainstream components is evident in *Redemption*. At an aesthetic level, though budget was reportedly low and filming is less than virtuosic, the markers of web video, including web cam shots, are replaced by a style that directly mimics the animations from the *Dragon Age* franchise. The game is brought into conversation with the world of web video, and both lend each other dimensions of prestige. As Indiewood films work as subsidiary capitalism for big studios, lending their prestige in place of profit, *Redemption* associates BioWare with the "indie" dimensions of web video and the celebrity of Day within gaming and geek circles, while Day gains association with a major video game release, potentially growing her audience beyond those circles. *Redemption* is both part of the franchise and part of Day's authorial aura as authentic gamer fan.

Another component of an "indie" culture is the implication that it is, economically, a smaller operation than major competitors within a given cultural industry. An "indie" film, like an "amateur" web video, is evaluated differently than major releases in terms of finances as well as aesthetics. Thus, though Day has been successful in web video, the scale of that success is undoubtedly several degrees below what might consti- tute success as the showrunner of a television series. The emphasis on the individual, seen in social media and in press coverage of *The Guild* and *Redemption*, further obfuscates the economic and labor realities of these productions.

Although Day's collaborators are not invisible, neither are they made central to understandings of these projects. Co-producer Kim Evey, in particular, has been part of both of Day's major online projects. She is listed in the credits, discussed in interviews, and has her own social media presence through which she engages with Day, fans, and other media producers. However, Evey is not granted the status of author of these texts; rather, she is positioned as secondary to Day's dominant, individual star text. Day, like film director Wes Anderson (Orgeron 2007), has made efforts to draw attention to her collaborators and their work, most commonly through interactive use of Twitter, discussion in published interviews, and participation in their other projects, such as *Guild* actor Sandeep Parikh's series *The Legend of Neil* (2008–2010). However, given the other factors that encourage individualist and auteurist interpretations of Day's work on the basis of her presentation of a celebrity self, displays of authenticity, and individual success narra- tive, such practices have not resulted in great attention to the collabora- tive nature of web series production.

A final element of Day's star text of connection that facilitates inter- pretations of her as an indie auteur is the tendency to position herself as a kind of underdog, perpetually surprised by success. This undoubt- edly builds on the elements of authentic geekery and individual cre- ativity that drive her star text. It is also, however, a routine narrative of celebrity; overcoming adversity is a simple story with great poten- tial for audience identification (Gamson 1994: 68). One of the key ways in which overcoming adversity is performed is through asking fans to aid in the promotion of her work. As previously discussed, Day asked fans to spread the word about *Redemption* via Facebook. Asking fans to "help us end with a BANG!" (Day 2011a) displayed excitement and a desire for, but not expectation of, success. Such posts have also characterized Day's promotion of *The Guild*. However, in the context of Microsoft's distribution of *The Guild* and BioWare's involvement with *Redemption*, it is perhaps more a performance of outsider status than an accurate reflection of need. Despite industrial relationships, the discourse of overcoming adversity both builds upon and reinforces the individual, authentic nature of Day's star text, furthering the development of a keenly managed "indie" professional persona.

Conclusions

This case study has demonstrated that the public presentation of an individual, authentic star text of connection via social media may overpower the industrial and material relationships at play in contemporary online entertainment media. In a figure like Day, who is both a subcultural celebrity and a new media entrepreneur, these tendencies are amplified, as the economics, labor relations, and collaborative nature of web video projects are subsumed into Day's star text. Day's persona, as actor, celebrity, writer, producer, geek, gamer, and social media user, is carefully managed in the service of particular goals. While some portion of this is likely conscious, I have argued that this managed "self" has broader effects upon the ways in which Day's work is understood. The unity of Day's biography, persona, and professional work fosters a seemingly natural auteurist reading of her star text and her productions; by publicly presenting as an authentic, "indie" individual via social media, Day facilitates a slippage between her persona and her work. Frequently, this slippage has benefited her as well as her creative and corporate partners, as she lends her aura as an approachable indie auteur to the corporations involved in these projects.

Thus, this case study also demonstrates the necessity of denaturalizing self-presentations in social media, and of reflecting upon them instead as constructed, onstage representations. New media often facilitates its own acceptance as truth through its perceived aliveness (White 2006) as well as through its interactivity. Approaching social media as not untruthful, but as both intentionally constructed and unintentionally suggestive of particular interpretations, allows for deeper investigation of the ways in which social media both does and does not challenge preexisting social and industrial structures. Many of the tactics described in this case study of Day recall the strategies used by film studios, gossip magazines, Hollywood agents, music industry professionals, and a range of other cultural producers and managers tasked with building and maintaining an audience. The locus and means of management may be different, but the process of self-management in social media draws on long histories of strategic presentation.

Finally, although powerful star texts have certainly long influenced reception, the similarity between celebrity use of social media for strategic self-presentation and the everyday practices of social media use amid neoliberal labor markets suggests that the ability to strategically manage and present an "authentic" individual self is an increasingly necessary skill across industries. Whether in Silicon Valley (Marwick 2010), new media labor (Gill 2010), among Hollywood agents themselves (Zafirau 2007), or in the mixture of work and play that constitutes much contemporary networked media use, the ability to craft and deploy an online self-presentation is central to the way in which individuals navigate their social and professional relationships. In conditions of uncertainty, the management of self as brand, as micro-celebrity, or as another form of salable resource allows for quick, flexible rearrangements of labor. The entrepreneurial self of new media labor is hailed in a variety of markets, including niche and, increasingly, major media industries. The potential of this self as text to gloss over crucial questions concerning capital and relations of power only call on us to become better equipped to critically engage with these texts and the work they do.

III

Tactics

9

"Selling Station Personality"

Managing Impending Change in Postwar Radio, 1948–1953

ALEXANDER RUSSO

Within radio lore, one of the most oft-told tales concerns the origins of Top 40 radio. In this story, which has a number of permutations, some night between 1953 and 1955, Todd Storz, the enterprising owner of KOWH in Omaha Nebraska, is sitting at a tavern waiting for one of the waitresses to get off duty. He notices that the customers and later the waitresses keep repeating the same songs on the jukebox. Asked by Storz why she kept playing the same songs again and again, an anonymous everywoman allegedly replied "I like 'em." Although KOWH was currently programming a range of specialty music shows to reach a wide audience, Storz immediately applied the observation that audiences prefer a limited playlist to trim his own station's focus and provide only a narrow range of pop tunes to housewives. Thus were the origins of the Top 40, which flew in the face of prevailing wisdom and programming practice during the postwar period. This story embodies one of the enduring myths of radio history, one that concerns the origins of the all-music formats that would replace a faltering network system in the 1950s.[1] Although the veracity of this tale has been repeatedly called into question, it persists because it resonates with powerful claims about the entrepreneurial insights of Storz and deejays like Alan Freed who supposedly anticipated and met audience needs. However, this focus on an individual's lightning-strike revelations (long the currency for radio lore) elides structural dynamics that better explain industrial efforts to manage the transition from network to post-network broadcasting. A series of conferences organized by rights management organization Broadcast Music Incorporated (BMI) and designed to discuss the future of the radio industry provides a contrast to the traditional tale of program innovation and forms the topic of this chapter. Convened across the country and bringing together national and local figures, the BMI program clinics suggest the importance of intermediary groups in generating and disseminating conventional wisdom for an industry undergoing significant change.

The seemingly smooth transition between radio's network golden age and its postwar incarnation stands out as a relatively unexamined era within the historiography of broadcasting. Within this body of literature, American radio broadcasting is neatly divided into two distinct eras, a network period and a locally oriented period. In the early 1950s, locally oriented, musically programmed stations supplanted national networks that had been decimated by competition with television for audiences and sponsors. Formatted radio supposedly arose "up from the middle," the product of pioneering entrepreneurs like Storz and Gordon McLendon, who were unencumbered by the centralizing policies of national networks, the restrictions faced by high-profile urban stations, and the failure of networks to respond to television (McFarland 1972). However, this narrative obscures the complex ways that the radio industry responded to changes in its own structure—with the rise of small stations and the development of new technologies such as the 45 rpm and 33 rpm "format wars," as well as the influence of new audience reception patterns. The latter included programming to specific demographic markets, such as teen, working class, and African American, as well as dispersed listening patterns created by multi-set homes and television/radio homes.[2]

This chapter examines the role of BMI program clinics in order to complicate narratives of radio history that posit the centrality of certain "great men" like Storz and McLendon as owners as well as disc-jockeys like Allen Freed and Bill Randle. Too often, histories of management slide into hagiographic accounts that amplify the supposed powers of "great managers" at the expense of other causal factors. The account in this chapter stresses the multiple, conflicting forces at a moment of transition.[3] It shifts the focus to that of "cultural economy," a term used by Paul du Gay and Michael Pryke, who note that "techniques of 'economic management' do not come ready made. They have to be invented, stabilized, refined, and reproduced; they have to be disseminated and implanted in practices of various kind in a range of different locales" (2002: 8). du Gay and Pryke argue for breaking down a distinction between cultural and economic accounts of media industries in order to understand how the economic decisions that drive organizational priorities and decision-making are "built up, or assembled from, a range of disparate, but inherently cultural, parts" (12). At a moment of transition, as the radio industry struggled to redefine itself, it relied on rationales, criteria, and models that were manifestly economic but were assembled from cultural preferences and biases. In the BMI program clinics, different sets of cultural values and valuations were brought to bear on the problem of what to do with radio.

One way to illustrate this process is to follow Keith Negus' suggestion that we examine the ways in which "industry produces culture" and also how "culture produces industry" (1999; 2002a: 118). Drawing on Pierre Bourdieu (1993) and Richard Peterson (1976), Negus charts how internal rules or organization (their institutional culture) influence decision-making procedures in the production processes of cultural forms. Negus is interested in how record label personnel choose which artists to sign, develop, and promote, but the issues he explores—aesthetic value and commercial potential—apply equally well to station and program managers. Because BMI established sites of inter-industry dialogue, it is possible to read their comments as representative of a set of beliefs and assumptions, or what Pierre Bourdieu (1979/1984) calls a "habitus," about programming strategies and content. Viewed in this way, the comments serve as an index of both received sets of cultural valuation and the industrial values of success that allowed the clinic participants to speak with authority. The choices made by various broadcasters as they responded to the chaotic postwar radio environment were part of a diffusion and articulation of standards of judgment, taste, and best practices at a particular moment of crisis in the radio industry. The changing habitus of station and program managers underwrote decisions that responded to systemic crisis as a structural condition that produced formatted radio.

BMI Management and Postwar Radio

BMI's program clinics demonstrate the value in studying the activities and orientation of "management," as seen elsewhere in this volume. The organization is neither a producer nor a consumer of culture. It is an intermediary, managing the rights of a subset of writers/composers and collecting aggregated payments from radio stations on behalf of those musicians. This intermediary managerial position creates overlapping interests. Radio interests formed it in 1939 to compete with ASCAP (American Society of Composers, Authors, and Publishers). A long established music and performance rights publisher, ASCAP focused on older, more traditional Tin Pan Alley and pop standards. Its reporting system and organization favored more established performers and, at least through the 1950s, its revenues were triple that of BMI. BMI artists tended to represent less established musical genres, most notably hillbilly (now country) and rhythm and blues ("Rock 'n' Roll" 1956: 75; Shepard 1956: 31; Haverlin 1956: 135).[4] Throughout the 1940s and 1950s, ASCAP and BMI fought an ongoing battle for control over performance rights for music broadcast on the radio, which intensified as recorded music became an ever more important source of programming for radio stations in the postwar period (Ennis 1992; Sanjek and Sanjek 1991). In conducting these programming clinics, the organization acted as a kind of management consultant to both the crop of new stations emerging via the postwar license expansion and the more established network affiliates which were planning their responses to the threat posed by television.

BMI wanted broadcasters to embrace the economic virtues of programming based on recorded music—practices that broke with the then-dominant model of dependence on network-supplied programs. This meant not just disc-jockeys playing records but also the value of certain kinds of music that would fill these formats. These economic and cultural considerations were deeply intertwined as broadcasters were filled with "common sense" knowledge about long-established broadcasting practices and generationally-enshrined concepts of good culture (not classical symphonic music, but rather established middle-of-the road big band and pop standards of the 1940s). Broadcasters had to be convinced that musical tastes of audiences demographically dissimilar to themselves would provide a solution to their economic problems.

Postwar broadcasters were concerned about the impact of television and increased competition among stations. The threat of television is well documented, and it looms in the background of the minds of postwar radio personnel (Schwoch 1990; Rothenbuhler and McCourt 2004; Douglas 1999; Boddy 1992). However, the BMI clinics were conceived at a time when, for many stations, television was a vague threat rather than an actual competitor. In 1948, less than one half of 1 percent of American households owned a set. It was at this moment that the program clinics had their genesis. Even during the year of the greatest number of clinics, 1951, less than one quarter of American homes had access to television (Sterne 1999). For many stations there was a more pressing need to respond to the rapid increase in the number of small, independent stations in late 1940s and their impact on intra-radio competition. Between 1946 and 1951, the number of radio stations in the United States tripled from just over one thousand stations to nearly three thousand. Moreover, in 1946, 93 percent of AM stations were affiliated with a national network (881 out of 948). In 1951, this had fallen to 54 percent (1247 out of 2331) (Sterling and Kittross 1978: 510–12). Because many of these stations either did not have a network affiliation or were affiliated with the Mutual Network, which exerted much less strict control over affiliate programming, they sought out and programmed differently than major network affiliates, and their strategies acted as bellwethers for the decisions made by those affiliates after the collapse of networks.

The rise of small, independent stations caused rifts within the broadcasting industry. They were regarded by networks as irritants, and even dangerous for counter programming and ignoring public service obligations to sell more time. Many of these independent stations relied heavily on transcribed programs or records, considered by the networks to be lower forms of programming. Following the "blue book"

controversy of 1945–1947, in which an FCC study led to significant public debate about public interest in commercial radio, the networks used
their clout to revise the National Association of Broadcasters' (NAB)
Code to restrict overt commercialization and protect their own interests (Socolow 2002: 282–02; Russo 2010: 144–49). This caused severe
financial problems for owners who had viewed stations as a "license
to print money." By 1948, irrespective of television, the average station
audience was half of what it had been just three years earlier, declining
from sixty thousand sets to thirty thousand sets (Ennis 1992:136). At the
1948 annual meeting, NAB President Justin Miller and NAB Research
Director Kenneth Baker warned that the outlook for AM was gloomy
due to competition from smaller stations and multiple station ownership ("Radio Warned" 1948: 6). Even though, and perhaps because,
nearly half of the new stations were unprofitable, they were perceived as
a threat to the industrial status quo.[5]

Independent stations objected to being depicted as spoilers and
exerted their newfound clout at the September 1947 NAB convention
over revisions to the NAB Code that restricted the use of spot com-
mercials, a guideline they perceived as favoring networks ("Station
Managers" 1947: 32). During this debate, Ted Cott, the program director of pioneering New York City independent station WNEW, played
an important role as an advocate for independent stations. Cott rose to
prominence within the industry while working for two powerful New
York City independents, first as dramatic director of WNYC from 1934
to 1943 and then as vice-president and program director of WNEW.[6] He
argued that the NAB's revisions to its code would disproportionately
harm unaffiliated stations. Cott and Ben Strouse of Washington, D.C.'s
WWDC negotiated for independent stations' representation within the
NAB to give them a voice in the organization's policy decisions and its
definitions of standards of practice ("NAB in Peace" 1948: 3).

Less than a year after this incident, Cott proposed the idea for industry-wide program clinics in the 1948 edition of *Radio Daily's Shows
of Tomorrow*. *Shows of Tomorrow* was a catalog of network and independently produced programs available for sponsorship and was an
important reference for program directors of local stations looking
for transcription, cooperative, or other programming types. Because it
was universally read, it also served as a forum for discussing the future

of programming. Conversely, because many popular press and trade articles on the future of radio featured no small amount of puffery and prognosticating, Cott's "Plea for Recognition," stands out. He wrote:

> The radio prophets are racing like Paul Reveres [sic] through the countryside announcing that the redinks [sic] are about to invade radio. Cries of alarm and warning proclaim the invasion of television coming to conquer the land of the AMers. Hastily the radio leaders are consulting their bankbooks; may we respectfully urge that they consult with their program directors. (1948–1949: 24)[7]

Cott noted that despite intense competition, and in contrast to radio engineers and salesmen, the nation's program directors had no public forum in which to "gather, discuss, instruct, learn or exchange information":

> We need a place for the program people of radio to get together and saturate themselves . . . with the stimulation of programming tools, techniques, and ideas; to carry back home and plant the seed of an idea that was grown in New York, [to] put into practice the gimmick that made for new listeners in Des Moines (24).

Cott's call for dialogue was based on mutual exchange and the role of program manager. No single type of station had the complete solution to the threat of television, it assumed, but by using ideas generated by different types of stations, multiple solutions could be found.

Cott found an ally in BMI President Carl Haverlin. Haverlin had become the first paid president of BMI the prior year, taking over duties that had been performed unpaid by Justin Miller, the head of the NAB. Although BMI was closely linked with the NAB, Haverlin's background placed him somewhat outside the norms prescribed by NBC and CBS. Haverlin rose to prominence in the 1930s as program director for KFI and KECA, Earl Anthony's Los Angeles stations. He later was station relations director for Davis and Schwegler, a transcription firm, and had the same role in the newly formed BMI in 1940. He stayed at BMI until 1943, when he left to serve as vice president of Mutual, but returned in 1947 ("Haverlin First" 1947: 13; "Our Respects" 1947: 46). Unlike NBC and CBS, Mutual allowed recorded programming, which suggests that Haverlin may not have shared the larger networks' antipathy toward transcriptions.[8]

As recorded music became more important for all radio stations, BMI sought to get its artists played. One strategy was to educate station personnel in how to manage their growing music libraries. To this end, starting in 1948, the organization sponsored an ongoing series of clinics that brought station librarians to New York and taught them various aspects of rights clearance, choosing music, and cataloging and caring for discs ("BMI Library" 1948: 1); it also conducted meetings at the NAB annual convention. The popularity of the clinics, however, convinced BMI to expand their focus to include general programming questions as well as take the clinics "on the road" across the country ("Radio Meggers" 1949: 4; "Program Problems" 1950: 27). As network radio faltered, the clinics grew in popularity and stature and went on the road to attract participants from smaller market stations ("New Series" 1951: 5). In 1951, the organization partnered with state broadcasters' associations, establishing links to the professional networks that operated at local levels ("BMI Thanks" 1951a: 21).[9] That year there were thirty-five clinics and in subsequent years there were forty-two and then fifty. By the end of 1953, over 12,000 broadcasters had attended a radio clinic. While the clinics continued after this point, they shifted their focus to television (Dolberg 1951–1952: 14).

In addition, program clinics fit BMI's strategy of client service as means of differentiating itself from ASCAP. Although BMI had successfully performed its role as an alternative to ASCAP, its costs were higher than its competitors'. In response, BMI offered an array of services to its clients, a service *Billboard* described as "say [ing] it with flowers." In practice, this meant that BMI and such organizations provided consultants, script services, catalogs of licensed songs, promotions, market research, transcriptions of individual songs, and complete programs. BMI representatives were charged with responding to station problems by providing BMI-based solutions to programming issues (Marvin 1945: 12).[10] As I have argued elsewhere (2010), a variety of program services provided aid to stations throughout the 1930s and 1940s in ways that served mutual interests. BMI, ASCAP, SESAC, and AMP extended this model (77–114). Still, in so doing, they suggest ways in which national organizations engaged and responded to local concerns.

Program Clinics as Venue for Managing Industrial Change

Clinics were not one-way lectures; rather, they represented an extended dialogue between "the middle" and the coasts. BMI was careful to foreground the clinics as a space for exchange of productive ideas, which could come from local, as well as, national stations. As Cott noted in a speech before a clinic in Portland, Oregon, in March 1951, "I'm not a guy from New York who comes around and tells you what to do. You do what you do as well as I can do. We have tremendous competition in New York. We have licked it and we are winning . . . but so are you" (BMI Program Clinic 1951h). Later that year, BMI's head of station relations Glenn Dolberg reminded his audience that the speakers were "Not here to tell you things. We are here to remind you and let you contribute from your wealth of experiences" (BMI Program Clinic 1951c). This dynamic of reciprocity was recognized by other individuals in the music industry. In the introduction to a special sixteen-page wrap-up of that year's sessions, Joe Csida, the editor-in-chief of *Billboard*, commented in May 1952,

> we've said previously that radio, in these critical evolutionary days, can only maintain its greatest position by sticking together, by freely exchanging ideas and experience, by programming, promoting, and selling with an aggressiveness, a vitality, and an ingenuity never before attained. The BMI clinics themselves are a living exciting example of radio doing all of those things. ("The BMI Clinic" 1952: 11–27)

That year, in response to participant demand, the clinics had been restructured to allow more time for "bull sessions" and Q&A with the speakers ("Programming Way" 1952: 13).

The formal presentation and "bull sessions" referred to by Csida created a venue for "war stories" which demonstrate how these clinics functioned as a venue for defining, evaluating, and redefining industrial practices. The clinics' format consisted of presentations by national and regional broadcasters followed by a question and answer period. Both presenters and questioners relied on anecdotal evidence derived from their experiences as station managers and programmers, which, in turn, allowed the clinic audience to weigh competing strategies and evidence of success. Studies of organization communication, such as Julian Orr's study of photocopy repairmen, have found that such "war stories" perform important functions in maintaining social relationships within an occupational community, disseminating information for problem solving, and establishing a collective memory for that group. Orr notes that these stories are a crucial part of the diagnostic process (1996: 104). Likewise, in the BMI program clinics, stories of successes and failures became part of a larger diagnostic dialogue. Because presentations were made by both national and local figures and because the process was open to active question and answer sessions, they demonstrate how the clinics created a site for discussion and evaluation. The following sections will examine repeated themes within these stories to demonstrate how the clinics were part of a larger industrial discussion over programming strategies and authority within stations. Space prohibits a complete elaboration of all the potential solutions discussed, so I will discuss several important threads that highlight radio's attempts to transition away from a network-centric model toward a local, musical model. Not all these strategies were successful, but that does not diminish the importance of the clinics as evidence of ways that the broadcasting industry sought to respond to and manage changes to its economic model. Nor does the failure of some of these solutions reduce the significance of the clinics in BMI's strategy of client service and its competition with ASCAP.

Station Response: Block Programming

In the latter half of the 1940s, one popular response to the challenges of competitive programming was disc-jockey–based music and news block programming. Although already a part of the radio soundscape, in 1947 the disc-jockey exploded in popularity. Mid-year, *Sponsor* called disc-jockey–based block programming "the hottest trend in radio" and noted that 90 percent of the country's independent radio stations either already used or planned to adopt it in the next six months ("Guesswork" 1947: 22). Station managers surveyed in 1948 by *Radio Daily* overwhelmingly considered music and news the top two types of programs that gained audiences (Burke 1948–1949: 9). Disc-jockey–based music and the block news format represent an intermediate step toward a unified station sound and away from discrete, short programs. Because of their popularity and their deviation from a network-era model of programming variety, block programming formats were a frequent topic of discussion in the program clinics.

Block programming of music depended on the disc-jockey to tie together still relatively disparate musical types into a uniform whole within increasingly larger segments of time in the schedule. For example, in 1947, Cincinnati station WCKY embraced this programming philosophy by replacing a single overall program director with several program directors, each of whom was responsible for a schedule segment. These directors worked with the segment deejay to develop a coherent presentational style for that block that also meshed with the overall station identity. They used the tone and style of the announcer personality to distinguish themselves from one another, rather than any specific musical genre (Keith 1989: 36). This conflation of program type and audience construction was possible because WCKY's segments lasted several hours, instead of the fifteen- minute or half-hour periods that characterized traditional programming. Repeated program events punctuated these blocks to draw their distracted audiences back to the station, but the deejays remained central.

In February 1947, *Sponsor* magazine noted that deejays were successful because they were "the perfect example of mood programming" in blocks that lasted several hours long. "This means that the listener who wants music knows he can have it without shifting his dial during an extended period" ("Music Sells" 1947: 21). Programming predictability was an innovation distinct from the fifteen-minute segments of varied program types and appeals that characterized network programming. It was, as WNEW owner Bernice Judis quipped in 1949, programming where "you can leave the room and, when you come back, you've missed nothing" (quoted in McFarland 1972: 101).[11] Residual programs and sponsors meant that not all stations were willing to use block programming for their entire schedule. Although it extended the time frame of the individual show, with a few notable exceptions, block programming continued the network era programming philosophy of "variety," wherein stations sought to appeal to a wide cross section of individuals. Shows and deejays had individual personalities but the station's identity was constituted by multiple blocks rather than a single overarching programming philosophy. Despite the hopes invested in it, block programming was not a panacea for radio's ills. Indeed, Eric Rothenbuhler and Tom McCourt argue that the elimination of block programming and embrace of a middle-of-the-road station-wide strategy was central to Todd Storz's success with KOWH (2004: 6). That success was based on another strategy of developing station personality with a schedule integrated by music, tone, and style. Although Storz is heralded for pioneering music formats, the BMI program clinics suggest that he was part of a larger, industry-wide conversation regarding the development of station personality as an alternative model of station identity.

Station Response: Network Identity to Station Personality

Station personality was a frequently mentioned strategy for stations to improve ratings, one that represented a shift away from then-dominant conceptions of program identity linked to the network to which the station was affiliated. Station managers and program directors often felt that many local stations could not compete on "quality"—a proxy for network-provided programs. At the same time, as networks began transferring their most popular entertainers to television, managers realized that existing identities based on network affiliation could soon lose their relevance (MacFarland 1972: 95–96). J. Leonard Reinsch, a manager of several radio stations, articulated this philosophy of variety in the 1948 book on *Radio Station Management.* As he noted, "you have an obligation as a licensee to provide a well-rounded program schedule for all segments of your potential audience. Your program schedule should mirror the area which you serve" (25). During the network era, the consensus within the radio industry was that total audience size was the best indicator of programming success. Networks and their affiliates rejected the idea of a single format for a station because they viewed this as a restriction on potential audience size. However, managers recognized that this model would not survive the end of network programming and searched for alternatives.

One of station personality's most forceful adherents was Ted Cott, whose frequent presence at clinics ensured this programming and promotion strategy was heavily repeated. In multiple venues, Cott cited his experience as the manager for independent stations in the highly competitive New York market as the origin for his evangelizing for station personality. His WNEW "war stories" were central to establishing his credibility and for demonstrating the success of station personality as a programming strategy in a competitive environment. Having a unique quality that allowed listeners to recognize the station in terms of its programs was, as Cott termed it, a way of "letting people know where to come back to" (BMI Program Clinic 1951h). Station personality was based on the development and maintenance of a distinct identity throughout the broadcast day with distinct audience segments and patterns in mind. It involved developing techniques for viewing the station's schedule as a singular unit, rather than as a collection of independent elements. The means to accomplish this switch was a central theme for many of the program clinics. At one clinic held at the 1949 NAB convention, Cott and several other large independent station program directors held a panel called "How to Steal an Audience" in which they discussed block programming, niche audiences, the process of selecting a station specialty, and music selection—all as solutions to increased competition with television and other stations ("Independents' Day" 1949: 26; "Sales Clinic" 1949: 29).

One frequently discussed route to station identity was program specialization, to be understood less in terms of our contemporary narrowcasting, but still as a clear movement away from a variety model. For example, George Perking of WHDH-Boston, argued in a September 1951 clinic that by specializing in a few types of programming— music, news, and sports—stations could compete with networks during specific hours and for specific audiences (BMI Program Clinic 1951a). "Specialized" was not a single audience; it was simply not every audience. As Allan Page, General Manager of KWSO, Lawton, Oklahoma, and KRHD, Duncan, Oklahoma, noted in an October 30, 1950, clinic:

> We need to give up the idea that you can program music for the average person. As individuals, people pick their music listening based on the mood they are in at the moment. . . . Music plays an essential role in developing that station personality. A station should determine what its station market should be and program its music to appeal to the greatest segments of that market. (BMI Program Clinic 1951g).

Many speakers advised stations to make local appeals and to become an integral part of the community. And as part of the outreach process, the clinics produced impacts in precisely those smaller, locally oriented stations ("BMI Program Clinics" 1951: 33). The idea of exchanging individual program identities for a station-based identity was received by the industry as a revolutionary and "shackle breaking" concept (75). A 1952 *Billboard* article on "Programming Way to Renounce Fear," which described the clinics, noted,

> The emphasis was variously put on stronger public service, the right kind of program blocking, more local news, judicious selection of recordings, and a minimizing of crime, hysteria, and bad news. But whatever direction the speaker took, he usually emphasized that the most important thing was to build and maintain the station's personality. (13)

Additionally, station personality was articulated through deejays. In a May 1951 clinic in Milwaukee, Wisconsin, Bud Bickel of Detroit station WJR noted that even large 50-kilowatt clear channel stations needed to develop personalities that were independent of the network identity so that audiences could identify with them: "The local personality can be more important than the big name simply because he is real, flesh and blood, approachable. If you're smart make sure he is seen as well and not on television" (BMI Program Clinic 1951e). Bickel recognized not only that local appearances by station announcers were effective and necessary, but that, as will be discussed below, the station manager needed to carefully monitor staff to prevent them from becoming so popular that they left the station.

Station Response: Musical Selection

A third technique used by independent stations was greater care in choosing musical selections used to both establish station personality and appeal to distinct audience segments. On network programs during the swing era, the sponsoring ad agency of the song plugger and bandleader chose the songs. The secondary status of recorded programming and the restrictions of transcription-provided content meant that program managers often delegated song selection to disc-jockeys or broadcast engineers (Ennis 1992: 110). With increased competition for audience attention this began to change. Dick Pack, WNEW's program director after Cott had been recruited to NBC, described the station's strategy in a talk entitled "Care and Feeding of Disc-Jockeys" at the September 1951 BMI clinic in Boston. He pushed stations to recognize that musical programming had to be "thought out, not just a few records slapped on turntable." He advised program directors to use the five W's of journalism "Why . . . what kind of music? What . . . any can be good. . . . When, what time of day[?] . . . Who . . . is the music for[?] . . . Where . . . what is the audience doing[?]" Still, for Pack, the ideal schedule featured a blend of popular hits and standards. At WNEW, each fifteen-minute period included at least one "well known" song—either a current Top 10 hit or an established standard. Foreshadowing what became Middle of the Road, or MOR formats, he noted that "Music can't be monochromatic but care must be taken that [it have] contrast of some sort but not too much clash. Don't go to extremes" (BMI Program Clinic 1951a). In a similar vein, repetition was considered a foundation of good deejay programming practice. As one trade magazine noted in 1947, "His listeners hear him at the same hour every day. They know he'll play Crosby at five, [and] Goodman at 5:15" ("Music Sells" 1947: 41). While Todd Storz may claim to have been inspired to understand the audience's desire for repeated songs by a diner waitress, his peers in the industry recognized the importance of repeated familiarity several years prior to his famed late-night encounter. Indeed, Pack demonstrates a model of contextual, companionate listening that was shaped around what he believed were audiences' daily activities and taste preferences and that would in turn shape the future of music formatting.

Other program directors, like WJLB-AM's George Kendall, urged clinic participants to divorce their own tastes from their professional choices, lamenting lost opportunities when program directors alienated audiences by refusing to air certain artists they did not like. Kendall's station illuminates some of the nascent developments of music formatting. Another 250-watt station, it was mostly known for its foreign-language programming aimed at Detroit's myriad ethnic groups. Then, in 1948, it abruptly switched strategies and retained only a few key personnel. Kendall was one, as was Bill Randle, a disc-jockey who later rose to fame in Cleveland and New York alongside Alan Freed, and also by programming rhythm and blues songs to suburban white youth. It is significant that three years before *Billboard* officially announced the birth of rock and roll, Kendall was speaking of the tremendous increase in interest in race music by both African Americans and white youths. He highlighted this as one of the hottest trends in the future and one that was not reflected in the playlists recorded in New York and Los Angeles–based trade publications. Kendall was certainly not alone in regularly visiting record stores to ascertain the best-selling records, but his comments are contemporary with Freed playing rhythm and blues on Cleveland station WJW (although Freed had first been hipped to crossover music a few years earlier when in Akron by local record store owner Leo Mintz).

These accounts demonstrate the ways that deejays (and potentially program directors) served as tastemakers for new audiences. As Diane Pecknold, among others, argues, the emergence of the deejay, as opposed to the announcers who had preceded them, operated as a "chief fan, expert consumer, and independent critic" whose job was to ratify the taste preferences of his or her audience (2007: 65). Extending this argument, Elena Razlogova argues that late 1940s and early 1950s disc-jockeys mediated between listeners and the music industry, offering what she, via Carlo Ginzburg, terms "conjectural knowledge" of the radio audience (2011: 143). Their position as intermediaries, she concludes, "blurred the lines of ownership and control in music radio" and made the disc-jockey the "key cultural institution of the period" (133). Yet, as Razlogova acknowledges, this process was a contested one with fault lines between program, sales, and on-air staff.

Addressing new audiences with formerly marginalized musical genres like hillbilly and rhythm and blues could create tension between program managers and the sales staff. Traditional pop music not only provided the greatest range of potential sponsors but also sponsors that more closely matched the habitus of the salesmen. Sales staff resented having to sell programs with what they viewed as limited cultural value. In a 1951 clinic, Harry McTigue of WINN in Nashville discussed the pressure he received from his salesmen when he committed the station to country and western and hillbilly strip programming. McTigue is also notable because he embraced deejays who had extensive musical knowledge of the genres they played. For him, their expertise gave them their personalities (BMI Program Clinic 1951d). Consequently, many successful deejays began selling their own programs, and, their successes created conflicts with station program directors.

Station Response: Retaining or Regaining Control over Programming

Disc-jockeys were not the only intermediaries grappling to make sense of the new radio soundscape. At the same time as they tried to do so, the unpredictable vicissitudes of taste (and the uncontrollability of deejays) led many in the industry to rationalize music's newfound importance in terms of programming. In the clinics, there was a marked reluctance to cede too much control to deejays, whom some program and station managers did not trust.

Indeed, one clear prerogative of the clinics was to develop ways for program managers to both circumvent and control disc-jockeys. In one of the earliest clinics held in January 1950, Murray Arnold, the program director of WIP in Philadelphia, warned his audience that deejays should not be in control of their own programs because of payola in the form of "gifts, cash, and dates . . . if you know what I mean." Arnold insisted that deejays were interchangeable and that with "a three month build-up" any announcer could equal the performance of their predecessors. During that same clinic, WINS disc-jockey Jack Lacey largely agreed with Arnold, but stressed the proper choice of deejay, one who "can keep his feet on the ground and not be swayed by synthetic fame" ("Widespread Payola" 1950: 4).

Other program managers saw deejays who put their own identity first as a threat to station identity. For example, in the March 27, 1951 clinic in Columbia, South Carolina, Dave Baylor, the program manager of WJMO in Cleveland, Ohio, advised clinic attendees to counterprogram (he called it "cross programming") against deejay-based programming. He noted that in the late afternoon hours, seven out of eight Cleveland stations already had youth-oriented disc-jockey stations. WJMO was an independent, relatively low-powered, daytime-only, and newly licensed station. It exemplifies the kind of stations that proliferated in the postwar period—stations that did not look to networks for programming in the same manner that many prewar stations did. However, Cleveland was a market that was already crowded with deejays oriented toward teens and African Americans. Therefore, although many trade publications and some other clinics embraced deejays and their audiences as the solution to increased intramedia competition and as a way to counteract the popularity of television, Baylor displayed a suspicion of deejays. He saw the tendency for deejays to seek out the first and exclusive songs as counterproductive—other deejays would simply purchase and air a hit record as soon as it was available. "I get a little tired of having seven deejays [in the 3–5 p.m. slot] all telling the kids playing the same records because [unintelligible] with a boogy beat is going to set the town on its ear.[Laughter from crowd]." Instead, Baylor noted that in a multiple station situation "You don't have to be a whole lot better just a little bit different" (BMI Program Clinic 1951b).

Thus, Baylor represents a move toward managing station personality and differentiation by consolidating power around the program director (though he did not use this terminology). He also advised program managers to "compromise their ideals" in terms of music. Referencing the smash hit "Tennessee Waltz" became a touchtone for giving the audience what they wanted, not what an older generation of program managers preferred. While Baylor expressed a personal preference for Cole Porter, "The listener doesn't care. He likes the Tennessee Waltz and you've damn well got to give him the Tennessee Waltz as often as he wants or you aren't going to sell Hedacol [a patent medicine known for its high alcohol content]" (BMI Program Clinic 1951b). Baylor's musical reference is significant. Published by Acuff-Rose Music, the "Tennessee Waltz" was the most successful record of 1951, and as James Manheim (1992) has argued, it should be understood as a coalescence of tremendous changes occurring in the music industry in the postwar era. These changes involved the incorporation of Tin Pan Alley aesthetic and economic structures to country music, thereby providing the possibility for country-pop crossovers that linked emergent markets with mainstream popular success. This "waltz" emerged out of an oral performance tradition rather than a Tin Pan Alley sheet music tradition.

Likewise, it is significant that "Tennessee Waltz" was not aimed at teenagers. McCourt and Rothenbuhler (2004) argue that the commonly held contention that teenage audiences listened to Top 40 stations in the 1950s is ahistorical. While rock and roll is remembered as the most vibrant music of the era, Top 40 stations were reluctant to focus on the teen audience because they were available for only part of the day— the afternoon. Not until the early 1960s did teen- oriented pop music dominate the Top 40. In Storz-managed stations, program schedules were aimed not at specific markets but to a mass market. According to McCourt and Rothebuhler, they sought to follow rather than lead popular taste (11). This echoes the advice given by Baylor that sought to convince program directors that their own taste categories were irrelevant, and potentially detrimental, to the success of their stations. At the same time, Baylor's advice represents a rearguard action that embraced new musical genres only once they became popular and rejected a model of a musical vanguard.

Indeed, a frequently voiced opinion was that it was the job of the station manager to control the station talent. In another BMI clinic held in August 1951, WJMO's Baylor admonished his fellow managers for failing to ensure proper diversification in a schedule without too much deejay-based programming: "It isn't the deejay's fault if he is ruining the station. It's your fault if you are letting him" (BMI Program Clinic 1951d). In a similar vein, in a 1952 article on the clinics in *Broadcasting*, BMI President Carl Haverlin advised broadcasters to "start program concepts in the front office, rather than in the programming office" ("BMI Session" 1952: 48). By this, he suggested that sales and station managers' policies, not deejays, should drive programming choices. There are numerous such examples of tensions between program managers and disc-jockeys, but a particularly useful one is a survey of station managers published in the February 28, 1953 issue of *Billboard*. In comparison with previous years' surveys, 1953 saw a trend toward reliance on trade paper chart listings and increased control over the make-up of disc-jockey shows ("Billboard 1953" 1953: 50). Thus while BMI was known for featuring artists in the hillbilly and rhythm and blues genres who could not gain representation from ASCAP, it was not always able to convince program directors and sales mangers that the audiences who listened to these genres were valuable.

Conflicts were not limited to program directors and deejays, as not all program directors were receptive to the advice offered by either BMI or the speakers. For example, in a clinic held in Boston, BMI representative Glenn Dolberg solicited opinions on sponsoring a young composer contest, part of the organization's classical music initiative. The response was awkward silence, derisive groans, and quick backpedaling by Dolberg (BMI Program Clinic 1951a).[12] In another example, some program directors obstinately reaffirmed the value of network programming and rejected trends toward musical programming. Ralph Sims, program director for Baton Rouge, Louisiana NBC affiliate WJBO, displayed a disdain for disc-jockeys and musical programs in particular. Sims stated that he "never thought much" of the teen audience and had recently banned disc-jockeys from WJBO's airwaves. For him, station identity came from network affiliation, so he retained the network-era conception of brief fifteen- to thirty-minute programs and substantial shifts in mood and genre from one show to another. In one example, he spoke highly of an early morning pop music show that was followed by a classical program as a means of cultivating musical appreciation in an audience that may not enjoy classical music, even as he recognized much of that audience would immediately change the channel (BMI Program Clinic 1951f). Assertions like this, and other predictions proven wrong by history, further demonstrate how management is not always successful.

A Portrait of an Industry in Flux

In conclusion, the BMI program clinics serve as a lens through which to understand media management at a moment of transition. Increased competition generated by the explosion of small stations in the immediate postwar years and fears of the future impact of television pushed the industry to reevaluate its existing programming and economic models. As musical programming moved from scarcity (live band remotes) to abundance (records), the managers were torn between their desire to maintain control over their schedule and the problem of how to successfully program their stations in a newly competitive environment. Developed by a national organization and the former head of a nationally recognized independent station, the BMI clinics represent multiple sites where the present and future of the medium was actively debated.

Through a diagnostic dialogue, attendees discussed a variety of solutions: block programming, developing distinctive station identities, embracing formerly marginalized musical genres, and more judicious programming choices. At the same time that they served as a site for exploration, the clinics also were a venue to articulate the contests for authority—BMI versus ASCAP, program managers versus deejays, old models versus new—that defined the parameters of the broadcasting industry's response to changing economic models. These contests demonstrate the ways that the existing habitus of accepted station practice and assumptions about programming, audiences, and personnel were in flux. This tension between new ideas and the desire to maintain control helps explain radio's attempts to transition from the network to the Top 40 eras.

NOTES

1. I took this version from Fong-Torres (1988: 37–39). But is has been retold repeatedly and called into question. At other points Storz said he drew upon noticing the repeated song preference in bars during World War II.
2. For an extended discussion of these factors, see Russo (2010).
3. To her credit, Razlogova's work on disc-jockeys in *The Listener's Voice* (2011) is an exception in that it focuses on a variety of deejay practices, rather than well-known figures like Alan Freed, as well as industry responses. For a broader application of this idea, see Altman's discussion of "crisis historiography" in *Silent Film Sound* (2005) as well as Gitelman's expansion of this notion in *Always Already New* (2008).
4. See also Sanjek and Sanjek (1991) and Ryan (1985).
5. Of the 249 stations that began broadcasting between October 1945 and April 1947, nearly half were unprofitable as of late 1947. See FCC (1947: 47).
6. Significantly, in 1950 he was hired away from WNEW by NBC to manage the transition for the network's flagship New York stations as general manager of WNBC and WNBT-TV.
7. Other accounts ("BMI Program" 1951a: 32) stress the involvement of BMI President Carl Havelin and BMI directors of station relations first Roy Harlow and later Glen Dolberg. These former figures are important for their earlier work with independent radio stations—Harlow with the Yankee Network and Havelin with Mutual. Even network vet Dolberg was active on the West Coast with KHJ and KFI, all of which suggests an orientation toward alternative ways of thinking.
8. For more on the major networks' culture of opposition to recorded programming, see Russo (2010: 106–14).
9. See also "BMI Colorado" (1951: 5) and "BMI Thanks" (1951b: 63).

10. See also Sanjek and Sanjek (1991: 103).
11. However, as Goodman (2010: 15–46) notes, this represented a radical proposition in the network era.
12. Additionally, Russell and David Sanjek note that BMI's promotion of young composers was part of the organization's attempts to court Aaron Copeland and the American Composer's Alliance (Sanjek and Sanjek 1991: 98).

10

Tweeting on the BBC

Audience and Brand Management via Third Party Websites

ELIZABETH EVANS

In spring 2011, Twitter was at the center of two very different but ulti-mately related media storms. In April, *Glee* executive producer Brad Falchuck was outraged when an extra tweeted the characters due to be named prom king and queen, threatening her that she would never act again (Andrew 2011). A month later, a much larger storm erupted in the United Kingdom when Manchester United footballer Ryan Giggs was identified on Twitter as being the subject of a high court "super-injuction" forbidding any news outlet from revealing his extramarital affair. Giggs demanded that Twitter reveal the identity of the user nam-ing him so that he or she could be charged with breaching the injunc-tion. In response, 75,000 Twitter users retweeted his identity, the story became public knowledge, and the injunction was lifted. Both cases demonstrated two key issues concerning Twitter and its relationship to "traditional" media. The first involves the shifting boundaries of the media industries in terms of *who* becomes part of them. *Glee*'s tweeter suddenly became an unwelcome part of the *Glee* publicity machine.

Injunctions of the kind held by Giggs had previously only related to the professional media of newspapers, magazines, and broadcasters. Now, Twitter and its ordinary users were seen as an integral part of the media landscape, on a par with the professional press or the BBC. This leads to the second issue the cases raise: the daunting prospect of the unruly audience and its impact on a celebrity or institution's public image. If your audience's (or fans') knowledge and opinions, good or bad, could suddenly be available for anyone to see, then managing those audiences and their opinions becomes not just a case of maintaining loyalty from that individual audience member but also maintaining a broader brand image.

Catherine Johnson recognizes the centrality of concrete, connected branding strategies now that television companies are increasingly operating outside of broadcast space:

> New developments in the use of the Internet and mobile phone technology to deliver audio-visual content is likely to extend and complicate further the range and function of television's ancillary texts. This will increase the need for strong brand identities for television programmes in order to provide a coherent identity across the range of media platforms and products that will form the texts of television. (2007: 20)[1]

Beyond this, however, the development of television-related online activities complicates *who* is a part of that branding process. Adam Arvidsson argues that "brand management is still essentially about putting public communication to work in ways that either *add to* or *reproduce* the particular qualities that the brand embodies" (2005: 67, original emphasis). Branding is about managing the conversations around a brand as much as the visible signs of that brand such as logos. As Arvidsson also argues, "it is what consumers think of or *do with the brand* that is the source of its value" (7, emphasis added). The Internet makes the cultural and social exchanges surrounding both television and branding public to a greater extent than in the twentieth century. Websites such as Twitter ensure that viewing habits and discussions that were once hidden in the home or the semi-private spaces of interpersonal relationships are now becoming visible online. The elements of branding and marketing that a company (or broadcaster) cannot directly control (audience conversations) are increasingly just as public as those elements they can (idents, trailers, logos, and press releases). In response, both well-known figures and media institutions are increasingly turning to social networks such as Twitter (Deller 2011) to manage their brand identities within an "attention economy" that offers countless alternative options for audiences' time (Goldhaber 1997; Grainge 2011; Dovey 2011).

The BBC makes use of a number of social network websites, including YouTube and Facebook. Twitter, however, is the most prominent third-party site both as featured throughout the BBC's own website and in television content via the promotion of hashtags. This chapter will focus on how the BBC uses Twitter both to create a more "humanized" brand identity than the paternal, Reithian "Auntie" metaphor of its past and to manage its audience's role in maintaining that identity. This brand identity works to create a more visibly two-way relationship with its audience and functions with respect to multiple stakeholders. The fact that Twitter is not owned or controlled by the BBC speaks to the Corporation's image within the broader U.K. media industry. By not creating a similar service of its own, the BBC presents itself as knowing its boundaries. This works to defuse tensions evident in the early 2000s and 2010s between the securely funded BBC and not only a U.K. television industry suffering due to increased economic pressure and audience fragmentation, but also a broader society and culture undergoing extreme spending cuts in the fallout of the 2008 financial crisis. Elsewhere in this volume, James Bennett and Niki Strange also explore how these tensions have resulted in shifts (and failures) in the BBC's multiplatform commissioning strategies. In many ways, the Corporation's adoption and development of third party social media websites has intensified at the same time as the "360-degree" multiplatform production discussed by Bennett and Strange has been largely abandoned, and can be linked to many of the same economic tensions. In addition, however, these sites allow for the cultivation and management of brand-enhancing audience behavior such as gossip and participation that similarly aid in reinforcing the BBC's position within the U.K. television market.

These issues will be explored though an analysis of policy documents from the BBC and the BBC Trust, the Corporation's independent governing body, which explicitly indicate how the Corporation and its personnel should use online spaces. This document analysis will be twinned with quantitative and qualitative analysis of the Twitter feeds for two program case studies, *Strictly Come Dancing* (*SCD*; BBC One, 2004–) [2] and coverage of the FIA Formula One World Championship (F1; BBC One, 2009–). Both are amongst the Corporation's highest rated programs and sit at the forefront of the BBC's development of online spaces. They approach Twitter in different ways, but ultimately serve the same audience and brand management aims. This dual methodology allows a consideration of the alignment between policy and practice and an examination of how social media sites prove useful for the BBC's brand and audience management. "Management," in this case, functions in two respects. The first is in the BBC and its personnel making use of online spaces that are an increasingly central part of cultural discourses to foster a positive, cooperative image of its relationship with external stakeholders, namely other U.K. media institutions and its audiences. The second is the use of such spaces to shape audience behavior by encouraging activities that enhance that brand image and, in turn, solidify the Corporation's position in an increasingly turbulent media ecology. These two forms of management, brand and audience, become intertwined.

From Castle to Portal: The BBC, Third Party Sites, and Digital Public Service Broadcasting

Although the BBC has not yet seen the kind of Twitter storm surrounding *Glee* and Giggs, the Corporation is increasingly turning to third-party websites and social networks to manage its broader brand identity amidst continuing debates over its position within the U.K. television industry. The decision to use social networking, and to do so on third-party sites rather than creating a BBC-version that the Corporation can have greater control over, can be seen as a result of the wider cultural and political context in which the BBC has operated in the late 2000s and early 2010s. On the one hand, the BBC is playing catch-up to audience habits that have already changed (Evans 2011b: 43–44). In the BBC's five-year strategy paper, *Creative Future*, Director General Mark Thompson (the BBC's then chief executive and editor-in-chief) identified "Martini Media" that is "available when and where you want it with content moving freely between different devices and platforms" and "the audience who doesn't want to just sit there but to take part, debate, create, communicate, share" (Thompson 2006). Thompson went on to comment, "we need a new relationship with our audiences—they won't simply be audiences anymore, but also participants and partners—we need to know them as individuals and communities." The turn towards Twitter can be seen within these changes; rather than trying to marshal audiences into their own space, the BBC has chosen to follow them. The BBC's role as "trusted guide" to the web, which emerged in its 2006 Charter Review (BBC 2006c: 5), becomes something that expands beyond BBC-owned online space. [3] Not only do they use their own content to demonstrate the potential of the web; they now also point outwards and use their own brands to offer examples of what viewers can do on the rest of the web.

The use of non-BBC sites also allows the BBC to manage its position within the broader U.K. media industry. The decision to *not* create something new has become an increasingly prevalent feature of BBC discourses surrounding its role as a public service broadcaster. In 2008 the BBC was criticized by its governing body, the BBC Trust, in its review of BBC Online for limited click through to external sites (Graf 2004: 9).[4] The Trust argued that

> the BBC has a role in linking users of bbc.co.uk to external sites which provide content and services which contribute to the BBC's public purposes. We are therefore asking BBC Management to bring to the Trust its plans for improving linking and other functions which help users navigate beyond bbc.co.uk. (BBC Trust 2008: 53)

Victoria Jaye, Head of Fiction and Entertainment Multiplatform Commissioning at the BBC, describes this as a shift in the Corporation's self-conceptualization of its online role:

> there was a time when BBC Online was like a castle, it just didn't link out. But now it absolutely wants to be part of the web and be smart and be credible; you're not smart and credible on the web if you don't link to anybody else or you only link to yourself.[5]

The BBC's shift to "portal," however, is tinged with concerns over its place within the U.K. media market. The Corporation's editorial guidelines for the use of microblogs by its employees states:

> If we add a BBC presence, we are joining their site rather than the opposite. . . . We should 'go with the grain' and be sensitive to user customs and conventions to avoid giving the impression that the BBC is imposing itself on them and their space. (BBC 2010a)

There is a risk for the BBC of appearing to be trying to colonize the web and threaten the sovereignty of the commercial industry.

The relationship between public service broadcasters and their commercial counterparts has long been a complex mix of competition and mutually beneficial arrangements. Henrik Søndergaard has argued that public service broadcasting is increasingly inseparable from the market forces that so directly affect commercial institutions:

> The inclusion of commercial enterprises means not only that the duties of public service broadcasting are spread over, or shared by, different kinds of institutions, but also that they become embedded in the market economy and thus have to be regulated differently than has been the practice to date. This latter point means that public service broadcasting, once conceived as an alternative to the market, tends increasingly to be regarded and judged in market-economic terms. (1999: 25)

The mixed public service economy of the United Kingdom, and the BBC especially, has always had to work through the balance between commercial interests and public service ethos (Johnson 2009; 2011). Twitter has in fact provided space for direct, public dialogue, however brief, between the BBC and key industry rivals. Ben Ayers, at the time Social Media Manager at U.K. commercial broadcaster ITV, tweeted interest in the soon to be released "Strictly Social": "Looking forward to seeing what the BBC have up their sleeves for @bbcstrictly online— apparrently [sic] it's called strictly social or summink [sic]" (October 2, 2010). The series then responded, directing him to the service's website (October 2, 2010).

Whilst this is a relatively benign, and basic, way in which the BBC's use of third-party sites is concerned with intra-industrial relations, elsewhere it is more complex and less benevolent. The BBC has a guaranteed source of income in the license fee, which gives it a particularly privileged position within the market (Evans 2011a: 106). Often this is articulated in terms of services the BBC should provide, services that commercial broadcasters are less able or willing to offer (certain kinds of programming, education services, technological development, and so on). Concerns over what the BBC should *not* do have tended to focus on issues surrounding commercial strategy or impartiality of content. Increasingly, however, key BBC players are acknowledging that the Corporation's status as a publically funded broadcaster means that there are some services that it should not provide. In 2009, Victoria Jaye commented on the role the BBC should take in the wider media industry:

> The BBC is in a unique position, because it has confirmed funding (not just for its network output but for online as well), to be a catalyst for the market as well as having a responsibility for delivering public value in a digital world.[6]

She went on to say that "Twitter does something very well already . . . we're not interested in reinventing what's already out there." This is reflected elsewhere in BBC policy. The BBC Trust's response to the Corporation's *Putting Quality First* service review in 2010 outlined the need for focus, especially in relation to online services: "[The BBC should] pursue a new strategy for BBC Online where BBC activity in individual online markets is clearly defined and justified in terms of its distinctiveness and its focus on the BBC's public purposes" (BBC Trust 2010: 5). The Trust went on to call for

> A BBC that works more openly with the market, trailing significant new investments, communicating directly with others in the industry, identifying and setting clear boundaries around "no-go" areas where there are particular sensitivities, building a range of partnerships with a bias towards non-exclusive arrangements. (BBC Trust 2010: 9)

Subsequently, concrete strategies have been developed. As Erik Huggers, Director of BBC Future Media and Technology, announced in

January 2011, "the relationship with the wider industry is also important. Focus creates clarity on what BBC Online will and won't do—and we'll be taking a more open approach on what we are doing" (Huggers 2011). The BBC's unique position within the U.K. media market, as a public service broadcaster that is not at the mercies of a volatile advertising market, has resulted in a conservatism that can embrace the development of services that exist beyond its own boundaries.

Discourses concerning the limits of the BBC are ironically also tied to the construction of the BBC as a threatened institution. Whilst the BBC has a secure funding source in the license fee, the size of that source is less secure, and since the 2008 financial crisis, the Corporation has been subjected to the same kinds of cuts in public spending that have affected other public sectors in the United Kingdom. In March 2010, anticipating funding cuts that would follow later that year, the BBC's *Putting Quality First* review focused on streamlining the Corporation and included a 25 percent cut of BBC Online's budget. This was then followed in October with a license fee freeze until 2016 and the Corporation's taking on responsibility for international news radio and television service from the World Service (previously funded by the U.K. Foreign Office) and for Welsh-language channel S4C (previously funded by Channel 4). The year 2010 saw the BBC's budget reduced in real terms whilst its responsibilities increased and the need to save £140 million over two years was stipulated (BBC Trust 2010: 7). These institutional changes were, however, merely a symptom of the pressure that the U.K. media industries had been under for a number of years due to the impact of changing audience habits and advertising revenue. ITV suffered significant losses in 2008–2009, and the funding of Channel 4 had been debated for a number of years in light of similarly falling advertising revenue. The BBC had been required to justify its seemingly secure position within a struggling market for a number of years amongst calls for its funding model to be fundamentally changed (Beckett 2008; Smith 2010). Twitter allows the BBC to develop the image of a benefactor to the industry—one that is consciously looking to reduce its budget in a shrinking economy and to foster relationships with other industry partners—rather than appearing to trample on other institutions' commercial interests.

Whilst the initial development of third-party sites predates some of these later developments, the speed at which Twitter in particular has been taken up complements these concerns. Twitter is cheap. Program brands that previously had complex online social networking tools now primarily focus on Twitter. *The Apprentice* (BBC One, 2005–present), for instance, once had an interactive voting system, whereby viewers could say who they thought would be voted off as the program aired. For the 2011 season, the equivalent service became a Twitter feed integrated into the website's homepage. Not only does the BBC's adoption of third-party sites allow it to focus and limit its activities to prevent any perception that it is constricting the commercial sector of the industry, it also allows them to expand the services branded as "BBC" with minimal extra cost (Debrett 2009: 813). Twitter also allows the BBC to develop its "brand personality," which, as Traci H. Freling and Lukas P. Forbes argue (calling on S. D. Carr 1996), "elicits an 'emotional rather than an intellectual response' that arouses passion and incites an 'affinity without rationale' for the brand" (2005: 150). As I shall go on to explore, the BBC's actual use of Twitter has been focused on creating a more personal, "humanized" relationship between key personnel or programs and its audiences. Such emotional attachment in its audience can only help the BBC promote its existence; if those who pay for it love it, surely it should not be threatened.

When "Auntie" Tweets: Managing the Audience, Humanizing the Brand

If the policy of using third-party sites allows the BBC to manage its relationship with various industrial and political stakeholders, the practice of such usage has the additional potential to extend that management into its relationship with audiences. The BBC's historical brand image as "Auntie," linked to the "Auntie knows best" approach and the Corporation's first Director General John Reith's foundational philosophy to "inform, educate and entertain" (Thompson 2004), separates the BBC from its audience by presenting itself as authoritative and overtly paternalistic. By contrast, Twitter allows the BBC to generate and maintain an image that is based on openness and dialogue with its audiences. The BBC has always maintained a certain amount of dialogue with its audiences through audience review programs such as *Points of View* (1961–present) and regional "audience councils" that bring BBC

executives and audiences together. However, these are carefully controlled, "special" occasions. Twitter takes these conversations into the
everyday. Rather than contact the BBC to complain about or praise a
program, audiences can engage in a more mundane form of dialogue
through Twitter and receive a more immediate response. Whereas
Auntie may, or may not, respond to a plea, Twitter sustains a dialogue
between friends

The BBC first began using Twitter in 2007 with feeds for news and
sport. Since then, feeds have been developed across a range of programming from factual to drama programs. Many, such as the news feeds,
function as information sources, complementing the main BBC website's content. However, the *SCD* and F1 feeds offer greater integration of
Twitter, BBC-owned online space, and television content than is found
in other BBC programming. Both the *SCD* and F1 feed are prominently
integrated into their corresponding websites, but offer very different
approaches to Twitter use.[7] Whereas *SCD* is focused on the program,
with a single account operating only during a season run, F1 Twitter
coverage is a series of individual feeds. Most of the onscreen and online
production team, including then host Jake Humphrey, commentator
Martin Brundle (2009–2011), and website writer Andrew Benson, have
individual Twitter feeds that appeared automatically on the BBC F1
homepage. The two approaches of *SCD* and F1 demonstrate alternative
ways in which Twitter's ability to present a more open relationship with
audiences not only humanizes the BBC brand but also encourages positive audience behavior.

The combination of audience and brand management is evident in
the editorial guidelines for the use of micro-blogs. Predominantly concerned with maintaining the integrity of the BBC brand, these guidelines call attention to the ways in which BBC presence on such sites
could lead to being perceived as approval of them:

> You may wish to make "friends" on a third party web page. But remem-
> ber that approving a "friend" may make other users of the site think
> they are more trustworthy. . . . If you want to make "friends" with an
> organisation . . . consult your interactive Editor/senior editorial figure
> first. Remember that this is likely to give the impression that the BBC is
> endorsing the organisation. (BBC 2010a)

Such concerns relate directly to the specific position of the BBC and its public service remit as impartial and devoid of commercial associations: reinforcing the broader image of the BBC as a public service broadcaster remains paramount. However, at the same time, these guidelines demonstrate the potential use of social networks for audience management and for marshalling audiences into more overtly BBC-branded space:

> This [strategy] is partly so that users who may consume little or no BBC content can discover for themselves more of what we have to offer. So we should always link back to BBC Online. We can then encourage users to consume more BBC content on our site. (BBC 2010a)

Central to the use of non-BBC sites is their ability to act as a conduit to BBC content in the age of "Martini Media." Moreover, as audience habits shift to include online and mobile platforms, these platforms allow the BBC to catch audiences wherever they are. Together, these spaces are tinged by discourses concerning the management of the Corporation's brand image amid changing audience behaviors and expectations.

The differences and similarities between the *SCD* and F1 feeds demonstrate the complexities and overarching strategy of the BBC's Twitter policy.[8] The *SCD* feed functions primarily as an information source for the program. One single feed runs from mid-August to early January. It begins as a form of initial marketing for the series, providing information on when contestants will be announced and how viewers can apply for tickets. It then runs throughout the series, providing episode commentary, links to extratextual online content, such as rehearsal videos and dress designs, and behind-the-scenes gossip, ending shortly after the series' end. A significant portion of the tweets (47.2 percent for the 2009 season) are some form of news, predominantly concerning the celebrities or dancers involved in that season, with another portion (26.5 percent) providing commentary on episodes. However, the most popular reason for a *SCD* tweet was to encourage "productive" audience behavior that supports the program's marketing and brand strategies. Thus, 48.4 percent of the tweets were either a response to an audience member's question or a direct call for some form of participation.[9] Questions ranged from technical problems with transmission to how particular songs are chosen or how to get tickets, and on through to gossip about the progress of each couple. Viewers who use their Twitter account to ask such questions not only demonstrate an attachment to the program beyond its broadcast hours, but also promote the program's existence on their personal feeds. In turn, they are rewarded in the production's acknowledgement of their interest when their question is answered. The participation calls include posing questions to the Twitter community about events in the program and encouraging them to take part in *Strictly Social*, which, in turn, allow viewers to react online to events in the program and guess how the onscreen judges will respond. The feed has a clear objective to encourage discussion around the program, develop word of mouth promotion, and encourage more engagement with the program's transmedia elements.

The F1 Twitter feeds are slightly more complex in that they are focused on individuals, rather than on the production as a single unit, and the feeds are updated all year long, regardless of whether the championship is running or not. They seem, in fact, to partially contradict the section of the editorial guidelines that concerns transparency:

> We should avoid creating or endorsing "hybrid" sites . . . which are likely to cause confusion, editorial problems and brand damage. For example, a presenter's personal profile should not have a URL or username or avatar which contains a BBC brand or programme name. (BBC 2010b)

The guidelines go on to say: "It should be clear to users whether the site they are interacting with is a BBC page run by the BBC for BBC purposes or whether this is a personal page run by an individual for their own purposes." Some of the F1 Twitter feeds, however, do act as such hybrid sites. Thus, whereas BBC website writer Andrew Benson's is focused in scope, containing only information about BBC coverage, commentaries on practice, qualifying, and race sessions, links to interviews with Formula One personnel, and news about developments within the sport, Jake Humphrey's and Martin Brundle's feeds are not so clear cut in that both merge their personal and professional lives.[10] Humphrey's feed, for instance, includes not only commentary on the production process and race-related issues, but also a number of tweets (10 percent) relating to his personal life, including holidays with his wife, and a further 9 percent on his support of Norwich City Football Club (NCFC), something that, whilst sport-related, has little to do with his core BBC role.

Despite the apparent ambiguity in how "official" the feed is, Humphrey's in particular was given status within the on-screen programming, originally included "F1" in his online name, and was used as a key method of audience management.[11] Unlike the *SCD* feed, which rewards contributors only within Twitter itself or other online spaces such as web videos, the F1 feed was brought into television coverage. During each qualifying session or race, Humphrey encouraged audiences to tweet him with questions or comments, giving out his personal Twitter feed address on screen. He was constantly seen holding an iPad, which he used to connect to the feed, and asked questions that had been tweeted to onscreen guests. This audience interaction was a key part of the *F1 Forum*, the extension to the main programming that takes place on the BBC's red-button digital television service and consists of interviews and question and answer sessions with key Formula One personnel. Humphrey's personal Twitter feed became part of the program's overall strategy of audience management. Viewers were encouraged to interact directly with those on screen, to ask them questions, and offer commentary on events. Those who did were "rewarded" with either a personal reply by production personnel or onscreen recognition.

For *SCD* and F1, Twitter offers a space where both brand identity and audience behavior can be shaped simultaneously, with each aspect feeding off and reinforcing the other. Rather than managing via more disciplinary actions, such as chastising "negative" behavior, both *SCD* and F1 use Twitter to encourage beneficial, brand-enhancing audience behavior (mainly gossip and interaction). Audience members become marketing tools themselves, as their questions and gossip become part of the BBC's public image. Both programs encourage the use of the hash tags #scd and #bbcf1. When included in a tweet, these tags identify it as relating to a particular topic and allow users to find all the tweets relating to a specific hash tag. If enough people use them, then the topic gains "trending" status and appears on Twitter's homepage. By tweeting about particular programs, viewers are in turn advertising it to their network of friends; when these programs reach "trending" status, that network becomes the global Twitter population. This has often happened during races, with Humphrey thanking viewers for giving the program such status, and thereby adding an additional layer of "reward" to those viewers taking part in positive, brand-enhancing behavior.

By encouraging gossip and interaction, the BBC Twitter feeds invite a more personal relationship between audience and the programs by emphasizing the dialogic potential of Twitter. In research conducted in January 2008 (only fifteen months after Twitter's founding), Courtenay Honeycutt and Susan C. Herring found that "some users are already taking advantage of Twitter for informal collaborative purposes, and conversation is an essential component of collaboration" (2009: 9). Of course, this dialogue is something that can be controlled, and negative comments can be ignored or criticized. However, the very act of opening up such interaction contributes to an image of the BBC as approachable and personable, as the overseeing manager of numerous conversations between its staff and its audience rather than the impenetrable and uncommunicative fortress of "Auntie." In the F1 feeds, the emphasis on individual personnel constructs the production as a group of individuals, with whom viewers can potentially have conversations and form sustained relationships (however controlled they may be). The presence of more personal information in Humphrey's feed only enhances this, despite the potential "hybridization" and confusion it may create. Tweets such as "Well done Chelsea [football club], still not quite like watching Norwich though! #ncfc" (March 1, 2011) and "Big day in the Humphrey household. Time team tonight, Ch4 9pm, comes from the Roman Village at the end of our road, where I got married!!" (May 4, 2011) position him as more than just an information source on Formula One and the BBC's coverage of it. He becomes a more rounded human figure with a personal life that the audience is (partially) brought into. His role within the production as host, the audience's key entry point into the program, is reinforced by the more personal image he presents via Twitter.

The *SCD* feed demonstrates the importance of personalizing feeds in terms of successfully managing an open "humanized" relationship with audiences. When the feed began, it presented itself as coming from an unnamed production source; the program tweeted, rather than any individual. Throughout the 2009 season, the style of tweets changed, suggesting that several different individuals were involved. Episode commentaries, for instance, varied from in-depth descriptions to cursory phrases that merely acknowledged the appearance of each couple. However, throughout the season, audiences began to investigate who was behind the feed. During the series finale, the tweeter provided his name in response to a request from a viewer: "My name's Paul, and I'm the senior producer on the Strictly website! :)" (December 19, 2009). In the 2010 season, the figures behind the tweets became more visible. Paul returned and identified himself as the author of a number of tweets; when asked why his name was now appearing, he responded, "Because there's going to be a team of us Tweeting this year (in between our other jobs!)—now you'll know who's said what!" (August 26, 2010). Although the 2010 tweets were not all linked to an author, many were written by a second member of the online production team, Gemma, and the nature of the responses became more friendly and personable, with a greater use of first person:

> Morning tweeps! Gemma here. Flown down from scdHQ to bring you some Blackpool goss. Heading down to the ballroom soon. See what I can find . . . (November 18, 2010)

> Thanks for all your wonderful messages tonight guys, Loving your tweets, as ever! Night all—Gemma (November 27, 2010)

> Not [tweeting] on the Christmas special I'm afraid. I'll be at home having turkey with my family! (December 17, 2010)

Such first-person identification was absent throughout the 2009 season, indicating a shift in tone for SCD's use of Twitter. The SCD feed became increasingly a feed from an individual, on behalf of the program, rather than an anonymous, unnamed facet of the production team.

The BBC's use of Twitter to present a more humanized brand image directly reflects the social network's form. Victoria Jaye describes the importance of understanding how a third party site works and, most importantly, what audiences expect from it. It is, she says, crucial to understand the nuances of sites and realize that an institution like the BBC cannot have a "one size fits all" policy:

> If you're engaged in an activity that is focused on harnessing crowds or fans out there in the blogospheres and the social networks, you're actually involved in a conversation with your audience—it's a subtle form of promotion or marketing. And this "conversation" can't simply comprise of pushing a video promo out to the audience; it needs to be more rewarding, more "two way" than that.[12]

This remark demonstrates the importance of considering Twitter's unique characteristics compared to other sites such as YouTube, the BBC's most prominent other third-party website. YouTube is primarily a distribution avenue with some limited space for audience discussion; there is little sense of audience comments forming a dialogue with producers. Twitter, however, is focused on short snippets of conversation that may be one-to-one or may be one-to-many. These "two-way" conversations are a key structuring feature of the BBC's use of Twitter for audience management and the ultimate consequence of shaping its brand image. Honeycutt and Herring's research found that, whilst most Tweets took the form of monologues, the use of the @ symbol rapidly facilitated more conversational dialogues (2009: 6). It is this @ symbol that allows anyone's tweet to reach a BBC personality or program (and so be replied to) and thus provides the *opportunity* for audience members to ask the BBC a question and get a personalized reply or onscreen recognition, even if this doesn't necessarily occur for every tweeter.

At the same time, Twitter constructs any statement or conversation as simultaneously public and personal. Each user's homepage contains all tweets posted by anyone whom the user is "following." Even though any tweet may be going to thousands if not millions of followers, it is also sent directly, and individually, to each and every one, appearing on each follower's home screen as if it were a direct, personal message. This individualization also extends to those behind the tweets and ties directly to the importance of personalities to audience engagement with media content. Victoria Jaye discussed the need to think through what added value the BBC can provide in online spaces:

> We ask ourselves, "What is our role in social media? What are we bringing to the discussion around our content?" . . . We're saying, "What is it that we can bring into the discussion that will really add value, and

make it more meaningful and impactful than it would be if we weren't involved?"[13]

She went on to identify this as access to individuals: "one of the key triggers for audience interest in and around our shows is talent—presenters, celebrity participants, personalities, fictional characters. This is absolutely what the audience wants to get closer to." What Jaye described relates to what Sharon Marie Ross calls "tele-participation." By facilitating direct conversations, Ross argues, the Internet creates "*literally social* audiences that increasingly include the voices of creative professionals, critics and industry executives in tandem with the voices of viewers" (2008: 257, original emphasis). Amanda D. Lotz similarly recognizes community as a key part of the post-network era in US television (2007: 245). Both F1 and *SCD* offer their Twitter audiences access to individuals, either through personal feeds or through developing individual identities for those behind program feeds. Twitter allows the BBC to humanize otherwise corporate discourses, to respond to viewers on a seemingly more individual basis, and ultimately, to offer a personal, rather than mass, form of communication.

Conclusion

While Ryan Giggs' affair and *Glee*'s spoiler may have brought Twitter's uneasy role in the creation and maintenance of brand image and audience behavior to the fore, the BBC's embrace of the website demonstrates the potential of that role. For the BBC, Twitter offers a step towards solving a number of issues facing the Corporation in a time of financial and industrial uncertainty. As audience habits change, and potentially threaten the sovereignty of broadcasters to control both their content and their brand image, moving into online spaces already populated by their audiences has allowed the BBC to develop strategies of brand management that also serve as strategies of audience management. By using Twitter to create the perception of personalized dialogue with its audience, the BBC presents itself as a collection of approachable individuals, rather than a monolithic, powerful media institution. Twitter allows the BBC, and individual BBC productions, to create the *appearance* of a more direct, personal, and arguably more intimate relationship with its audience. The Corporation is then simultaneously able to encourage behavior that supports its own marketing strategies via word of mouth and make use of the increasingly important and valuable online communities that emerge independently around its key program titles. Of course, the actual nature of the relationships between BBC personnel and their audiences is carefully controlled and balanced in favor of the Corporation. However, despite the limited nature of these relationships, they contribute to the construction of the Corporation as relevant in a media environment defined by increased competition for audiences' attention and continued scrutiny by external stakeholders. The BBC is subsequently able to respond to financial threats in the form of reduced budgets, ideological threats in concerns over their power and the future of public service broadcasting, and industrial fears of their competitors.

NOTES

1. See also Grainge (2010).
2. Known globally as *Dancing with the Stars*.
3. The Royal Charter review, which is run by the U.K. government's Department of Culture, Media and Sport, takes place every ten years and sets out what services the BBC should provide in return for receiving license fee funding, paid for by all U.K. television viewing households.
4. The BBC Trust was formed in 2007. It is independent of BBC management and the government and oversees the BBC's activities, determining key strategies to ensure that it fulfils its Royal Charter in the best interests of license fee payers.
5. Victoria Jaye, personal interview by author, September 2009.
6. Jaye, personal interview.
7. The sites are: www.bbc.co.uk/strictlycomedancing; and news.bbc.co.uk/sport1/hi/motorsport/formula_one/default.stm.
8. Tweets were collected and categorized throughout the 2009 and 2010 seasons for the SCD feed (@bbcstrictly) and from the individual Twitter feeds of Jake Humphrey (@jakehumphreyf1), Andrew Benson (@andrewbensonf1), and Martin Brundle (@martinbrundlef1) between the 2010 Belgian Grand Prix (28 August 2010) and the 2011 Malaysian Grand Prix (9 April 2011). They were categorized according to their subject matter and purpose (for instance, to promote onscreen content or to encourage audience participation).
9. Some tweets, despite only being 140 characters long, served two functions, hence the percentages totaling more than 100 percent.
10. This hybrid status became problematic when the BBC announced a partnership deal with Sky for broadcasting the Formula One season. Martin Brundle

tweeted that he was "not impressed," something that subsequently got picked up by the mainstream press as a sign of "discontent" within the on-air team (Carey 2001). Brundle subsequently moved to Sky's coverage.

11. In early 2011, Humphrey changed his Twitter name from @jakehumphrey1 to @mrjakehumphrey as a direct result of these tensions of hybridity, tweeting that he "will still Tweet like mad from races, but removing F1 from my name means I can tweet about other stuff" (February 10, 2011).

12. Jaye, personal interview.

13. Jaye, personal interview.

11

Market Research in the Media Industries

On the Strategic Relationship between Client and Supplier

JUSTIN WYATT

"This network is an industry joke. We had better start putting together one winner for next September. I want a show developed based on the activities of a terrorist group, Joseph Stalin and his merry band of Bolsheviks. I want ideas from you people. And, by the way, the next time I send an audience research report around, you all better read it, or I'll sack the fucking lot of you, is that clear?"

Diana Christensen, the ferocious TV programming executive in the classic *Network* (1976), pointed to the significance of market research within the media industries more than thirty-five years ago. Yet again, Paddy Chayefsky was amazingly prescient with his landmark film in telegraphing the role of market research as a guide for the media industries. Chayefsky's brief reference cannot encapsulate, however, the complexities of media market research in the current industry. Within contemporary business, market research is commonplace and accepted as a routine and expected part of business practice in most industries, from packaged consumer goods to pharmaceuticals, finance, and insurance. Across these industries, market research is used to assess the competitive environment, to anticipate shifts in consumer needs and demands, and to determine the optimal product offering and messaging for entering the marketplace with products and services. Given the importance of these functions for the maintenance and growth of business, market research is understandably treated as one of the key components in decision-making for top-level executives. Of course, the degree to which these executives turn to market research for guidance, recommendation, or merely information varies by industry and company. Nevertheless, market research is viewed as part of the battery of marketing assets at a firm, just as crucial as creative advertising, public relations, and media strategy or sales.

Within the media industries, however, market research occupies a more tentative and variable space. The creative nature of the film, television, or digital media "product" offers an initial hurdle for the inclusion of market research. The repercussions of this adjustment for the creative product are far-reaching, with impact on the structure, organization, and management of projects. In this chapter, I will analyze the relationship between the market research supplier and the client within the media industries. In detailing this relationship, I want to illustrate ways in which the supplier-client market research relationship can be defined, or at least, modeled. Through this supplier-client partnership, the media industries have morphed market research to suit their particular needs. Hence, understanding the strategic relationship between supplier and client within the media industries aids considerably in appreciating how the industry views market research, both positively and negatively.

Sketching the Landscape

Before tackling this relationship, I want to address the larger context for market research within the media industries. At the most global level, the divide between "commerce" and "art" continues to underpin much of what passes as creative "product," whether in film, TV, or digital media (Reiss 2009: 79–85). This divide is manifested differently in given industries: motion pictures, apart from strict genre and franchise items, tend to utilize market research primarily for fine tuning editing; television utilizes it more widely (especially in the niche world of cable television); digital media, with its lower production costs and evolving products, is tested less often in terms of content. Across all media, advertising-, marketing-, and positioning-testing are more prevalent, in part because market research is seen as gauging the effectiveness of communication strategies in these areas, in contrast to "judging" the entertainment value of the media product in the case of content-testing.[1]

Most conspicuously, the divide between art and commerce is reflected in the organizational structure of media companies. Creative executives are placed apart from the key elements of commerce; in the television industry, for example, departments like Development, Programming, and Current are divided from departments such as Marketing, Finance, Sales, and Research. This division may seem obvious, and needed, but it continues to reinforce the separation of so-called creativity from all matters of business. From another perspective, a traditional "Research & Development" unit within a packaged goods company is focused on product development informed by both research and an imperative to solidify or expand market position. This unit responds to creative and market impulses in a way that most media companies do not. With the division between art and commerce, the media creative executives tend to see market research as a part of the process of enhancing or molding their already existing product rather than as an integral guide for their show development and decision-making. Consequently, market research becomes one more stepping stone needed before a media product is released to the public, rather than a partner "at the table" helping to make decisions on what should be crafted and what should be dismissed.

The separation of creative vision from business imperatives is exacerbated by the nature of time frames within the media industries. In terms of market research, timeliness has two distinct aspects: the deadline for delivery of research and the limited shelf life of the product. While other industries operate with more flexible time frames, the media industries are ruled by strict schedules, with release and premiere dates for product announced to the public sometimes more than a year ahead of time. For the broadcast TV industry, timelines are even more pressing given the large number of hours a network must provide original programming to feed its schedule. With these firm public deadlines in place, all other factors supporting these deadlines must also "fall in line." Consider, for example, the broadcast networks' upfront announcement of their fall schedule of programming in early May each year. This announcement is made primarily to present the fall schedule to advertisers who then bid for ad space on new and returning shows for each network. Many production decisions, including testing the new show pilots, are based on the deadline of the upfront announcements. Consequently, market research follows these strict timelines, with very little latitude in terms of timing. Since the public release dates cannot be altered without extra cost for marketing and potential suspicion or embarrassment within the industry, if some aspect of a timeline gets "crunched," it will inevitably be an internal one, such as the market research schedule. So, if a pilot is delivered to the network behind schedule, the testing schedule is simply abbreviated since the upfront announcement cannot be pushed later, given the vast significance of its timing to all facets of the network. As a result, market research can face contracting timelines for projects, with little time for in-depth analysis of results. Several prominent research suppliers attest to this "time crunch." Vicki Cohen, Executive Vice-President of the research consultancy Frank N. Magid Associates, describes time frames as the major issue in market research for media: "You're dealing with a shorter time frame (compared to other industries). The issue usually is 'help me fix my program now.'"[2] David Smith, partner at the research firm SmithGeiger concurs, and adds another reason for the time crunch in TV market research in particular: "Timetables (for all research) have really been collapsed with overnight ratings and local PeopleMeters. Primary research needs to be very quick, but keep all of its quality to survive."[3]

The compression of market research timetables is also impacted by the shift in the industry toward mass releases and saturation campaigns (i.e., TV, print, audio, online, and social media). As Robert Marich describes the situation, "That perishable quality—that a film is unlikely to ever return once it is out of the theaters—makes movie research all the more important because there's really just one shot to get the sales pitch right" (2009: 33). The movie industry has further evolved from an opening weekend business to an opening day business. With social media spreading word-of-mouth more quickly than ever before, negative word of mouth can damage a film before its opening weekend is even completed. For instance, in 2009, *Brüno*, Sacha Baron Cohen's comedy about an Austrian fashion journalist, opened to $14.2 million on Friday, and then experienced a drastic downturn between Friday and Saturday, which resulted in its falling as much as $20 million short of some expectations for opening weekend. Màny experts speculated that *Brüno* could be the first movie defeated by Twitter, and that Friday could be the "new weekend" when measuring box office success ("Twitter Enabled" 2009).

Similarly, in the TV industry, the rise of "enfotainment"—entertainment industry news and information—privileges high performers in the Nielsen ratings. Finally, the explosion of alternative delivery systems—from DVR and VOD to mobile devices—has also intensified the time pressure, with product being served across a wide variety of windows across an increasingly brief time period. As a result, the always-limited shelf life of media product has been shortened even further in the current environment. The level of anxiety is raised even higher since these contracted time frames also mean that there are very limited possibilities for remarketing a media product post-opening. The ability to adjust, tweak, or reorient a campaign or the content of a media product is essentially non-existent in the current media landscape. The media environment presents few opportunities for "do-overs" given the greater distribution options and the tighter time frames.

Aligned with the issue of testing creative product and encouraged by the fragmentation of the marketplace, the final parameter setting the landscape for media market research is the specificity of media itself. *All* product testing is based on forming a bond or an emotional connection with the potential user/consumer/viewer. With consumer packed goods and many other products, this bond is created through brand building—that is, establishing and enhancing the image and promise of the brand for the consumer.[4] With media entertainment, this process is complicated substantially since the emotional connection is generally not to the corporate brand but rather to the individual media product: viewers base their consumption decisions on the individual media, not the studio, network, or company/corporation supporting it.

Consequently, media market research seeks to understand narration—more specifically, how viewers become connected to characters and the dramatic stakes of the media entertainment. The trickiness of this process is gauging this relationship through the prototype—pilot, commercial or clip—used in media market research testing. At the most fundamental level, the question becomes: what should be tested as representative of the media entertainment experience? Of course, testing audience response to a stimulus as close to the final product, in length and content, is preferable to testing responses to rough cuts or abbreviated clips. The respondent should be considering as close to a final product as possible to replicate the actual consumer experience. In actuality, research is sometimes conducted in a much rougher environment. For instance, web page usability with consumers may be enacted using paper page outlines of the web page, with respondents indicating verbally or with marks on the page their reaction to and potential usability of the online version. Of course, testing a live prototype of the page with fully clickable links creates a much richer experience since the respondent is interacting with a site very close to ones he or she uses in everyday life. Even when testing a full-length feature film or a TV show pilot, however, the issue of an appropriate stimulus stays on the horizon. Given the proliferation of windows for media products, it is now necessary to account for the experiential quality of the media entertainment (e.g., viewing in theater, at home, on a mobile device, online, etc.) as part of the consumer testing.[5] Viewers often cite this quality of the entertainment experience as important to their enjoyment, so understanding the parameters of the viewing context adds another layer of complexity to the testing process. Consequently, what used to be simple stimulus-response testing for media has become much more complex, given the growth of distribution outlets and the need for media entertainment to "play" across multiple outlets.

Admittedly, the divide between art and commerce has always made market research an uneasy partner in the media industries. However, the surge in technology and distribution options and their impact on timelines have created a more dire situation for market researchers engaged in the media business. The relationship between media and market research is, indeed, fragile. Looked at in terms of the most significant content testing—namely, that of pilot testing for TV and of recruited audience testing for movies—the issues are inflected by continually thwarted expectations for prediction of, for instance, box office gross or Nielsen rating. At best, the research methods used within the industry have offered broad indicators of appeal while faring less well in terms of prediction. This "holy grail" of prediction and accurate estimation for media market research has been elusive. Within the industry, work in the area was pioneered by James Spottiswoode at the National Research Group in the late 1980s, with the development of a model targeting box office gross through advanced analytics. The difficulties in accounting for specifics at the level of the individual film (beyond components such as star power and genre) proved to be thorny, despite the ability to account for a significant variance in box office results. Since that time, the approaches within advanced analytics have shifted from neural networks to media mix modeling, yet the ability to account for opening and total box office results remains, at best, rough. The additional modeling complexity presented by technology and distribution changes has made the task of prediction much more difficult and the results much less reliable. For many, media market research is useful only as a bellwether of general audience direction and attitudes rather than a predictive tool for assessing potential audience size, gross, or rating.

Market Research Project Structure within the Media Industries

This depiction of market research within the media industries is designed to illustrate the multiple constraints—or, more positively, challenges—faced by researchers. These challenges, both internal and external, are evidenced on the more granular level of the individual market research project. In considering management of media market research, it is necessary to recognize that two components are absolutely crucial and connected to each other: project management and relationship management. In media market research, business relationships are managed and negotiated through the execution of research projects. Through the process of initiating and engaging in the projects, these relationships are developed and solidified. The specific management structure and organization of market research illustrate how the industry has responded to the constraints and "threats" facing media research. By detailing this structure, I aim to make the functioning of market research within the media industry clear.

In terms of management, media market research is separated into two areas (primary and secondary) and three economic agents (end clients, client researchers, suppliers). Primary research involves custom viewer/user research, either qualitative or quantitative in design, to address a single business problem or issue. In most situations, this means that the project is designed to deepen engagement with the audience or to increase the size of the potential audience. Secondary research, on the other hand, is a "third-party" account of audience size, viewership, or revenue, usually without specific exploration of the reasons for engagement or audience sizing. In the TV industry, the Nielsen ratings are the "metric gods" of secondary research, with clients selling ad space and garnering press attention around ratings. In the movie industry, tracking services for awareness and intent-to-view of new releases entering the marketplace are key secondary research metrics guiding launch strategies and advertising budgets for the distributors. The relationship between client and supplier within secondary research is unidirectional: the client pays for the use of the secondary research, and the research is delivered to the client. As much of the secondary research is syndicated and available to multiple clients, there is usually limited ability to customize the content for specific or unique business needs by client. Primary research, on the other hand, involves a much greater exchange between client and supplier. These projects are custom by design and require, ideally, close collaboration in navigating the stages of a project's life. This collaboration starts with the definition of a research problem; it continues with the creation of the research instrument as well as with fielding, analysis, and presentation of results.

While this description refers to just two economic agents (the supplier, the client), in practice, primary research usually extends across three parties: the supplier, the client researcher, and the end client. The supplier is the third party research vendor, unaffiliated with the client and in the business of conducting quantitative and/or qualitative research projects. A supplier might, for example, be responsible for orchestrating a survey, focus group, or ethnography to help solve a business problem for a client. The leading suppliers of media research are either multinational research and/or brand consultancies with media as just one of many vertical spaces (e.g., TNS, Nielsen Entertainment Television, Hall & Partners, IPSOS/OTX, Lieberman Research) or a boutique research consultancy with media as a key specialty (e.g., Frank N. Magid Associates, SmithGeiger, Insight Express, Hypothesis Group). Within the media industries, clients are split between two groups: client researchers, who either conduct research directly or partner with suppliers for research, and end clients, who can use the research to inform decision-making on content, marketing, or communication for the

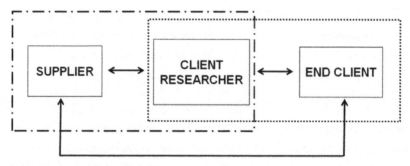

Figure 11.1. Economic Agents

media product (see figure 11.1). The end client is, in many instances, a creative executive in development, production, or marketing.

Given these economic agents, there are four basic scenarios outlining the management interaction for a market research project.

First, the supplier works directly with the client researcher. Here, the client researcher is the sole contact for the supplier. The supplier may not even know, in fact, who the end client is or what their specific goals are. All is conveyed by the client researcher to the supplier. An example of this relationship would be a cable television researcher hiring an experienced moderator to conduct a focus group as part of pilot testing for new shows. The moderator probably has extensive experience with show testing, and the client researcher can use this experience in formulating the findings from the project. In this (limited) case, the supplier/moderator may not even be privy to the full platform of research being conducted around the show pilot. Their only concern is the responsibility of leading the focus group for their portion of the research.

Second, the client researcher works solely with the end client. In these cases, the client researcher conducts their own research for the end client, and there is no role for the supplier. On the positive side, these projects allow for a greater exchange between the end client and the client researcher: the end client must become an active participant in the research project. Time and workload limitations, however, do not allow the majority of projects to be conducted in this manner. This can be the case when issues of confidentiality do not permit research to be conducted by a third party (e.g., a supplier). For instance, a network news production team may develop a series of new delivery means/techniques for news and information distribution. While they need feedback on these prototypes, involving an outside research supplier could present issues of confidentiality and could limit their competitive advantage. The solution is for the in-house client researcher to work directly with the client to limit this potential for information leakage.

Third, in the most typical case, client researchers often partner with a supplier to conduct research projects with a clear and direct connection to the needs of an end client. In this case, the supplier connects with the client researcher who relays the end clients' objectives and parameters for the project. The client researcher responds to the business questions and problems of the end client and is responsible for formulating a research platform to help answer these issues, while the supplier is a key component in meeting these goals. In this instance, the client researcher acts as both a supervisor to and research partner with the supplier. The client researcher "reports" to the end client to the extent that he or she is responsible for supplying and analyzing research data that addresses the key business problems faced by the end client. In this scenario, the supplier is often kept separate from the end client, with the substantive interaction occurring between the client researcher and the end client. An example of this scenario would be a brand tracking survey for a cable network. Since cable networks are usually niche oriented, decisions on programming, marketing, and communication are usually guided by a specific "brand filter." For instance, an upscale cable network with appeal to women and gay men might use the following words as brand filters: "upscale," "feel good," "sophisticated," "stylish," "connected," and "vivid." The brand tracker would need to gauge how viewers perceive the network in terms of these brand filters. The end client (in this case, probably a network president) would be telegraphing these brand filters to the client researcher. In turn, the development of the brand tracking survey would need the client researcher to relay to the supplier the brand filter and mission or goals of the network in a clear, direct manner. Consequently, the research project is based on the collaboration of the client researcher and supplier to meet the needs of the end client.

The fourth and final scenario presents the supplier creating a research project directly for the end client. In this case, the client researcher is elided from the situation, and the supplier interacts directly with the end client. From the perspective of the client researcher, this is the "cheat scenario" since both the supplier and the end client reject the value added of the client researcher to the project. The supplier has an incentive to pursue this scenario since they can form a bond with the end client, who can then insist on using this particular supplier for other projects. The end client benefits by eliminating the "objective" opinion and guidance of the client researcher. Correspondingly, the role of the client researcher as gatekeeper for the research is also scratched. The client researcher is usually versed in research methodology and the costs and benefits of various research approaches. By deleting the client researcher from the equation, the supplier is able to present their ideas for research to answer the business problem straight to the end client. The end client, usually unfamiliar with research methods, accepts the supplier's recommendations without attention to the method, sample, or rigor of the research. The supplier frequently is anxious to bond with the end client for multiple reasons: the chance to work directly with the user of the research, the chance to act as a research consultant (in lieu of the client researcher), and, most obviously, the opportunity to sell additional research or pitch projects to those unfamiliar with the parameters of the industry or normal business practice for market research. As would be expected, the client researcher dreads this scenario, in which they are omitted from the dialogue and management/supervision of the project. How might it occur? Sometimes it arises from a personal relationship between a supplier and end client (e.g., they worked together at a previous company or there is some interpersonal connection bonding them). The end client simply calls the supplier ("We're friends, after all"), and the discussion leads to the possibility of a research project for the end client. The supplier pitches the project as exploratory, and the end client has discretionary funds for pursuing it. As a result, the client researcher is sidelined as the project develops. This fourth scenario happens rarely, however, due to a most tangible reason: usually, the budget for research projects resides with the client researcher. If the end client wants to mount a research project, they must fund it from their own sources. In a large company, the sourcing and procurement department would then question why a market research project would be commissioned outside the research department.

Modeling Communication Strategy within Media Market Research

Management within media market research differs in each scenario. At the broadest level, management traces the flow of dollars through the system: those paying money (e.g., client researcher or end client) for research services are able to exert control over those conducting the research (e.g., supplier). In this case, management takes the form of first commissioning the project, then partnering on the research design and research instrument, and then disseminating the results from the project. Looking at the issue in a more granular fashion, we find that management of media market research is probably best judged in terms of the efficacy of the research project. Those projects deemed successful provide data, information, and insights that are useful for solving a business problem. Those deemed failures offer little or no useful data, information, or insights for the business unit. In this way, the success or failure of a research project has little to do with the technical competence of the researcher. Rather, the research project must be helpful in either a tactical or strategic way for the business. More specifically, the project is linked, directly or indirectly, to either a stabilization or growth in revenue, profit, or market share.

As a fundamental step toward a successful project, communication between the parties in the research project is absolutely necessary. While this may seem basic, the nuances of communication—and the strategies involved—are keys to establishing and building a successful research engagement. Communication, of course, is the first step in relationship building. As F. H. Buckley suggests, relationship maintenance is the salient factor in long-term business dealings: "What gives the relationship stability is not the individual contracts but rather the personal relationships and trust built over the years between firm and client" (2005: 45). This communication is multi-directional, with communication strategies enacted and developed by both supplier and client (client researcher, end client). Most crucially the communication is not dictated by the flow of cash; strategies develop that are motivated by factors other than revenue and payment.

To understand these communication strategies, the economic framework of game theory is illuminating.[6] Growing from seventy years of economic theorizing across a wide variety of applications, game theory involves considering the strategic thinking and principles in an interaction, exchange, or partnership. The most famous model in game theory is the prisoner's dilemma, in which the outcome for two prisoners interrogated separately depends on the behavior or actions of the other prisoner. Through this simple model, game theory shows that outcomes in situations are frequently based on inter-dependent actions (or inactions).[7] Tracing the potential outcomes through the logic and reasoning leading to each, the model demonstrates that strategic thinking can be helpful in "unpacking" the outcomes in any situation where the agents' actions are interdependent. While game theory's focus on strategy may suggest adversaries looking for competitive advantages, in fact, much of game theory is based on understanding *both* strategic and cooperative behaviors. With media market research, game theory helps us understand the management and communication flow existing in the different scenarios. Further, the success or failure of a market research project depends on the strategy, cooperation, and communication between the supplier and the client researcher/end client.

This communication flow is based on a series of decisions made by the supplier and the client researcher/end client. In each case, the economic agent can be either open or restrained in their communication (see figure 11.2). When open, the economic agents are fully transparent in their interactions, supplying all the information to all parties on the particular issue. There are no attempts to "spin" or manipulate the information for the benefit of only one party. In other words, open communication means that information is provided in an accessible fashion that does not discriminate against any party in the exchange. Restrained communication, on the other hand, implies that there is an imperfect flow of communication around a particular issue or exchange. Information may be withheld, misrepresented, or "spun" to the benefit of one party in the interaction. In this way, restrained communication is by design an attempt to maintain control or gain advantage over another party by being less than fully open in the communication flow.

Figure 11.2. Communication flow

Restrained communication can therefore be viewed as strategic rather than simply as "failed communication" between the two parties.

The choice of open versus restrained communication occurs at several key points in the life of the market research project. From the client side, the choice arises during discussion of the background of the project, at the "problem definition" meeting (i.e., the explication of the business problem to be addressed by the research project), while addressing issues that arise during the fielding and analysis of the project, and when identifying any next steps in light of the research findings and recommendations. From the supplier side, communication is usually related to the specifics of the project and less to the business motivation or impetus for the project in the first place. The supplier may be open or reserved regarding comparable studies or past findings from other studies in the same area, the specifics of sampling and fielding, the analysis of results, and, of course, the choice of what constitutes relevant findings. Some of these issues are shared by both supplier and client (e.g., deciding on the research design or sample frame) while others fall solely in the domain of either the supplier (e.g., monitoring fielding) or the client (e.g., disclosing past research studies which may inform the current study).

The motivations for open communication are multiple from both sides, supplier and client. In the best case, open communication allows for true partnership on the research project. The supplier brings a knowledge of market research design and techniques and a background of past findings from allied studies. The client is closer to the business problem in the research project. Consequently, the client is able to infuse the project with specific details and parameters of the industry and marketplace. Given proximity to the issue, the client is also assumed to keep the research project "on track," making the research design, instrument, and findings as actionable as possible. The client usually sets parameters on what is included and excluded in the project given their needs. It is incumbent, therefore, on the client to make sure that the project is able to proceed with as few constraints as possible.

While the reasons for open communication may seem obvious, the rationale for restrained or limited communication need greater explanation: after all, why would a business partner choose to have restrained communication if it is clear that open communication leads to a stronger research product? From the client side, there may be concern about losing a competitive advantage by revealing full information about an entertainment product or strategy. Given that most major media research suppliers work across multiple accounts and competing companies, clients are concerned about a research project compromising plans as a result of indiscretion on the part of a supplier or a respondent. Consequently, some clients are apt to cloud or mask their identity and even aspects of the media product tested to avoid this situation. For instance, in 2012, concept testing for a new music reality show at E! Entertainment entailed using three show concepts (actually green-lit projects at E!, CW, and ABC), all masked for network identity. The intention was to assess the competitive costs and benefits of each project, independently of its network affiliation. The networks were removed to retain the competitive advantage of E!'s project and to understand the value, beyond network affiliation, of each concept. This restrained approach to communication can limit the efficacy of the market research in many ways. Restrained communication also derives from, to invoke an economics term, imperfect information in the marketplace.[8] In this case, the client or supplier does not knowingly restrain information, but rather lack of knowledge creates the flaw in communication in the research project. An example would be specifying recruitment parameters and quotas in a qualitative research project to reflect a percentage of target viewers based on marketing projections rather than on the true percentage of actual viewers in the population (e.g., recruiting a target of 70 percent Caucasian/30 percent Non-Caucasian respondents for a qualitative group whereas the actual viewership skews 55 percent Caucasian/45 percent Non-Caucasian). The deviation in the sample due to the incorrect viewer sample quota presents an "incorrect communication" in the exchange between supplier and client. This, in turn, may negatively impact the outcome of the research project.

Returning to the realm of game theory and the prisoner's dilemma, we can sketch out the most typical media market research project. In this model, the client researcher and supplier are engaged in a research project. Each agent can be either open or restrained in their communication. Given this scenario, the four possible outcomes depend on the combination of actions from the supplier and client researcher. In the most desirable outcome, both the supplier and the client researcher operate with open communication (e.g., the supplier is transparent with research design, fielding, and analysis options; the client researcher provides all past studies informing the current project, articulates the business problem of the end client clearly and accurately, and works with the supplier to create a research instrument that reflects the needs of their client). Any secondary motives on the part of either the client researcher or supplier do not interfere with clear communication needed to design, field, and analyze the research project. With open communication between the supplier and the client researcher at each point in the research process, the project meets the goal of providing actionable information to help solve the end client's business issue. Most significantly, both parties, the supplier and the client researcher, really do partner on the project as a result of open communication on goals, method, fielding, data analysis, and results. What does each bring to the table? The client researcher offers an articulation of the business problem, while the supplier constructs a research platform to aid in answering it.

The alternatives to this model are less desirable. When one party is open in communication and the other is restrained, the outcome is either a qualified success or a qualified failure. For example, when the supplier is open with communication and the client researcher restrained, this imbalance of information is usually due to the client researcher limiting the information either for reasons of confidentiality or to maintain a competitive position for their end client. This tendency toward guarding information is infused through Hollywood. As Sherry Ortner describes it, "[Hollywood] is deeply invested in discourses and practices that both define and constantly construct insideness and outsideness" (2009: 176). Moreover, the client researcher may simply be multi-tasking and, due to handling several projects at one time, fails to create an adequate dialogue with the supplier on the research project. Regardless of the reasons, though, with the supplier open in communication and the client researcher restrained, the project can only be viewed as a qualified success: an opportunity for the supplier to build trust with the client researcher and to create solid ground for moving forward has not been maximized fully.

In the case when the supplier is restrained with communication and the client is open, the result is also clearly a missed opportunity and must be classified as a qualified failure. While it may be difficult to imagine a situation when the supplier is restrained in communication, this happens in cases when a "bait and switch" occurs in the project— when, for instance, an account executive who sells the project to the client researcher then hands off the project to a more junior analyst who actually services the project for the client researcher. The junior analyst either may not have enough experience or enough interest to create an adequate communication flow with the client researcher. Alternately, the junior analyst may follow the project outline or design too closely, while neglecting to recognize either pitfalls or benefits that arise during fielding. As a result, the research design, research instrument, analysis, or reporting may be compromised. At a minimum, the project is not being optimized due to this communication breakdown between supplier and client researcher. Another example of restrained communication on the supplier side would involve concealing or not revealing issues like sampling problems, survey programming glitches, and miscoded data. In these instances, the supplier is purposefully limiting communication in the interest of completing the project, even in a haphazard manner.

When both supplier and client researcher are restrained in their communication, the project is open to failure. Any number of issues may occur during the life of a research project: sampling problems, low incidence of respondents, data tabulation errors, timelines missed, objectives morphing mid-project, and internal priorities changing the focus of a project. A lack of communication between the two parties increases the chances that an issue during the life of the project will not be resolved to the satisfaction of both supplier and the client researcher. Given that the supplier is usually attempting to build a relationship with the client researcher (and end client), resolving these communication issues can often times be at the expense of the supplier's profit margin. For example, because of shifting internal demands, clients sometimes request additional data tabulations and analyses beyond the initial scope of the project. The supplier will be forced to absorb the cost of a project change in the interest of fostering the business relationship with the client researcher. The good will from this gesture helps to alleviate any bad feeling from the communication differences in the relationship. Clearly, though, these moments of "communication failure" are opportunities for both parties to learn about the parameters needed to launch an effective research project for both the client and the supplier.

The analysis above is based on the economic agents of the supplier and the client researcher. In the media industries, this is the most frequent kind of exchange for a market research project. In terms of the other scenarios (supplier/end client, client researcher/end client), while the outcomes from the communications quadrants may be the same as in the supplier/client researcher case, there are important differences in terms of emphasis. When the end client is directly involved in a project, either with the supplier or the client researcher, there is even more to be gained when both parties are open with their communication. Since it is atypical to have access to the end client in this way, these instances offer a chance to educate and inform the end client about the benefits of research, to warn them of the potential pitfalls or limitations, and to hear directly about the business issue or problem. Consequently, when both parties are open with communication, the research project has the potential for really developing both trust in the research process and growth in the relationship between those conducting the research project. It should be noted that by eliminating either the client researcher or the supplier from the dialogue, there is a greater need for the remaining research partner to bring to the table knowledge of research methods, design, and analysis. The excitement of working directly with the end client can be undone quickly with sloppy research that lacks rigor in design or analysis. Similarly, with restrained communication from the end client in one of these dyads, the result is more likely to be a qualified failure compared to times when a client researcher is included. If the end client is in direct communication with the client researcher or supplier yet is hesitant or restrained in communication, then the research project is in jeopardy.

This model of communication suggests that media market research depends on both the strategic and cooperative bases of game theory. While it may always be the intention to have open communication, the "pressure points" of a research project—when either the supplier or the client face an issue with the project—offer a chance to address the communication needs directly. These instances are crucial for building trust between supplier and client. In fact, weathering issues that develop is the most significant way to establish a solid relationship for future projects. As Edye Twer, President of Media Research at Phoenix Marketing International, comments, "When things go wrong? The key is making sure that the vendor is honest about it. They should call the client after they have a plan. They should offer the problem and a solution at the same time."[9] Although Twer refers to a problem from the supplier side, it is important to realize that these "problems" are multi-directional: they might derive from the client, supplier, or merely market forces at play in the fielding of the project. However they may arise, they create an opportunity for both sides to understand their respective problem-solving methods, Once established, this understanding is, of course, crucial to all future projects.

One method for ensuring that both parties work toward open communication is to conduct an ex-post analysis of the project. This analysis is designed to uncover the tactics and strategies that were effective and ineffective during the course of the study. The benefits are multiple: to gauge success of the project in meeting the business goal(s), to assess how both parties were able to communicate through moments of ambiguity and difference, and to establish parameters for future projects. Maria Stark, founder of media research company Hypothesis Group, adds that this dialogue is critical at the start of the relationship: "This analysis is really important, particularly when you're starting out. You need to ask two key questions: 'where were the areas where we added value?' and 'where are the areas where we can bring more to the table?"[10] For the supplier, an ex-post analysis should also evaluate the project in cost-benefit terms (i.e., did the revenue from the project off-set the cost and effort?) and decide whether the service team (e.g., analyst, statistician, account executive) matched well with the needs of the project. For the client, the ex-post analysis is a chance to understand how reasonable were the initial goals and expectations for the project. Given that the supplier wants to book more research business from the client, the onus is usually on the supplier to initiate these kinds of ex-post analysis meetings. Keep in mind, though, that the easiest route is to skip this step in the research project: clients can ignore any potential confrontation that developed over the course of the project, and suppliers can simply hope that their performance warrants a new project.

Despite the real or imagined pain of the ex-post analysis, the process also helps move both supplier and client into the quadrant of "open communication." In this phase, when the project has been completed, both parties have a chance to learn more about their own communication strategies and to adjust these strategies, if needed. The project management and the communication strategies behind it therefore lead to the relationship management. The goal is to become an entrenched supplier working in partnership with the media client. Through this collaboration and cooperation, both client and supplier finally have a chance to make an impression on the media landscape through innovative and purposeful market research platforms.

In my own career, I have functioned as both a client and a supplier. While I would like to think that I have always operated with a policy of open communication in both roles, the truth is that open communication has not happened as often as I would have liked. As a client, for example, I have sometimes been remiss in providing feedback on proposals that were not chosen to move forward. As a supplier, I have focused on developing and sharing innovative methods and approaches with those clients who occupy the largest amount of time (e.g., those with the greatest spend). Other clients may not be privy to the latest and most innovative methods, given their lower potential expenditure. Interestingly, these omissions are motivated by wanting to avoid a potentially negative interpersonal conflict between supplier/agent. Maintaining personal relationships in the industry seems key, given the mercurial nature of the media industries and the need to build a personal support network in them. If anything, my personal experience suggests that the framework of open versus restrained communication needs to be placed within the larger context of building strong interpersonal business relationships. At the end of the day, the media industries operate through these personal relationships, and communication, of any kind, cannot happen if the relationships are not present in the first place.

NOTES

1. Assessment of value in art, both aesthetic and economic, is explored in depth in the anthology *The Value of Culture: On the Relationship between Economics and Art*, edited by Arjo Klamer (1996).

2. Phone interview with Vicki Cohen, Executive Vice President, Frank N. Magid Associates, May 21, 2007.

3. Interview with David L. Smith, Founder, SmithGeiger Research & Consulting, May 19, 2007.

4. For an excellent review of the process of brand building within packaged goods, consult Anne Bahr Thompson (2003: 79–96).

5. David Lynch muses on the pros and cons of the shifted experience of moviegoing in his own exploration of creativity (2006: 155–57).

6. An alternative to conceptualizing this relationship through game theory would be to consider the role played by "exchange" in the transaction. This could also account for the issues of communication and strategy present in the game theory framework. John Davis (1992) offers a succinct analysis of the anthropological and economic structures of exchange in his monograph, *Exchange*.

7. Avinash K. Dixit and Barry J. Nalebuff explore a range of contemporary applications of the prisoner's dilemma in economic and non-economic contexts in *The Art of Strategy* (2008: 64–101).

8. There is a considerable literature within economics on the impact of imperfect information on the outcome of game theoretical structure. The most famous model of this type is the Harsanyi Transformation (Bierman and Fernandez 1998: 275–79).

9. Phone interview with Edye Twer, President, Media Research, Phoenix Marketing International, April 27, 2007.

10. Interview with Maria Stark, Founder, Hypothesis Group, May 12, 2007.

12

Listening and Empathizing

Advocating for New Management Logics in Marketing and Corporate Communications

SAM FORD

Among the managerial logics employed by corporate employees charged with creating media texts and communicating directly with external audiences, the actual communication experience of those audience members is rarely a primary focus. Instead, the "audience" is often discussed as an abstraction, a statistic, a target, a recipient, or even as a nuisance to be avoided, silenced, or otherwise dealt with as efficiently as possible. Soap opera writer Tom Casiello writes that, despite an obsession with focus group results and ratings, "there wasn't a lot of focus on The Audience" as actual human beings in his industry (2011: 275). Across corporate America, companies represent current or potential customers through spreadsheets, impressions, conversions, and other easily intelligible terms. This inclination to favor audiences as statistics rather than people is even more pervasive outside creative industries, where corporate leaders often rise from financial divisions of the business, rather than what might be considered creative or communications roles, and business performance is primarily discussed in numbers rather than words.

Currently, I work for Peppercomm Strategic Communications, a firm that advises companies on corporate communications strategy, including public relations. The company subsidizes a portion of my time being spent continuing to do independent academic research, writing, and speaking, as well as adjunct teaching, and I spend the rest of my time writing and speaking to industry audiences and consulting with the firm's current and potential clients on better understanding, listening to, empathizing with, and prioritizing the wants and needs of the audiences with whom they communicate and for whom they create content.

Through that consulting work, I've encountered companies facing managerial issues related to their communication on a regular basis. These companies typically employ earnest people who express an interest not only in helping their company make money but also in helping serve their customers or other constituencies through their communications work. However, as Mark Deuze writes, "The problem of contemporary media work, as felt and experienced by its practitioners, is management" (2010: x). In my consulting, employees regularly voice frustration with coordinating external communications efforts across the organization. While they are not always fully aware of it, employees often find such coordination difficult because of the divergent range of logics by which each department is governed.

This essay explores these internal tensions and challenges as companies seek to create new practices for managing external communications in response to the rise in communication on digital platforms, where more forms of corporate communications are becoming mediated and where customers and other external audiences are more frequently using media channels to communicate about companies. In the process, I draw on key debates happening among those who manage corporate media strategy across marketing, corporate communications, and customer service. Specifically, I will focus on my intervention in this conversation: why I see it as necessary and as part of my academic work. I will summarize strategies I advocate in my consulting and how they have been received (or ignored) by management teams, as an effort to demonstrate the potential such approaches afford for affecting change in corporate media policies, as well as the challenges this embedded approach faces.

In the process, I also hope to provide a more nuanced view of companies that are largely comprised of compassionate and dedicated individuals who truly do wish to serve their audiences but who face a variety of impediments—whether practical, infrastructural or as a result of restrictions caused by pervasive industry logics. My hope is that this exploration underscores a greater need for media studies scholars to understand the environments, processes, and relationships shaping communication and media strategy within companies outside the media industries and the profound effect internal communications processes have on external communication.

For the purposes of this essay, I'm describing "management" as the processes and logics by which a company's communication to external audiences is conceptualized, organized, and implemented across divisions. I contend that interdepartmental communication processes and competing conceptualizations of "the audience" among the various management teams charged with reaching that audience lead to internal tensions that manifest in external communication across media channels.

These challenges are infrastructural, and such questions of interdepartmental communication have long been the domain of organizational communication scholars and consultants. However, as an increasing degree of communication between companies and external audiences takes place online, these interactions are themselves becoming media texts. Thus, the processes for coordinating such communications should be examined through the lens of media management. Existing research on management processes governing "creative work" have typically focused on what are considered the "creative industries" (Hesmondhalgh 2007, Deuze 2009). As marketing, advertising, public relations, and other forms of corporate communications have been considered by media scholars, studies have often considered employees like myself who work for agencies, which themselves are wholly media companies. Instead, this reflective essay looks at those creating mediated communications texts within companies that are primarily not in the media sector. As such, concerns about how business logics and managerial processes constrain creative labor might be seen as especially restrictive on these professionals in organizations where, often, media and communications are not a priority among top corporate decision-makers.

Understanding Internal Managerial Tensions

Staying true to the focus I advocate in my consulting, I see the best place to begin examining internal managerial issues as the customer's perspective, where interacting with a given company is often a fractured communication experience. For example, consider the typical experience a person has with a cable provider. As a new customer, I set up service by talking to the local office staff. The technician who comes to my house to establish that service is a subcontractor who does not communicate directly with that local office. After my service is established, my primary interaction with the company is through paying my bill on the website once a month. If I have a service issue, the company's Twitter account is immediately responsive if I complain about that issue publicly online. Yet, a call to the company's 1-800 number results in an automated menu, a fifteen-minute hold time, and an agent talking off a script who tries to quickly address my issue. Meanwhile, the company mails, emails, and advertises to me on a weekly basis, and someone from the cable operator even calls every few weeks to tell me about a great deal on its "triple play service."

This range of communication experiences—across multiple media formats—illustrates why asking customers to describe their relationships with a company is a complicated query. Even if every employee involved in the scenario described above were fully motivated to serve the customer, that customer's experience would still be disjointed at best.

Businesses have identified a range of legal and tax benefits from having the corporation described as an individual in the United States, yet—if the cable company depicted above is to be understood as a single "person"—its identity is one suffering from the type of dissociative identity disorder one might expect from a soap opera character. The company is immediately responsive on one channel and difficult to connect with on another, garrulous in one format and terse in another. And customers are treated differently across channels or may even get different answers to the same question, depending on where the question is posed.

This picture of fractured corporate communication from the customer's perspective is due to splintered corporate managerial practices governing external communications. In the cable company example, customer "on-boarding" is managed locally; service set-up is out-sourced; the website is designed by the ".com" team; online complaints are handled by public relations; the call center is managed by customer care; promotional materials come from marketing; and calls are driven by sales. The employees of these various divisions often work in sepa-rate locations and report to different company leaders. In many organi-zations, these teams' managers do not coordinate frequently. And these various communication functions are not viewed equally, most often with those more directly responsible for creating revenue receiving higher priority from company leadership.

An even more fundamental challenge is that each division maintains its own understanding of the customer, operates by a different manage-rial logic, and measures success on its own terms. In the cable com-pany scenario, the sales team is measured by "conversion," charging its employees to, as they say in the 1992 real estate film *Glengarry Glen Ross*, "always be closing." The marketing team is tasked to "engage" cur-rent and potential customers and are often evaluated through measures of stickiness: how many current or potential customers view an ad or click a link, and how much time do those people spend with the com-pany's content? And call center operators are charged with getting from one call to the next as efficiently as possible, as customer service is often considered a "cost center" within the company—meaning any resources spent on it are considered only as a subtraction from the company's profits (Yellin 2009: 13).

Corporate infrastructure—and its related exponentially complex organizational charts—is built for a reason: to provide order and ensure a company weathers changes in the economy, the sector, workforce turnover, and other external forces. However, that structure can make it harder for organizations to be flexible in incorporating new processes or philosophies—particularly for those managing creative work such as the creation of media texts and the handling of communications and services. Deuze writes of the "gradual bureaucratization of workspaces in media organizations" (2009: 144)—a trend that is likely to be even more pronounced within the divisions who handle creative work within companies outside the media industries.

Staying true to Cartesian philosophy, employees in organizations begin to accept internal "truths" over time without ever returning to question them—meaning that tradition eventually begins to dictate how people organize, even if the world outside has changed. Amanda D. Lotz (2008) argues that the only way these outmoded "truths" are eventually uncovered is through pressure from disruptive external forces. For corporate communications in all its forms, the many new ways customers and other external audiences have found to communicate about companies and to access and directly compare media texts from and about the company provide that disruption (Ford 2010c). And, in response, companies are rapidly prioritizing the search for new structures for internal communication to better coordinate the production of external media content.

However, the competing internal logics described earlier are not the only barriers companies face in a quest for integration. Battles for budgets and higher positions in the corporate hierarchy also greatly shape the tone of internal collaboration. Within companies, there can be much talk about who "has a seat at the table" with the CEO and other members of the so-called "C-Suite." Again, this concern is particularly pronounced among those doing largely creative labor outside the media industries, where some or all forms of media development and communications are seen as necessary evils that take away from profit margins rather than as vital business functions.

Just within marketing and communications, such tensions are frequent. Conflicts rise as new processes surrounding digital communication have blurred the lines between what the "digital team," the public relations/corporate communications division, and marketing and advertising functions within a company are supposed to do (as well as the budgets they afford to agencies such as the one for which I work). Traditionally, the company sets a budget for how much will be spent on advertising, public relations, direct marketing, and other forms of marketing, and then each team develops a plan based on that budget. Thus, who "owns" digital communications becomes a sensitive question. For instance, Ken Payne finds through a survey of members of the Public Relations Society of America that "concern is growing within the industry that failure to assume a leadership role in the adoption and use of Web 2.0 technologies by public relations professionals will ultimately result in . . . encroachment from other disciplines such as marketing and advertising" (2008: 76). As Henry Jenkins, Joshua Green and myself write in *Spreadable Media*: "Such questions are more than just semantics. . . . Who 'owns' the customer relationship within a company is ultimately a question of who remains relevant and who keeps their job" (2013: 179).

Addressing a corporate workshop we facilitated together, Ed Moed (2010) writes:

> [C]orporate politics and turf battles are almost always a reality of day-to-day business. . . . One run-of-the-mill infrastructure issue we often see involves functional departments competing over budget sizes and resource allocations. And, within departments, managers often jockey for control over specific projects/campaigns or groups of employees.

In my consulting work, I have had clients agree with an idea but never share it across the organization for fear it would be a perceived encroachment of a relationship with some other external partner ("Great idea, but that's our ad firm's territory"), or for fear that the idea, if implemented, would end up owned by a different department and take budget away from their team. Such an environment is predicated on a mentality where corporate divisions are viewed simultaneously as collaborators and competitors, a dynamic that—as Moed suggests—is an everyday part of the corporate workplace and an omnipresent element in managerial strategies developed among those who fall under the broad marketing/communication umbrella.

Outside marketing and within a company's broader organization, these dynamics and struggles for power and budget become even more complex. I regularly lead workshops on social media/digital communication for organizations. At these events, I encourage all those charged in some way with managing external communications to join. Often, these employees from human resources, recruiting, information technology, customer service, legal counsel, governmental relations, investor relations, sales, research, and other corporate divisions are as much strangers to one another as they are to me. As a result, we spend the first part of the day helping people understand who everyone is and what it is they do.

The ability to get various functions within the company to have a conversation based on common language is daunting. Not only are these various divisions measured and understood differently within the company, but each employee's perspective is also guided by the professional culture of his or her field (Mierzejewska 2010: 18). Frequently, the training, focus, and philosophy of one field conflicts, implicitly or explicitly, with the concerns and interests of fellow employees in other departments.

Because of these cultural differences, employees at these workshops sometimes only know one another through prior internal conflicts. For instance, at several gatherings, marketing expressed that legal counsel only serves as a barrier to their ideas and that executives bow to the concerns of lawyers rather than listen to the marketing team's insights about why more open and responsive communication is now essential. Other times, legal counsel expressed frustration that, rather than be consulted at the point of ideation, they were called in as a project neared completion. The result, they said, were projects they had to oppose because certain elements of its execution raised legal red flags that could have been easily avoided. Overt animosity arose at one meeting between the marketing team who conceived of new ideas and the digital team who implemented them. The marketing team complained that digital designers were slow to respond, hard to reach, and unresponsive to deadlines. The digital team complained that marketing conceived of ideas without consulting them and then built detailed plans that were overly complicated to act on because they did not reflect the particulars of the company's digital platforms.

I've seen companies launch multiple almost identical Twitter accounts or Facebook pages because each function within the company wants to own its own version, with no one coordinating or even communicating internally about their efforts. I've heard of sales forces that actively ridicule and sell against their company's marketing when talking to potential customers but who never express their concerns to the marketing team. I've encountered digital communications teams who attempt to help customers complaining online without access to the detailed files their customer service departments keep on those customers' issues. I've seen tensions arise during meetings when the marketing department heard what call center employees were saying and became angry that it did not align with messaging on the website and in advertising. And I've heard of frustration from customer service professionals who know firsthand what customers want and need but who never have a chance to share that knowledge with those who design the company's mass media messages.

Production studies and media industries management research have given us a more nuanced understanding of how work is organized in the creative industries. Conversely, these observations point toward the many managerial fissures which shape media and message development within companies outside the media sector, where communication is typically less understood and less of a priority and where those tasked with creative labor may be especially constrained by managerial processes. Understanding how these pressures shape the work of professional communicators throughout a company's organizational chart is vital for understanding how those organizations relate to and communicate with external audiences.

The Need for Intervention

In *Technologies of Freedom*, Ithiel de Sola Pool (1983) presciently argues that the development of the Internet would challenge public media policy because the new communication medium is simultaneously printing press, broadcast platform, and common carrier—three distinct modes of communication that have their own regulatory histories. Similar to how the challenges he posed continue to vex internet regulation today, corporate policy for managing communications in distinct media formats has broken down because online communication blurs those formats. Is a blog a place for broadcasting material, publishing opinion, or facilitating dialogue? The answer, of course, is all three.

From a corporate perspective, whereas communications used to be aimed at one particular audience (current customers, potential customers, current employees, potential employees, former employees, investors, local communities, government regulators, etc.), that content is likely to be seen by multiple groups when distributed through online channels. And, from the perspective of a customer or other external audience, online media provide the means to access content directly from a company when we want it, rather than relying on an advertisement or news story finding us. Further, we can now directly compare online content to additional communication from the company and content from other primary sources.

However, as Poole argued from a regulatory perspective, it is not new technologies themselves that determine industry practice but rather the corporate policies and managerial processes developed to govern corporate communication in a "digital age." Here, I take the perspective that—just as public intellectuals have focused decades of work on advocating for regulatory paths forward which lead to a more open communication environment—it is important for some media scholars to take up an interventionist mantle to influence the policies being formed on corporate campuses and not just on Capitol Hill. After all, in a capitalist society which often relies on self-governing market forces, many aspects of the balance of power and information between companies and their external audiences are determined through the everyday implicit and explicit policies within these organizations (Jenkins, Ford, and Green 2013).

My primary academic affiliation is with a program called Comparative Media Studies (CMS) at MIT. William Uricchio and Henry Jenkins, co-directors of that program when I was a Master's candidate, developed this program in the humanities at an institution that prioritizes applied research with a range of public and private partners. In that spirit, CMS sought to create an "applied humanities" approach. The program's research projects partner with foundations, governments, and other institutions on subjects from "new media literacies" and "civic media" to the educational potentials of gaming and new digital humanities archival processes.

During my time at MIT, I helped conceptualize, launch, research for, and later manage a project called the Convergence Culture Consortium (C3). Created around the launch of Henry Jenkins' 2006 book *Convergence Culture*, C3 was funded by companies interested in how audiences were relating to and communicating around media content in a digital age. The project focused on finding ways for humanities academics and graduate students researching these issues to put that thinking into conversation with the companies shaping media practice, primarily through white papers, newsletters, retreats, conferences, and a research blog.

This "applied humanities" approach, especially when it comes to intervention within the industry, has been met with its share of cynicism. Cryptoxin, an active writer on fannish culture, suggests C3 is "a disturbing sign of the increasingly corporatized academy" and writes of his wariness about the project's corporate funding and "alienating" use of "corporate-speak" in an attempt to converse with corporations (2008). Researcher Juan Gonzales calls C3 "the exact opposite" of what academics should hope to achieve (2006). And an "MIT professor familiar with the consortium, who asked not to be named," said of C3 in a *Chronicle of Higher Education* profile on Jenkins, "One of the dangers of this is that the money can drive the program" (Young 2007).

Despite such criticism, however, the successes of our work have convinced me that collaborative industry/academic approaches aimed to intervene within industry discourse rather than to criticize from a removed distance is a key approach to media reform. Through C3's direct interaction with corporate partners, as well as the conferences the project organized and industry audiences attended, we have seen concepts that advocate for companies to create more equitable relations with their audiences take root in corporate discourse.

Jenkins argues that media reform must be a multi-subject and multi-pronged battle (2006: 247–48). Taking up that charge, my own career has been fueled by a conviction that distanced critical approaches con-stitute a crucial element of intervening in media but not the whole of media studies approaches to such reform. Since leaving my full-time position at MIT, I have worked directly within the corporate commu-nications space. While I suspect many academics might not go so far as to be embedded in an industry position to make such interventions (and that some scholars would discount my even using the mantle of "academic" to describe my work), it's crucial to see the value of not only critically examining media management logics as a system but also finding ways to intervene within that system, with the goal of affecting industry policy. I see this essay as a chance to reflect on that work and how these attempts at intervention have (and have not) been taken up within the managerial practices of companies with which I've worked.

Advocating Managing Communications from the Audience's Perspective

I have posed the question in industry publications as to whether inter-nal corporate discussions about social media might become a "Trojan horse" for bringing about more fundamental change in internal communications and for better connecting disparate parts of the company that have not traditionally spoken the same language (Ford 2010a). But what goals guide such integration?

As a consultant, my interest is in pushing companies to create more participatory, transparent, and equitable approaches to communicating to customers and other audiences. I see my role as advocating on behalf of external audiences and, ultimately, convincing all employees managing external communication to view their role in a similar fashion. However, I know that a company's primary motivation remains efficiency and efficacy: to find more effective ways to communicate with audiences for the purpose of selling a company's products and services. In a market economy, that goal is a given, and it is the marker by which employees will always in some way be measured.

Thus, my point of intervention has been to advocate that companies that manage their external communication strategies through more interpersonal (as opposed to distanced and corporate) logics will not just better address their audiences' wants and needs but find greater long-term business success as well. Occasionally, and especially in the short term, such audience-centered approaches may run directly counter to a company's business interests. But those organizations that consistently care about external audiences (including critics who are not part of their potential customer base) beyond profit margins build better reputations, stave off communication crises, and stay more attuned to the wants and needs of the customers and communities who keep them in business. My goal is to shift, in whatever incremental ways I can, corporate economic logics slightly toward social logics, at least in how companies communicate with their audiences (the area in which I can reasonably hope to have some small degree of influence).

These interpersonal or "human" approaches to managing corporate communication focus on putting the audience at the center of a company's way of thinking (Ford 2012b). Here, let me briefly profile two approaches that have been at the center of my efforts: prioritizing corporate "listening" and pushing all those in charge of managing communications and media content to empathize with their external audiences.

Listening

Word of mouth is the oldest and most influential form of marketing, and most businesses seem aware that customer testimonials—or rants—have substantial impact on a company's reputation. Today, however, online platforms maintain a textual trail of those conversations. That, in turn, transforms conversations into publications. In response, companies have developed a variety of monitoring tools to make sense of what people are saying online about them and their brands. Often, these tools seek to produce quantifiable results of customer conversations, measuring "share of voice" (how much a company is being discussed online vis-à-vis its competitors), "sentiment" (whether discussions are positive, negative, or neutral), and shifts in the volume of discussion over time. Such quantified "surveillance" techniques are regarded critically by Mark Andrejevic (2007), who redefines online spaces of presumed open communication online as digital enclosures where people are closely monitored and analyzed.

But, even within the profit-driven logics of corporate America, these efforts to simplify and quantify audiences are limiting. David Hesmondhalgh writes that, in the media industries, market research's reliance on quantitative data and focus groups have led to management processes that primarily seek to mitigate risk (2007: 196–97). The restrictive impact of these processes extends beyond media companies, however, repressing both the creative energies of employees and qualitative processes that seek to understand and connect with external audiences. In industry discourse, I have argued that online quantitative research tools act as "hearing aids," amplifying and recording that a noise has been made but giving a company little knowledge beyond recording the sound (Ford 2010b).

Conversely, my advocacy for "listening" strategies refers to processes that move beyond these acts of "hearing" in three fundamental ways:

First, these processes focus on the context of communication rather than just the mention of a company or its products. While quantitative monitoring can provide an overall snapshot at a high level, it does little to provide insight into what customers actually want, need, or think. Instead, listening requires focusing in detail on what audiences are actually saying, or at least a large sample of what audiences say. For instance, since the mid-1990s, Robert V. Kozinets has advocated for a research methodology he labels "netnography," which is "a form of ethnographic research adapted to include the Internet's influence on contemporary social worlds" (2009: 1). In short, Kozinets and others have worked to develop systems to help academic and marketing industry researchers investigate online communication within its original context. Kozinets' work advocates for more widespread adoption of the type of qualitative online community research techniques one might expect from fan studies—an area that Kozinets has explored on many occasions, from media fandom (Kozinets 1997) to "brand fandom" (Brown, Kozinets, and Sherry 2003).

Second, listening processes focus on companies paying attention to what external audiences are talking about beyond just their brands/products. Many companies that do invest in paying attention to what their audiences are saying unfortunately focus only on "reactive" monitoring, ignoring what their audiences are saying unless it is specifically about the company. (That's why corporations, were they actually people, would too often make for horrible cocktail party companions.) Instead, listening processes should focus on following what external audiences are discussing in relation to the larger issues, needs, and wants which the company's products and services are created to address; these processes focus on the audience's agenda and concerns rather than just on the company's. Further, Grant McCracken (2009) has strongly advocated that companies have to pay attention what's happening outside their industry—to listen to what's happening in the culture surrounding them and to pay attention to new trends and patterns that are developing in how people live and communicate.

Finally, listening processes demand "an active response: not just gathering data but doing something about it" (Jenkins, Ford, and Green 2013: 178). Externally, companies are known for focusing deeply on measurement but only lightly on engagement. Internally, hearing processes too often lead to myriad tables, charts, graphs, and statistics to forward up the chain of command but little knowledge about audience concerns that could be disseminated throughout the company. Customer service professionals might hear what's wrong with products, and sales teams might find out why customers are offended by a marketing campaign; however, that knowledge never gets shared across departments. And those in corporate communications handling online monitoring programs rarely spread the knowledge gathered around the company—or, if they do, they do so only as part of a measurement report months after the intelligence could have been useful.

In my attempts to advocate on external audiences' behalf in the face of implicit and explicit corporate communications managerial policies, I've argued that companies that are closely attuned to audiences' wants and needs should use that knowledge to better serve their customers. This difference between "listening" and "hearing" distinguishes companies that are attempting to be connected, responsive, and committed to those with whom they communicate from those that still view the people they communicate at in aggregate.

Empathy

Building on that emphasis on listening, my recent work focuses on empathy as a central approach for creating communications management processes that are more effective for businesses but also more equitable for their external audiences. This approach draws, in part, on the writing of consultant Carol Sanford (2011), who argues—through her work with Seventh Generation and a variety of other organizations—that companies that put a responsibility to their customers at the center of their everyday business practices and align all employees' way of working around this customer-centered approach become not just more responsible but more profitable over time. Applying Sanford's approaches to a company's media and communications strategy provides a means for all employees who manage some aspect of external communication for a company to find as their common ground a central desire to put themselves in their customer's shoes and to look at the company and its communications from that perspective.

Such a mindset draws heavily on the elements of "design thinking" (Ford 2012a). This concept has been driven by thinkers like Rolf Faste and David Kelley at Stanford University, where the d.school (the Hasso Plattner Institute of Design) has popularized a way of approaching design and business with its stated goal of creating an interdisciplinary environment to "make the lives of the people they're designing for better" (Stanford University 2010).

As Dev Patnaik (with Peter Mortensen, 2009) argues, a sense of empathy must pervade an organization in order for such an approach to be effective. Design thinking requires being able to solve problems by constantly putting one's self in the audience's shoes, an ability that can only be possible if employees feel connected to the lives of those audience members. David McQuillen's work at Credit Suisse provides an example of this approach (Yellin 2009: 248-249). In an effort to help the bank's senior executives better understand their customers' experiences, McQuillen put them on the phone as customers with the bank's call center and took them to stand in line for a teller. Credit Suisse made this way of thinking pervasive in the company, creating a team whose focus was helping people throughout the organization think about solving their everyday problems by putting themselves in their audience's shoes.

Emphases on ethnographic research and putting employees' in their audiences shoes have informed new processes for product design, website design, retail space planning, and (increasingly) customer service to approach everyday business objectives from the perspective of the end "user." Yet, such an approach has not often been applied to communications, where managerial processes are often guided by seeking to align audiences with what the company wants to say rather than moving the company's communication toward addressing what its audiences want and need (Jenkins, Ford, and Green 2013).

Currently, Peppercomm is consulting and conducting workshops aimed at helping clients put themselves in their audiences' shoes to experience communication with and about the company and the categories and issues surrounding that company's area of business. This way of thinking has become central to the way our company describes itself (Ford and Cody 2011). As journalist and customer experience expert Emily Yellin—our partner on the initiative—has said of this Audience Experience work, our goal is to help marketers and corporate communicators adjust to a world where marketing is increasingly "more about service than selling" (quoted in Peppercomm 2012). Projects have included helping an appliances manufacturer understand the communication experience their customers have when buying a new appliance and helping a financial services firm think about how students research potential employers and how the company's recruiting communications look from a graduating college senior's point of view, and using these processes to transform business practices. While the approach has occasionally led directly to improvements for businesses, the primary focus is on better communicating with customers in ways that only indirectly impact "the bottom line." Nevertheless, we strongly advocate that this mentality is vital to a business' longevity and reputation in the long term.

Success and Challenges of Intervening within an Industry Setting

Frequently, my work within marketing and communications has energized me about the potential such an embedded position has to transform media managerial practice. I've played a role in transforming the way my company thinks and how it counsels clients, and I've counseled and held workshops with a variety of media industries companies along the way. However, as this essay has detailed, I have also had many opportunities to moderate and guide discussions among corporate leaders working for companies outside the media industries; to present perspectives inside companies and at industry events that challenge prevailing corporate logics; and even to directly help shape corporate policies in relation to how their communications are understood, from social media guidelines for employees to processes for interdepartmental collaboration surrounding external communications. In the process, I've been fortunate to receive visibility within marketing and communications circles for that work.

However, for every success, I've met many more roadblocks. The disjointed and competitive environment within companies has frequently obscured or dampened the impact this advocacy can have. In some cases, business leaders in one division find such arguments to resonate but have no power to disseminate those ideas beyond their division. In others, the problems with internal communication are so vast that it has discouraged employees to act on new ways of thinking, even if the ideas resonate.

In several instances, the profit-generating logic of companies has gotten in the way. My attempts at intervention have been shrugged off with "nice-to-have but not essential" responses or else met with questions of how success can be measured for "feel good" priorities that don't generate hard numbers through which performance can be assessed. Most frustrating of all is when the conversation turns immediately to ROI—what "return on investment" does funding these audience-centered approaches give me? In such cases, I know immediately that a meaningful intervention could not possibly be made.

These difficulties are driven by the fact that managerial processes and logics are often especially restrictive on creative work outside creative industries. Those who manage communications are expected to conform to profit-driven forms of measurement—largely quantitative in nature—and often develop policies against their own creative and human instincts in an effort to maintain or gain respect within the prevailing business logic of their organization. Additionally, while many of the professionals I meet feel these are barriers and constraints, I have met several individuals who manage communications and media creation who lack concern about connecting with or serving audiences and who seem to have embraced a direct profit motivation at the expense of social considerations.

Perhaps worse than encountering those for whom my advocacy falls on deaf ears is to see ideas embraced only in a cursory way. Companies say they want to start listening but then do little more than assess how their messages are "resonating" with their "key audiences"—in other words, labeling as "listening" efforts to "hear," and creating reportable "results" that managers up the corporate hierarchy will immediately comprehend and value. Organizations express interest in developing relationships and prioritizing the wants and needs of their customers or other constituencies but then prove that they really care only about "the influencers" who might gain them some immediate clout for public relations purposes. Perhaps most frustrating is when people pick up some words and phrases of what I have said or new concepts that have been introduced into corporate communications and begin applying them to what becomes only a slightly altered version of what the company has long been doing.

The most frequent way in which companies take this surface-level approach is to prioritize responding to customers' wants and needs on a one-off rather than a systemic basis. Public relations and marketing teams often address customer service issues to silence customers' complaints rather than to transform their business. In the process, listening and empathizing are limited to mitigating the potential "damage" a customer might cause to a brand, on the negative end, or trying to turn people into "advocates," on the positive end. In short, communication is seen solely as advancing what the company wants to say rather than addressing audiences' concerns.

However, the most significant barrier to the potential impact my advocacy from within the communications industry could have is self-censorship. I vehemently reject the notion that my role compromises an ability to speak critically in general terms of the industry in which I now work; on the contrary, I have found all attempts to do so at a macro level embraced. Yet, on a micro level, my perspective is restrained both by my own sense of "picking my battles" and by the needs of my employer.

I provide frank counsel when it's sought and interject objections when I perceive violations of audiences' rights or needs. But the ideas shared will undoubtedly be shaped, whether consciously or unconsciously, by the degree to which a company seems willing to consider new ways of thinking and the need to maintain an ongoing relationship with a client (barring, of course, blatant and flagrant offenses to transparency or business ethics). And my ability to find opportunities for intervention at a company level is also shaped by the business needs of the company by which I am employed. For instance, while Peppercomm supports my participation in industry-wide events or publications where its visibility will be enhanced, I am less likely to find myself traveling to get in front of a company unless it is believed there is some chance for ongoing business with them as a potential client.

These various barriers point toward why it's critical to have scholars who maintain a critical distance to industry and who advocate for media policy changes that seek to revolutionize how corporations communicate with their external audiences and how access to media platforms is managed. Yet while calls for revolution help us explore new possibilities for corporate and governmental media policy, intervention at the level of evolution within industry can also achieve significant gains toward shifting formal and informal corporate policies in ways that are more equitable and empathetic to us all. Despite the limitations, barriers, and frustrations I encounter on a daily basis, I'm heartened by every minute change I see made. The work of policy intervention on the corporate level is worthwhile if we see attempts to better balance power between companies and their external audiences as ongoing; if we define those in corporate America not solely in oppositional terms of struggle but also—when appropriate—in terms of potential collaboration; and if we aim to try and change the world as it exists rather than to overturn the world for the sake of some utopian alternative.

Adalian, Josef, 2012, "Dan Harmon Is No Longer Showrunner on *Community*," *Vulture*, May 28. Retrieved July 17, 2012, from http://www.vulture.com/2012/05/dan-har-mon-community-future-nbc-sony.html.

Adam Smith Institute, 2010, "Scrap the License Fee and Reform the BBC," August 2. Retrieved May 20, 2011, from http://www.adamsmith.org/blog/media-and-culture/scrap-the-tv-licence-fee-and-reform-the-bbc/.

Albarran, Alan B., 2010, *Management of Electronic Media*, Wadsworth Publishing, Boston.

"All This and Sadie, Too," 1940, *Warner Club News*, December 3, 12.

Altman, Rick, 2005, *Silent Film Sound*, Columbia University Press, New York.

Anderson, Chris, 1994, *Hollywood TV: The Studio System in the Fifties*, University of Texas Press, Austin.

Andrejevic, Mark, 2007, "Surveillance in the Digital Enclosure," *The Communication Review* 10 (4), 295–317.

Arrow, Jennifer, 2011, "Identity of *Glee*'s Prom King Spoiled in Twitter Scandal!" *E!Online*. Retrieved April 28, 2011, from http://uk.eonline.com/uberblog/watch_with_kristin/b236985_identity_of_glees_prom_king_spoiled_in.html.

Arvidsson, Adam, 2005, *Brands: Meaning and Value in Media Culture*, Routledge, London.

Autran, Arthur, 2010, "O pensamento industrial cinematográfico brasileiro: ontem e hoje," *Cinema e Mercado*, Escrituras, São Paulo.

Azenha, André, 2010, "2010: O ano do *blockbuster* brasileiro," *CineZen*, December 29. Retrieved March 15, 2011, from http://cinezencultural.com.br/site/2010/12/29/2010-o-ano-do-cinema-brasileiro/.

Bandler, Michael J., 1982, "Casting Is His Lot," *American Way*, November 22.

Banks, Mark, 2007, *The Politics of Cultural Work*, Palgrave, Basingstoke.

Banks, Miranda, 2009, "Gender Below-the-Line: Defining Feminist Production Studies," in Miranda Banks, John Caldwell, and Vicki Mayer, eds., *Production Studies: Cultural Studies of Media Industries*, Routledge, London, 87–98.

Barbosa, Livia Neves de H., 1995, "The Brazilian Jeitinho: An Exercise in National Identity," in David J. Hess and Roberto A. Damatta, eds., *The Brazilian Puzzle:*

Cultures of the Borderlands of the Western World, Columbia University Press, New York, 35–48.

Barnett, Kyle, 2006, "Furniture Music: The Phonograph as Furniture, 1900–1930," *Journal of Popular Music Studies* 18 (3), 301–24.

——, 2009, "The Recording Industry's Role in Media History," in Janet Staiger and Sabine Hake, eds., *Convergence Media History*, Routledge, New York, 81–91.

Barns, Lawrence, 1981, "TV's Drive on Spiraling Costs," *Business Week*, October 26, 199.

Barthes, Roland, 1972, "The Great Family of Man," *Mythologies*, Annette Lavers trans., Hill and Wang, New York, 100–16.

Bastin, Bruce, and John Cowley, 1974, "Uncle Art's Logbook Blues," *Blues Limited* (June), 12–16.

BBC, 2006a, *Creative Future: Detailed Press Briefing*, April 25. Retrieved May 22, 2006, from http://www.bbc.co.uk/pressoffice/pressreleases/stories/2006/04_april/25/creative_detail.shtml.

——, 2006b, *BBC Vision Launches with a Promise to Audiences*, November 20. Retrieved November 20, 2006, from http://www.bbc.co.uk/pressoffice/pressreleases/stories/2006/11_November/20/vision.shtml.

——, 2006c, "Statement of Programme Policies 2006/2007." Retrieved April 12, 2011, from http://www.bbc.co.uk/aboutthebbc/statements2006/.

——, 2007, "BBC and YouTube Partner to Bring Short-Form BBC Content to Online Audiences." Retrieved April 14, 2011, from http://www.bbc.co.uk/pressoffice/pressreleases/stories/2007/03_march/02/you_tube.shtml.

——, 2008, "Formula One Returns to BBC Television." Retrieved April 28, 2011, from http://www.bbc.co.uk/pressoffice/pressreleases/stories/2008/03_march/20/formula1.shtml.

——, 2010a, "BBC Use of Social Networking, Microblogs and Other Third Party Websites," Retrieved April 12, 2011, from http://www.bbc.co.uk/guidelines/editorialguidelines/page/guidance-blogs-bbc-full.

——, 2010b, "Social Networking, Microblogs and Other Third Party Websites: Personal Use," Retrieved April 12, 2011, from http://www.bbc.co.uk/guidelines/editorialguidelines/page/guidance-blogs-personal-full.

BBC Trust, 2010, *Putting Quality First: Final Conclusions,* Retrieved April 6, 2011, from http://www.bbc.co.uk/bbctrust/assets/files/pdf/reviewreportresearch/strategicreview/finalconclusions.pdf.

Beauchamp, Cari, 1997, *Without Lying Down: Frances Marion and the Powerful Women of Early Hollywood*, University of California Press, Berkeley.

Beckett, Charlie, 2008, "Bashing the BBC," July 4. Retrieved May 20, 2011, from http://www.charliebeckett.org/?p=732.

Beckett, David, 1984, "The Politics and Practice of 'Crossover' in American Popular Music, 1963–1965," *Musical Quarterly* 78 (4), 774–97.

Bedell, Sally, 1981, *Up the Tube: Prime-Time TV and the Silverman Years*, Viking Press, New York.

Beller, Jonathan, 2006, *The Cinematic Mode of Production: Attention Economy and the Society of the Spectacle*, University Press of New England, Lebanon, NH.

Bennett, James, 2008, "Interfacing the Nation: Remediating Public Service Broadcasting in the Digital Television Age," *Convergence* 14 (3), 277–94.

Bennett, James, and Niki Strange, 2008, "The BBC's Second-Shift Aesthetics: Interactive Television, Multi-Platform Projects and Public Service Content for a Digital Era," *Media International Australia* 126, 106–19.

Bennett, Tony, 1998, *Culture: A Reformer's Science*, Sage, Thousand Oaks, CA.

Bergman, Anne, 2002, "Shattering the Casting Couch Myth: Contrary to Popular Notions, Women Dominate the Field," *Variety: Women in Showbiz Issue,* November 18, A8.

Bielby, Denise, and C. Lee Harrington, 2008, *Global TV: Exporting Television and Culture in the World Market*, New York University Press, New York.

Bierman, Scott, and Luis Fernandez, 1998, *Game Theory with Economic Applications*, Addison-Wesley, New York.

"The Billboard 1953 Disk-Jockey Poll" 1953, *Billboard*, February 28, 50.

Bilton, Chris, 2006, *Management and Creativity: From Creative Industries to Creative Management*, Wiley-Blackwell, London.

BioWare 2011, "Dragon Age 2—Felicia Day," *Bioware—Dragon Age*. Retrieved July 26, 2012, from http://dragonage.bioware.com/da2/feliciaday.

Blakeley, Kiri, 2006, "Tyra Banks On It," *Forbes*, July 3, 120–26.

"The BMI Clinic Story," 1952, *Billboard*, May 17, 11–27.

"BMI Colorado Clinic Draws Goodly Crowd," 1951, *Radio Daily*, March 21, 5.

"BMI Library Course Proves to be Popular," 1948, *Radio Daily*, November 11, 1.

BMI Program Clinic, 1951a, Boston, MA, September 18, AU RL 379, Library of American Broadcasting, College Park, MD.

———, 1951b, Columbia, SC, March 27, AU RL 307, Library of American Broadcasting, College Park, MD

———, 1951c, Gainesville, FL, March 26, AU RL 307, Library of American Broadcasting, College Park, MD.

———, 1951d, Harrisburg, PA, August 20, AU RL 356, Library of American Broadcasting, College Park, MD.

———, 1951e, Milwaukee, WI, May 16, AU RL 324, Library of American Broadcasting, College Park, MD.

———, 1951f, New Orleans, LA, June 29, AU RL 338, Library of American Broadcasting, College Park, MD.

———, 1951g, Oklahoma, OK, October 30, AU RL 399, Library of American Broadcasting, College Park, MD.

———, 1951h, Portland, OR, July 24, AU RL 107, Library of American Broadcasting, College Park, MD.

"BMI Program Clinics a Bonanza for Sponsors," 1951, *Sponsor*, May 7, 32.

"BMI Session Covers Programming, Clinics," 1952, *Broadcasting*, April 23, 48.

"BMI Thanks the Presidents of the State Broadcasters Associations for Endorsing the BMI Program Clinics," 1951a, *Broadcasting*, May 7, 21 [Ad].

"BMI Thanks the Presidents of the State Broadcasters Associations for Endorsing the BMI Program Clinics," 1951b, *Sponsor*, May 21, 63 [Ad].

Boddy, William, 1992, *Fifties Television: The Industry and Its Critics*, University of Illinois Press, Urbana.

Boltanski, Luc, and Eve Chiapello, 2005, "The New Spirit of Capitalism," *International Journal of Politics, Culture and Society*, 18 (3–4), 161–88.

Bordwell, David, Janet Staiger, and Kristin Thompson, 1985, *The Classical Hollywood Cinema*, Columbia University Press, New York.

Born, Georgina, 2003, "Uncertain Futures: Public Service Television and the Transition to Digital. A Comparative Analysis of the Digital Television Strategies of the BBC and Channel 4," *Media@LSE*. Retrieved January 8, 2005, from http://www.lse.ac.uk/collections/media@lse/pdf/EWP3.pdf.

———, 2005, *Uncertain Vision: Birt, Dyke and the Reinvention of the BBC*, Vintage, London.

Bourdieu, Pierre, 1977, *Outline of a Theory of Practice*, Cambridge University Press, Cambridge.

———, 1979/1984, *Distinction: A Social Critique of the Judgement of Taste*, Richard Nice trans., Routledge, New York.

———, 1993, *The Field of Cultural Production*, Randal Johnson trans., Columbia University Press, New York.

Boyer, Peter J., 1986, "Production Cost Dispute Perils Hour TV Dramas," *New York Times*, March 6, C26.

Broadfoot, Kristen, Stanley Deetz, and Donald Anderson, 2004, "Multi-Levelled, Multi-Method Approaches in Organizational Discourse," in David Grant, Cynthia Hardy, Cliff Oswick, and Linda Putman, eds., *Sage Handbook of Organization Discourse*, Sage Publications, London, 193–212.

Brophy-Warren, Jamin, 2009, "How the Web Series 'The Guild' Stays Successful," *Wall Street Journal*, August 25. Retrieved July 26, 2012 from http://online.wsj.com/article/SB10001424052970203706604574371032925896794.html.

Brown, Les, 1971, *Television: The Business Behind the Box*, Harvest Books, New York.

Brown, Stephen, Robert V. Kozinets, and John F. Sherry, Jr., 2003, "Teaching Old Brands New Tricks: Retro Branding and the Revival of Brand Meaning," *Journal of Marketing* 67 (3), 19–33.

Brown, Wendy, 2003, "Neoliberalism and the End of Liberal Democracy," *Theory & Event*, 7 (1).

———, 2005, *Edgework: Critical Essays on Knowledge and Politics*, Princeton University Press, Princeton.

Bruns, Axel, 2008, *Blogs, Wikipedia, Second Life and Beyond: From Production to Produsage*, Peter Lang Publishing, New York.

Buckey, F. H., 2005, *Just Exchange: A Theory of Contract*, Routledge, London.

Burgess, Jean, and Joshua Green, 2009, *YouTube: Online Video and Participatory Culture*, Polity, London.

Burke, Frank, 1948–1949, "Program Directors Survey," *Radio Daily Shows of Tomorrow*, New York, 9.

Butler, Judith, 1999, *Gender Trouble*, Routledge, London.

Caldwell, John Thornton, 2008, *Production Culture: Industrial Reflexivity and Critical Practice in Film and Television*, Duke University Press, Durham, NC.

———, 2009, "Cultures of Production: Studying Industry's Deep Texts, Reflexive Rituals and Managed Self-Disclosures," in Jennifer Holt and Alisa Perren,eds., *Media Industries: History, Theory, and Method*, Wiley-Blackwell, New York, 199–12.

Carey, Tom, 2011, "BBC F1 Commentator Martin Brundle 'Not Impressed' by the Corporation's Handling of Controversial Switch to Sky," *Telegraph,* July 30. Retrieved August 2, 2011, from http://www.telegraph.co.uk/sport/motorsport/formulaone/8672623/BBC-F1-commentator-Martin-Brundle-not-impressed-by-the-corporations-handling-of-controversial-switch-to-Sky.html.

Carr, S. D., 1996, "The Cult of Brand Personality," *Marketing News* 30 (10), 4–9.

Casiello, Tom, 2010, "The Role of 'The Audience' in the Writing Process," in Sam Ford, Abigail De Kosnik, and C. Lee Harrington, eds., *The Survival of Soap Opera*, University Press of Mississippi, Jackson, 275–78.

"Casting Directors: Under their Expert Eyes, Aspirants Go from Glossies to Glory," 1991, *People Weekly*, March 27, 71.

Caves, Richard, 2000, *Creative Industries: Contracts between Art and Commerce*, Harvard University Press, Cambridge, MA.

Charles, Harry, 1968, Interview, Gayle Dean Wardlow Collection, Center for Popular Music, Middle Tennessee State University, Murfreesboro, TN.

Chin, Bertha, and Matt Hills, 2008, "Restricted Confessions? Blogging, Subcultural Celebrity, and the Management of Producer-Fan Proximity," *Social Semiotics* 18 (2), 253–72.

Christian, Margena A., 2003, "Tyra Banks: Says 'It's a Lot More than Just Looks' to Become 'America's Next Top Model," *Jet*, May 26.

Cinema: A Practical Course in Cinema Acting, 1919, Standard Art Book Co., London.

Cohen, Noam, 2009, "When Stars Twitter, a Ghost May Be Lurking," *New York Times*, March 27, A1. Retrieved July 26, 2012, from http://www.nytimes.com/2009/03/27/technology/internet/27twitter.html?_r=1.

Collins, Glenn, 1990, "For Casting, Countless Auditions and One Couch, Never Used," *New York Times*, January 30, C15.

Cook, David A., 2002, *Lost Illusions: American Cinema in the Shadow of Watergate and Vietnam, 1970–1979*, University of California Press, Berkeley.

Cott, Ted, 1948–1949, "Pleas for Recognition: Would Organize Directors," *Radio Daily Shows of Tomorrow*, 24.

Couldry, Nick, 2008, "Reality TV, or The Secret Theater of Neoliberalism," *Review of Education, Pedagogy, and Cultural Studies*, 30 (1), 3–13.

Cryptoxin, 2008, "Sexing and Selling 'Convergence Culture,'" *LiveJournal*, May 21. Retrieved May 21, 2008, from http://cryptoxin.livejournal.com/42223.html.

"C.S.A. Searches for Respect, Identity in 'New' Hollywood," 1989, *Daily Variety*, June 26, I32.

Curtin, Michael, 2007, *Playing to the World's Biggest Audience: The Globalization of Chinese Film and TV*, University of California Press, Berkeley.

Davies, Margery W., 1982, *Woman's Place Is at the Typewriter: Office Work and the Office Worker, 1870–1930*, Temple University Press, Philadelphia.

Davis, Howard, and Richard Scase, 2000, *Managing Creativity*, Open University Press, Buckingham, UK.

Davis, John, 1992, *Exchange*, University of Minnesota, Minneapolis.

Davis, Ronald L., 1993, *The Glamour Factory: Inside Hollywood's Big Studio System*, Southern Methodist University Press, Dallas.

Day, Felicia, 2011a, "Episode 5 of Dragon Age," *Facebook*, November 8. Retrieved November 8, 2011, from http://www.facebook.com/FeliciaDay.

———, 2011b, "I uploaded a video playing with myself . . . as Tallis from @dragonage. You should def watch it ;) http://www.youtube.com/watch?v=3DxsVzYUleo," *Twitter*, November 29. Retrieved November 29, 2011, from http://twitter.com/feliciaday/statuses/141550750840012800.

———,2011c, "@davidgaider I'm excited I keep bragging up the DLC writing. I'm a lore whore so I was so excited with all the new info!" *Twitter*, September 27. Retrieved September 27, 2011, from https://twitter.com/#!/feliciaday/statuses/118759979237912576.

———, 2011d, "Just ate half a bag of tortilla chips at 9am. This day of writing is not starting off with the self-discipline I would like, haha," *Twitter*, February 4. Retrieved February 4, 2011, from https://twitter.com/#!/feliciaday/statuses/33584223176622080.

de Certeau, Pierre, 1984,*The Practice of Everyday Life*, Steven Rendall trans., University of California Press, Berkeley.

De La Fuente, Anna Marie, and Marcelo Cajueiro, 2011, "Padilha, Meirelles back Nossa," *Variety*, October 11. Retrieved July 25, 2012, from http://www.variety.com/article/VR1118044243?refCatId=19.

de Sola Pool, Ithiel, 1983, *Technologies of Freedom*, Belknap Press, Cambridge, MA.

Debrett, Mary, 2009, "Riding the Wave: Public Service Television in the Multi-Platform Era," *Media, Culture and Society* 31 (5), 807–27.

———, 2010, *Reinventing Public Service Television for the Digital Future*, Intellect, Bristol, UK.

Deller, Ruth, 2011, "Twittering On: Audience Research and Participation using Twitter," *Participations: Journal of Audience and Reception Studies* 8 (1). Retrieved August 9, 2011, from http://www.participations.org/Volume%208/Issue%201/deller.htm.

Deuze, Mark, 2007, *Media Work*, Polity Press, Cambridge, UK.

———, 2009, "Convergence Culture and Media Work," in Jennifer Holt and Alissa Perren, eds., *Media Industries: History, Theory, and Method*, Wiley, West Sussex, UK,
144–56.

———, 2010, "Preface," in Mark Deuze, ed., *Managing Media Work*, Sage, London,
ix–xi.

Deuze, Mark, and Brian Steward, 2010, "Managing Media Work," in Mark Deuze, ed.,
Managing Media Work, Sage, London, 1–10.

DiMaggio, Paul, 1977, "Market Structure, the Creative Process and Popular Culture:
Toward an Organizational Reinterpretation of Mass Culture Theory," *Journal of
Popular Culture* 11, 436–52.

Dixit, Avinash K., and Barry J. Nalebuff, 2008, *The Art of Strategy*, Norton, New York.

Dolberg, Glenn, 1951–1952, "Program Clinics Prove Helpful," *Radio Daily Shows of
Tomorrow*, New York, 14.

Donoghue, Courtney Brannon, 2011a, "Globo Filmes, Sony, and Franchises Film-
Making: Transnational Industry in the Brazilian Pós-Retomada," in Cacilda Rêgo
and Carolina Rocha, eds., *New Trends in Argentine and Brazilian Cinema*, Intellect,
Bristol, UK.

———, 2011b, "'Lighting Up Screens around the World': Sony's Local Language Production Strategy Meets Contemporary Brazilian and Spanish Cinema," Ph.D. diss.,
University of Texas, Austin.

Douglas, Susan, 1999, *Listening In: Radio and the American Imagination*, Times Books,
New York.

Dovey, Jon, 2011, "Time Slice: Web Drama and the Attention Economy," in Paul
Grainge, ed., *Ephemeral Media: Transitory Screen Culture from Television to You-
Tube*, BFI, London.

Down, Kathleen Morgan, and Patrick Huber, 2004, *The 1920s*, Greenwood Press,
Westport, CT.

Draper, James Jr., 2012, "Negotiating the 'Lavender Whiff': Gay and Straight Masculini-
ties in Men's Lifestyle Magazines, 1990–2010," Ph.D. diss., University of Michigan,
Ann Arbor.

Drucker, Peter, 1999, *Management Challenges for the 21st Century*, Harper Business,
New York.

Duffy, Mike, 2001, "Forward," to Brian Wilson, *Soft Systems Methodology: Conceptual
Model Building and Its Contribution*, John Wiley & Sons, New York, ix.

du Gay, Paul, 1997, "Introduction," *Production of Culture/Cultures of Production*, Sage,
London, 1–11.

du Gay, Paul, and Stuart Hall 1997, *Doing Cultural Studies: The Story of the Sony Walk-
man*, Sage, London.

du Gay, Paul, and Michael Pryke, 2002, "Cultural Economy: An Introduction," in Paul
du Gay and Michael Pryke, eds., *Cultural Economy: Cultural Analysis and Commercial Life*, Sage Publications, London, 1–20.

Duggan, Lisa, 2004, *The Twilight of Inequality: Neoliberalism, Cultural Politics and the
Attack on Democracy*, Beacon Press, Boston.

Dyan, Steve, 2005, "Casting Directors Cast Their Fate with Teamsters," *Daily Variety*, June 24, 55.

Dyer, Richard, 1991, "*A Star Is Born* and the Construction of Authenticity," in Christine Gledhill, ed., *Stardom: Industry of* Desire, Routledge, New York, 132–40.

Ellcessor, Elizabeth, 2012, "Tweeting @feliciaday: Online Social Media, Convergence, and Subcultural Stardom of Felicia Day," *Cinema Journal* 51 (2), 46–66.

Ennis, Phillip H., 1992, *The Seventh Stream: The Emergence of Rock 'n' Roll in American Popular Culture*, Wesleyan University Press, Hanover, NH.

Ettema, James S., 1982, "The Organizational Context of Creativity: A Case Study from Public Television," in James S. Ettema and D.C. Whitney, eds., *Individuals in Mass Media Organizations: Creativity and Constraint*, Sage, Beverly Hills, CA, 91-106.

"Europe's 'Other' Channels: Numbers Double Every Three Years," 1997, *Screen Digest*, March 1, 57–64.

Evans, Elizabeth, 2011a, "The Evolving Ecosystem: Interview with Victoria Jaye, BBC," in Paul Grainge, ed., *Ephemeral Media: Transitory Screen Culture from Television to YouTube*, BFI, London, 105–121.

———, 2011b, *Transmedia Television: Audiences, New Media and Daily Life*, Routledge, London.

Fahey, John 1997, "American Quick Fix Religion," liner notes, *American Primitive, Vol. 1*, Revenant Records.

FCC, 1947, "An Economic Study of Standard Broadcasting," Government Printing Office, Washington, DC, October 31, 47.

"Felicia Day Interview," 2011, *Late Night with Jimmy Fallon*, NBC Television, New York, February 16. Retrieved July 26, 2012, from http://www.hulu.com/watch/216843/late-night-with-jimmy-fallon-felicia-day.

Feuer, Jane, 1985, "MTM Enterprises: An Overview," in Jane Feuer, Paul Kerr, and Tise Vahimagi, eds., *MTM Quality Television*, BFI Press, London, 1–31.

Fick, Jeff, 2011, "Brazil's Economic Boom Advances in First Quarter," *Wall Street Journal*, June 3. Retrieved January 15, 2012, from http://online.wsj.com/article/SB10001424052702303745304576363382440798462.html.

Filene, Catherine, ed., 1934, *Careers for Women: New Ideas, New Methods and New Opportunities—To Fit a New World*, Houghton Mifflin, Boston.

"Film Secretary Promoted," 1936, *Los Angeles Times*, October 4, 4.

Fine, Lisa, 1990, *The Souls of the Skyscrapers: Female Clerical Workers in Chicago, 1870–1930*, Temple University Press, Philadelphia.

Fiske, John, 1996, *Media Matters: Race and Gender in U.S. Politics*, rev. ed. University Of Chicago Press, Chicago.

Fleissner, Jennifer L., 2005, "The Stenographer's Stake in Dracula," in Leah Price and Pamela Thurschwell, eds., *Literary Secretaries/Secretarial Culture*, Ashgate Publishing Limited, Hampshire, UK, 63–90.

Fong-Torres, Ben, 1988, *The Hits Just Keep on Coming: The History of Top 40 Radio*, Miller Freeman, San Francisco.

Ford, Sam, 2010a, "Does Social Media Give Us the 'Trojan Horse' to Fix Corporate Communication?" *Fast Company*, August 20. Retrieved August 20, 2010, from http://www.fastcompany.com/1684032/does-social-media-give-us-the-trojan-horse-to-fix-corporate-communication.

———, 2010b, "For Best Brand-Building Results, Listen Up!," *PR News*, August 2, 8.

———, 2010c, "Truly Tackling 'Social Media' Will Require a Deep Shift in Corporate Logic," *Fast Company*, July 6. Retrieved July 6, 2010, from http://www.fastcompany.com/1667436/truly-tackling-social-media-will-require-a-deep-shift-in-corporate-logic.

———, 2012a, "Reports of Design Thinking's Death Were an Exaggeration," *Fast Company*, January 27. Retrieved January 27, 2012, from http://www.fastcompany.com/1811688/the-report-of-design-thinkings-death-was-an-exaggeration.

———, 2012b, "Tip Sheet: Put the Humanity Back in Communications," *PR News*, January 9. Retrieved January 9, 2012 from http://www.prnewsonline.com/free/Tip-Sheet-Put-the-Humanity-Back-in-Communications_15879.html.

Ford, Sam, and Steve Cody, 2011, "Tip Sheet: Match Your Brand Promise to the Brand Experience," *PR News*, June 27. Retrieved June 27, 2011, from http://www.prnewsonline.com/free/Tip-Sheet-Match-Your-Brand-Promise-to-the-Brand-Experience_15069.html.

Foucault, Michel, 1969/1979, "What Is an Author?" in Paul Rabinow, ed., *The Foucault Reader*, Pantheon, New York, 101–20.

———, 1972, *Archaeology of Knowledge*, Pantheon, New York.

———, 1979, *Discipline and Punish: The Birth of the Prison*, Alan Sheridan, trans., Random House, New York.

———, 2008, *The Birth of Biopolitics: Lectures at the College de France, 1978–1979*, Palgrave Macmillan, New York.

Francke, Lizzie, 1994, *Script Girls: Women Screenwriters in Hollywood*, BFI, London.

Freling, Traci H., and Lukas P. Forbes, 2005, "An Examination of Brand Personality through Methodological Triangulation," *Brand Management* 13 (2), 148–62.

Gamson, Joshua, 1994, *Claims to Fame: Celebrity in Contemporary America*, University of California Press, Berkeley.

Gans, Herbert, 1979, *Deciding What's News: A Study of CBS Evening News, NBC Nightly News, Newsweek, and Time*, Pantheon Books, New York.

Gardiner, Michael, 2000, *Critiques of Everyday Life: An Introduction*, Routledge, New York.

Garver, Robert, 1949, *Successful Radio Advertising with Sponsor Participation Programs*, Prentice-Hall, New York.

Gennis, Sadie, 2012, "*Community* Creator Dan Harmon on His Firing: 'Maybe I Am Just a Jerk,'" *TV Guide*, July 11. Retrieved July 25, 2012, from http://www.tvguide.com/News/Community-Dan-Harmon-1049802.aspx.

Georgakas, Dan, and Kevin Rabalais, 2000, "Fifty Years of Casting: An Interview with Marion Dougherty," *Cineaste* 25 (2), 26.

Giddens, Anthony, 1984, *The Constitution of Society: Outline of The Theory of Structuration*, University of California Press, Los Angeles.

Gill, Rosalind, 2010, "'Life Is a Pitch': Managing the Self in New Media Work," in Mark Deuze, ed., *Managing Media Work*, Sage, London, 249–62.

Gitelman, Lisa, 2006, *Always Already New: Media, History and the Data of Culture*, MIT Press, Cambridge, MA.

Gitlin, Todd, 1983, *Inside Prime Time*, Pantheon Books, New York.

Goffman, Erving, 1959, *The Presentation of Self in Everyday Life*, Doubleday, New York.

Goldhaber, Michael H., 1997, "The Attention Economy and the Net," *First Monday* 2 (4). Retrieved May 24, 2011, from http://firstmonday.org/htbin/cgiwrap/bin/ojs/index.php/fm/article/viewArticle/519/440%20#dep.

Gonzalez, Anique, 2007, "BBC YouTube reach Partnership Agreement," *LawCrossing*. Retrieved April 14, 2011, from http://www.lawcrossing.com/article/2678/YouTube-BBC-Reach-Partnership-Agreement/.

Gonzales, Juan, 2006, "The Exact Opposite," *Global Culture*, June 26. Retrieved July 1, 2012, from http://global-culture.org/the-exact-opposite/.

Goodman, David, 2010, "Distracted Listening: On Not Making Sound Choices in the 1930s," in David Suisman and Susan Strasser,eds., *Sound in the Age of Mechanical Reproduction*, University of Pennsylvania Press, Philadelphia.

Gordon, Colin, 1991, "Governmental Rationality: An Introduction," in Graham Burchell, Colin Gordon, and Peter Miller, eds, *The Foucault Effect*, University of Chicago Press, Chicago, 1–52.

Graf, Phillip, 2004, Report of the Independent Review of BBC Online. Retrieved April 14, 2011, from http://www.news.bbc.co.uk/nol/shared/bsp/hi/pdfs/05_07_04_graf.pdf.

Grainge, Paul, 2010, "Elvis Sings for the BBC: Broadcast Branding and Digital Media Design," *Media, Culture, Society* 32 (1), 45–61.

———, 2011, "Introduction," in Paul Grainge, ed., *Ephemeral Media: Transitory Screen Culture from Television to YouTube*, BFI, London, 1–19.

Gray, Herman, 1995, *Watching Race: Television and the Struggle for "Blackness,"* University of Minnesota Press, Minneapolis.

Gray, Jonathan, 2010, *Show Sold Separately: Promos, Spoilers, and Other Media Paratexts*, New York University Press, New York.

Green, Archie, 1965, "Hillbilly Music: Source and Symbol," *Journal of American Folklore* 78 (309), 213.

Gregory, Mollie, 2002, *Women Who Run the Show: How a Brilliant and Creative New Generation of Women Stormed Hollywood*, St. Martin's Press, New York.

Guback, Thomas, 1969, *The International Film Industry: Western Europe and America Since 1945*, Indiana University Press, Bloomington, IN.

Guerini, Elaine, 2010a, "The Land of Promise," *Screen International*, August 5. Retrieved January 15, 2011, from http://www.screendaily.com/reports/territory-focus/the-land-of-promise/5016534.article.

———, 2010b, "Rio Film Commission to Unveil Inward Investment Plan," *Screen Daily*, September 27. Retrieved April 15, 2011, from http://www.screendaily.com/news/production/rio-film-commission-to-unveil-inward-investment-plan/5018738.article.

——, 2011a, "Brazil Has Record Box Office Year Drive by Elite Squad 2," *Screen Daily*, January 13. Retrieved March 1, 2011, from http://www.screendaily.com/territories/us-americas/brazil-has-record-box-office-year-driven-by-elite-squad-2/5022306.article.

——, 2011b, "Top Brazilian Filmmakers Launch New Distribution Company," *Screen Daily*, October 14. Retrieved November 15, 2011, from http://www.screendaily.com/5033348.article.

"Guesswork Is Skipped with Block Programming," 1947, *Billboard*, May 17, 13.

Hagstrom Miller, Karl, 2010, *Segregating Sound: Inventing Folk and Pop Music in the Age of Jim Crow*, Duke University Press, Durham, NC.

Harding, Nancy, 2003, *The Social Construction of Management*, Routledge, New York.

Harmon, Dan, 2012, "Hey, Did I Miss Anything," *Dan Harmon Poops*. Retrieved July 17, 2012, from http://danharmon.tumblr.com/post/23339272200/hey-did-i-miss-anything.

Harris, Alice Kessler, 2003, *Out to Work: A History of Wage-Earning Women in the United States*, Oxford University Press, Oxford, UK.

Harvey, David, 2007, *A Brief History of Neoliberalism*, Oxford University Press, Cambridge, UK.

Hasinoff, Amy Adele, 2008, "Fashioning Race for the Free Market on *America's Next Top Model*," *Critical Studies in Media Communication*, 25 (3), 324–43.

Havens, Timothy, 2003, "Exhibiting Global Television: On the Business and Cultural Functions of Global Television Fairs," *Journal of Broadcasting and Electronic Media*, 47 (1), 18–35.

——, 2006, *Global Television Marketplace*, British Film Institute Press, London.

——, 2007, "Universal Childhood: The Global Trade in Children's Television and Changing Ideal of Childhood," *Global Media Journal* 6 (10), Retrieved September 1, 2012 from http://lass.purduecal.edu/cca/gmj/sp07/gmj-sp07-havens.htm.

——, 2011, "Inventing Universal Television: Restricted Access, Promotional Extravagance, and the Distribution of Value at Global Television Markets," in Brian Morean and Jesper Strandgaard Pedersen, eds., *Negotiating Values in the Creative Industries: Fairs, Festivals and Competitive Events*, Cambridge University Press, Cambridge, 145–68.

——, 2013, *Black Television Travels: Media Globalization and Contemporary Racial Discourse*, New York University Press, New York.

Havens, Timothy, and Amanda D. Lotz, 2012, *Understanding Media Industries*, Oxford University Press, New York.

Havens, Timothy, Amanda D. Lotz, and Serra Tinic, 2009, "Critical Media Industry Studies: A Research Approach," *Communication, Culture & Critique* 2, 234–53.

Haverlin, Carl, 1956, "A Reply to Mr Celler from B.M.I.," *New York Times*, October 21, 135.

"Haverlin First BMI Paid President," 1947, *Broadcasting*, April 7, 13.

Hazelton, John, 2011, "A New Approach to International," *Screen Daily*, November 6. Retrieved November 15, 2011, from http://www.screendaily.com/reports/in-focus/a-new-approach-to-international/5033960.article.

"Henry Whitter, Okeh Artist, Real Hill Country Type," 1925, *Talking Machine World*, May 15, 35.

Herman, Edward, and Robert McChesney, 1997, *The Global Media: The New Missionaries of Global Capitalism*, Cassell, London and Washington, DC.

Hesmondhalgh, David, 2006, "Bourdieu, the Media, and Cultural Production," *Media, Culture & Society*, 28 (2), 211–31.

———, 2007, *The Cultural Industries*, 2nd ed., Sage Publications, London.

———, 2011, "Media Industry Studies, Media Production Studies," in James Curran, ed., *Media and Society*, 5th rev. ed., Bloomsbury, London,

Hesmondhalgh, David, and Sarah Baker, 2011, *Creative Labour: Media Work in Three Cultural Industries*, Routledge, London.

Highfield, Ashley, 2001, Speech given at The Production Show, London, October 13.

Hills, Matt, 2002, *Fan Cultures*, Routledge, London.

———, 2010, *Triumph of a Time Lord: Regenerating Doctor Who in the Twenty-First Century*, I. B. Tauris, London.

Hills, Matt, and Rebecca Williams, 2005, "'It's All My Interpretation': Reading Spike through the Subcultural Celebrity of James Marsters," *European Journal of Cultural Studies*, 8 (3), 345–65.

Hirschberg, Lynn, 2005, "Giving Them What They Want," *New York Times Magazine*, September 4. Retrieved July 25, 2012, from http://www.nytimes.com/2005/09/04/magazine/04MOONVES.html?pagewanted=all.

Hochschild, Arlie, 2003, *The Managed Heart: Commercialization of Human Feeling*, University of California Press, Berkeley.

Holt, Jennifer, and Alisa Perren, eds., 2009, *Media Industries: History, Theory, and Method*, Wiley-Blackwell, Malden, MA.

Honeycutt, Courtenay, and Susan C. Herring, 2009, "Beyond Microblogging: Conversation and Collaboration via Twitter," paper presented to the 42nd Hawaii International Conference on System Science. Retrieved May 20, 2011, from http://www.computer.org/portal/web/csdl/doi/10.1109/HICSS.2009.602.

Hoskins, Colin, Stuart McFadyen, and Adam Finn, 1997, *Global Television and Film: An Introduction to the Economics of the Business*, Oxford University Press, New York.

Huggers, Eric, 2010, *BBC Online: Putting Quality First.* BBC Blogs. Retrieved January 3, 2014, from http://www.bbc.co.uk/blogs/aboutthebbc/posts/bbc_online_putting_quality_first.

———, 2011, "Reshaping BBC Online." BBC Blogs. Retrieved April 13, 2011, from http://www.bbc.co.uk/blogs/aboutthebbc/2011/01/delivering-quality-first.shtml.

"Independents' Day: Meet in Chicago," 1949, *Broadcasting*, April 18, 26.

"Informe de Acompanhamento de Mercado: 2009," 2010, ANCINE (Agência Nacional do Cinema). Retrieved July 15, 2011, from http://www.ancine.gov.br/media/SAM/Informes/2009/InformeAnual2009.pdf.

"Informe de Acompanhamento de Mercado: 2010," 2011, ANCINE (Agência Nacional do Cinema). Retrieved July 15, 2011, from http://www.ancine.gov.br/media/SAM/Informes/2010/Informe_Anual_2010.pdf.

Inman, Phillip, 2011, "Brazil Overtakes UK as Sixth-Largest Economy," *Guardian*, December 25. Retrieved January 15, 2012, from http://www.guardian.co.uk/business/2011/dec/26/brazil-overtakes-uk-economy.

"Interviewing Helen Gregg," 1941, *RKO Studio Club News*, February, 8, 9.

"Interviewing Wynn Haslam," 1941, *RKO Studio Club News*, April, 9, 12.

Jenkins, Henry, 1995, "'Infinite Diversity in Infinite Combinations': Genre and Authorship in *Star Trek*," in John Tulloch and Henry Jenkins, eds., *Science Fiction Audiences: Watching Doctor Who and Star Trek*, Routledge, London, 173–94.

———, 2006, *Convergence Culture: Where Old and New Media Collide*, New York University Press, New York.

Jenkins, Henry, Sam Ford, and Joshua Green, 2012, *Spreadable Media: Creating Value and Meaning in a Networked Culture*, New York University Press, New York.

Jenkins, Henry, Xiaochang Li, and Ana Domb Krauskopf, 2009, "If It Doesn't Spread, It's Dead (Part Five): Communities of Users," *Confessions of an Aca/Fan*, February 20. Retrieved November 28, 2009, from http://henryjenkins.org/2009/02/if_it_doesnt_spread_its_dead_p_4.html.

Jewell, Richard B., 2007, *The Golden Age of Cinema: Hollywood 1929–1945*, Blackwell Press, Oxford.

Johnson, Catherine, 2007, "Tele-Branding in TVIII," *New Review of Film and Television Studies* 5 (1), 5–24.

———, 2009, "Trading Auntie: The Exploitation and Protection of Intellectual Property Rights during the BBC's Monopoly Years," *New Review of Film and Television* 7 (4), 441–458.

———, 2011, *Branding Television*, Routledge, London.

Johnson, Derek, 2007, "Inviting Audiences In: The Spatial Reorganization of Production and Consumption in 'TVIII,'" *New Review of Film and Television Studies*, 5 (1), 61–80.

———, 2013, *Media Franchising: Creative License and Collaboration in the Culture Industries*, New York University Press, New York.

Johnson, Randal, 1987, *The Film Industry in Brazil: Culture and the State*, University of Pittsburgh Press, Pittsburgh, PA.

———, 2005, "TV Globo, the MPA and Contemporary Brazilian Cinema," in Lisa Shaw and Stephanie Dennison, eds., *Latin American Cinema: Essays on Modernity, Gender and National Identity*, McFarland, Jefferson, NC,

Johnson, Randal, and Robert Stam, eds., 1995, *Brazilian Cinema*, 2nd ed., Columbia University Press, New York.

Kane, Michael, 2010, "Role Player: With Credits from 'Goodfellas' to 'Gump,' Casting Director Ellen Lewis Is a Great Judge of Characters," *New York Post*, September 20, 37.

Kay, George W., 1953, "Those Fabulous Gennetts," *Record Changer* (June), 4–12.

Keane, Michael, and Albert Moran, 2008, "Television's New Engines," *Television and New Media* 9 (2), 155–169.

Keith, Michael, 1989, *Broadcast Voice Performance*, Focal Press, Boston.

Kemper, Tom, 2009, *Hidden Talent: The Emergence of Hollywood Agents*, University of California Press, Berkeley.

Kepley, Vance Jr., 1990, "From 'Frontal Lobes' to the 'Bob-and-Bob' Show: NBC Management and Programming Strategies, 1949–65," in Tino Balio, ed., *Hollywood in the Age of Television*, Unwin Hyman, Boston, 41-62.

King, Geoff, 2009, *Indiewood, USA: Where Hollywood Meets Independent Cinema*, I. B. Tauris, London.

Klamer, Arjo, ed., 1996, *The Value of Culture: On the Relationship between Economics and Arts*, Amsterdam University Press, Amsterdam.

Klinger, Barbara, 2006, *Beyond the Multiplex: Cinema, New Technologies, and the Home*, University of California Press, Berkeley.

Kompare, Derek, 2011, "More 'Moments of Television': Online Cult Television Authorship," in Michael Kackman et al., eds., *Flow TV: Television in the Age of Media Convergence*, Routledge, New York, 95–113.

Kozinets, Robert V., 1997, "'I Want to Believe': A Netnography of The X-Philes' Subculture of Consumption," *Advances in Consumer Research* 24 (1), 470–75.

———, 2009, *Netnography: Doing Ethnographic Research Online*, Sage Publications, London.

Kraidy, Marwan, 2009, *Reality Television and Arab Politics: Contention in Public Life*, Cambridge University Press, Cambridge.

Kung, Lucy, 2008, *Strategic Management in the Media: Theory to Practice*, Sage, London.

Kyvig, David E., 2004, *Daily Life in the United States, 1920–1940: How Americans Lived through the Roaring Twenties and the Great Depression*, Ivan R. Dee, Chicago.

Lampel, Joseph, Jamal Shamsie, and Theresa Lant, 2000, "Balancing Act: Learning from Organizing Practices in Cultural Industries," *Organization Science* 11 (3), 263–69.

Leaver, Tama, 2010, "FlashForward or FlashBack: Television Distribution in 2010?" *Flow* 11 (5). Retrieved April 6, 2011, from http://flowtv.org/2010/01/flashforward-or-flashback-television-distribution-in-2010-tama-leaver-curtin-university-of-technology/.

Lee-Wright, Peter, 2008, "Virtual News: BBC News at a 'Future Media and Technology' Crossroads," *Convergence* 14 (3), 249–60.

Lesia, Lara, 2006, "Discursive Struggles within Social Welfare: Restaging Teen Motherhood," *British Journal of Social Work* 36 (2), 283–98.

Lieb, Sandra, 1983, *Mother of the Blues: A Study of Ma Rainey*. University of Massachusetts Press, Amherst.

Likert, Rensis, 1967, *The Human Organization: Its Management and Value*, McGraw-Hill, New York.

Lotz, Amanda D., 2007, *The Television Will Be Revolutionized*, New York University Press, New York.

———, 2008, "Television's Industrial Practices in Crisis: Industry Lore and the Post-Network Era," paper presented to the 2008 Society for Cinema and Media Studies conference, Philadelphia, PA.

Lustyik, Katalin, and Philippa K. Smith, 2010, "From *The Simpsons* to '*The Simpsons* of the South Pacific': New Zealand's First Primetime Animation, *bro'Town*," *Television & New Media*, 11 (5), 331–49.

Lynch, David, 2006, *Catching the Big Fish: Meditation, Consciousness, and Creativity*, Penguin, New York.

Mahar, Kathleen Ward, 2006, *Women Filmmakers in Early Hollywood*, Johns Hopkins University Press, Baltimore, MD.

Manheim, James M., 1992, "B-Side Sentimentalizer: 'Tennessee Waltz' in the History of Popular Music," *The Musical Quarterly* 76 (3), 337–54.

Mann, Denise, 2009, "It's Not TV, It's Brand Management TV: The Collective Author(s) of the *Lost* Franchise," in Vicki Mayer, Miranda Banks, and John Caldwell, eds., *Production Studies: Cultural Studies of Media Industries*, Routledge, New York, 99–114.

Marich, Robert, 2009, *Marketing to Moviegoers*, Southern Illinois University Press, Carbondale.

Marshall, P. David, 2010, "The Promotion and Presentation of the Self: Celebrity as Marker of Presentational Media," *Celebrity Studies*, 1 (1), 35–48.

Martindale, Hilda, 1988, *Women Servants of the State, 1830–1938*, Oxford University Press, Oxford.

Marvin, Wanda, 1945, "License Orgs Say It with Flowers," *Billboard*, January 20, 12.

Marwick, Alice E., 2010, *Status Update: Celebrity, Publicity, and Self-Branding in Web 2.0*, New York University Press, New York.

Marwick, Alice E., and danah boyd, 2011, "I Tweet Honestly, I Tweet Passionately: Twitter Users, Context Collapse, and the Imagined Audience," *New Media & Society*, 13 (1), 114-133.

Maslin, Janet, with Martin Kasindorf, 1977, "Finders Keepers," *Newsweek*, March 14, 92.

Mayer, Vicki, 2009, "Bringing the Social Back In: Studies of Production Cultures and Social Theory," in Vicki Mayer, Miranda Banks, and John Caldwell, eds., *Production Studies: Cultural Studies of Media Industries,* Routledge, New York, 15–24.

———, 2011, *Below the Line: Producers and Production Studies in the New Television Economy*, Duke University Press, Durham, NC.

Mayer, Vicki, Miranda J. Banks, and John Thornton Caldwell, eds., 2009, *Production Studies: Cultural Studies of Media Industries*, Routledge, New York.

———, 2009, "Introduction—Production Studies: Roots and Routes," in Vicki Mayer, Miranda Banks, and John Caldwell, eds., *Production Studies: Cultural Studies of Media Industries,* Routledge, New York, 1–13.

McChesney, Robert, 2008, *The Political Economy of Media: Enduring Issues, Emerging Dilemmas*, Monthly Review Press, New York.

McCracken, Grant, 2009, *Chief Culture Officer: How to Create a Living, Breathing Corporation*, Basic Books, New York.

McFall, Liz, 2002, "What about the Old Cultural Intermediaries?: An Historical Review of Advertising Producers," *Cultural Studies* 16 (4), 532–52.

McFarland, David, 1972, *The Development of the Top 40 Radio Format*, Arno Press, New York.

McGraw, Phillip, 1999, *Life Strategies: Doing What Works, Doing What Matters*, Hyperion Books, New York.

McHugh, Kathleen, 1999, *American Domesticity: From How-to Manual to Hollywood Melodrama*, Oxford University Press, New York.

McRobbie, Angela, 2002, "Holloway to Hollywood: Happiness at Work in the New Cultural Economy," in Paul du Guy and Michael Pryke, eds, *Cultural Economy: Cultural Analysis and Commercial Life*, Sage, London, 97–114.

———, 2005, *The Uses of Cultural Studies*, Sage, London.

Mierzejewska, Bozena I., 2010, "Media Management in Theory and Practice," in Mark Deuze, ed., *Managing Media Work*, Sage Publications, Thousand Oaks, CA, 13–30.

Miller, Toby, Nitin Govil, John McMurria, Richard Maxwell, and Ting Wang, 2005, *Global Hollywood 2*, British Film Institute, London.

Mittell, Jason, 2005, "Exchanges of Value," *Flow* 3 (4). Retrieved April 14, 2011, from http://flowtv.org/2005/10/exchanges-of-value/.

———, 2012, "*Community* and Dan Harmon's Imploding Author Function," *Just TV*, May 19. Retrieved July 27, 2012, from http://justtv.wordpress.com/2012/05/19/community-and-dan-harmons-imploding-author-function/.

Moed, Ed, 2010, "Can Social Media Bring Divided Factions Together?" *Measuring Up*, March 11. Retrieved March 11, 2010, from http://www.measuringupblog.com/measuring_up/2010/03/can-social-media-bring-divided-factions-together.html.

Muntean, Nick, and Anne Helen Petersen, 2009, "Celebrity Twitter: Strategies of Intrusion and Disclosure in the Age of Technoculture," *M/C Journal*, 12 (5). Retrieved July 26, 2012, from http://journal.media-culture.org.au/index.php/mcjournal/article/viewArticle/194.

"Music Sells . . . When a Disk-Jockey Spins Records," 1947, *Sponsor*, February, 21.

"NAB in Peace Pip Confab" 1948, *Billboard*, May 29, 3.

Neff, Gina, Elizabeth Wissinger, and Sharon Zukin, 2005, "Entrepreneurial Labor among Cultural Producers: 'Cool' Jobs in 'Hot' Industries," *Social Semiotics*, 14 (3), 307–34.

Negus, Keith, 1998, "The Production of Culture," in Paul du Gay, ed., *Production of Culture/Cultures of Production*, Sage, London, 67–118.

———,1999, *Music Genres and Corporate Cultures*, Routledge, London.

———, 2002a, "Identities and Industries: The Cultural Formation of Aesthetic Economies," in Paul du Gay and Michael Pryke, eds., *Cultural Economy: Cultural Analysis and Commercial Life*, Sage Publications, London, 115–31.

———, 2002b, "The Work of Cultural Intermediaries and the Enduring Distance Between Production and Consumption," *Cultural Studies* 16 (4), 501–15.

Negus, Keith, and Michael Pickering, 2004, *Creativity, Communication, and Cultural Value*, Sage, London.

"New Series of Clinics of Programming Set," 1951, *Radio Daily*, June 6, 5.

Newman, Michael Z., 2011, *Indie: An American Film Culture*, Columbia University Press, New York.

NMA Staff, 2010, "Red Button is Thriving (Not that you'd know it)," *New Media Age*, July 29, http://econsultancy.com/us/nma-archive/38091-red-button-is-thriving-not -that-you-d-know-it

"O Mercado: Gráficos e tabelas," 2011, *Filme B*. Retrieved December 1, 2011, from http:// www.filmeb.com.br/portal/html/graficosetabelas.php.

Oakley, Kate, 2009, "The Disappearing Arts: Creativity and Innovation after the Creative Industries," *International Journal of Cultural Policy* 15 (4), 403–13.

O'Connor, Justin, 2007, *The Cultural and Creative Industries: A Review of the Literature*, HPM and Arts Council England, London.

Orgeron, Devin, 2007, "La Camera-Crayola: Authorship Comes of Age in the Cinema of Wes Anderson," *Cinema Journal* 46 (2), 40–65.

Orr, Julian, 1996, *Talking about Machines: An Ethnography of a Modern Job*, ILR Press, Ithaca, NY.

Ortner, Sherry, 2009, "Studying Sideways: Ethnographic Access in Hollywood," in Vicki Mayer, Miranda J. Banks, and John Caldwell, eds., *Production Studies: Cultural Studies of Media Industries*, Routledge, New York, 175–89.

———, 2010, "Access: Reflections on Studying Up in Hollywood," *Ethnography* 11 (2), 211–33.

Osborne, David, and Ted Gaebler, 1993, *Reinventing Government: How the Entrepreneurial Spirit Is Transforming the Public Sector*, Plume, New York.

Ouellette, Laurie, 2011, "Real Justice: Law and Order on Reality Television," in Austin Sarat, ed., *Imagining Legality: Where Law Meets Popular Culture*, University of Alabama Press, Birmingham, 152–76.

Ouellette, Laurie, and James Hay, 2008, "Makeover Television, Governmentality and the Good Citizen," *Continuum* 22 (4), 471–84.

———, 2009, *Better Living through Reality TV: Television and Post-Welfare Citizenship*, Blackwell, Malden, MA.

Ouellette, Laurie, and Julie Wilson, 2011, "Women's Work: Affective Labor and Convergence Culture," *Cultural Studies*, 25, (4–5), 548–65.

"Our Respects to: Carl Haverlin" 1947, *Broadcasting*, August 4, 46.

Özbilgin, Mustafa, and Ahu Tatli, 2005, "Book Review Essay: Understanding Bourdieu's Contribution to Organization and Management Studies," *Academy of Management Review* 30 (4), 855–77.

Patnaik, Dev, with Peter Mortensen, 2009, *Wired to Care: How Companies Prosper When They Create Widespread Empathy*, FT Press, Upper Saddle River, NJ.

Payne, Kenneth, 2008, "Much Ado about Something: Web 2.0 Acceptance and Use by Public Relations Practitioners," in Tina McCorkindale, ed., *Public Relations Society of America Educators Academy 2008 Proceedings*, Detroit, Michigan, October 25, 2008.

Pecknold, Diane, 2007, *The Selling Sound: Country Music, Commercialism, and the Politics of Popular Culture*, Duke University Press, Durham, NC.

Peer, Ralph, 1958, interview by Lillian Borgeson, Hollywood, California, January 13 and May, Southern Folklife Collection, University of North Carolina, Chapel Hill, NC.

Peppercomm, 2012, "Peppercomm Launches Audience Experience," press release, January 25. Retrieved January 25, 2012, from http://www.Peppercomm.com/articles/1562.

Peters, Tom, 1997, "The Brand Called You," *Fast Company*, 10 (August), 8.

Petersen, Anne Helen, 2009, "'We're Making Our Own Paparazzi': Twitter and the Construction of Star Authenticity," *Flow*, May 28. Retrieved November 18, 2009, from http://flowtv.org/?p=3960.

Peterson, Richard A., 1976, "The Production of Culture: A Prolegomenon," in Richard A. Peterson, ed. *The Production of Culture*, Sage, Beverly Hills.

Peterson, Richard A., and N. Anand, 2004, "The Production of Culture Perspective," *Annual Review of Sociology*, 30, 311–44.

Pickford, Mary, Charlie Chaplin, Kenelm Foss et al., 1919. *Cinema: A Practical Course in Cinema Acting*, Standard Art Book Company, London.

"Program Problems Airs at BMI Clinic in Chicago," 1950, *Broadcasting*, October 10, 27.

"Programming Way to Renounce Fear," 1952, *Billboard*, May 17, 13.

"Radio Meggers to Hear Talk by Musickers," 1949, *Billboard*, May 28, 4.

"Radio Warned of Future," 1948, *Billboard*, May 29, 6.

"Ralph S. Peer Visits Important Points South," 1925, *Talking Machine World*, May 15, 85.

Raphael, Chad, 2009, "The Political Economic Origins of Reali-TV," in Susan Murray and Laurie Ouellette, eds., *Reality TV: Remaking Television Culture*, New York University Press, New York, 125–40.

Razlogova, Elena, 2011, *The Listener's Voice: Early Radio and the American Public,* University of Pennsylvania Press, Philadelphia.

Reade, Jason, 2009, "A Genealogy of Homo-Economicus: Neoliberalism and the Production of Subjectivity," *Foucault Studies*, 6, 25–36.

Reed, Adam, 2005, "'My Blog Is Me': Texts and Persons in UK Online Journal Culture," *Ethnos* 70 (2), 220–42.

Rêgo, Cacilda, 2005, "Brazilian Cinema: Its Fall, Rise, and Renewal (1990–2003)," *New Cinemas: Journal of Contemporary Film* 3(2), 85–100.

Reinsch, J. Leonard, 1948, *Radio Station Management,* Harper & Brothers, New York.

Reiss, John, 2009, *Think Outside the Box Office*, Hybrid Cinema Publishing, Los Angeles.

Richter, Paul, 1986, "Networks Get the Picture of Cost-Cutting," *New York Times*, October 26, sec. 5, 1.

Robertson, Peggy, 1995, "Peggy Robertson Oral History," interviewed by Barbara Hall, Margaret Herrick Library, Beverly Hills, CA.

"Rock 'n' Roll Laid to B.M.I. Control," 1956, *New York Times*, September 19, 75.

Rose, Nikolas, 1996, "Governing 'Advanced' Liberal Democracies," in Andrew Barry, Thomas Osbourne, and Nikolas Rose, eds., *Foucault and Political Reason:*

Liberalism, Neo-Liberalism and Rationalities of Government, University of Chicago Press, Chicago, 37–64.

Ross, Sharon Marie, 2008, *Beyond the Box: Television and the Internet*, Blackwell Publishing, Oxford.

Rothenbuhler, Eric, and Tom McCourt, 2002, "Radio Redefines Itself, 1947–1962," in Michele Hilmes and Jason Loviglio, eds., *The Radio Reader: Essays in the Cultural History of Radio*, Routledge, New York, 367–88.

——, 2004, "Burnishing the Brand: Todd Storz and the Total Station Sound," *The Radio Journal—International Studies in Broadcast and Audio Media* 2 (1), 3–14.

"Roundtable: Casting Directors," 2006, *Hollywood Reporter*, December 7. Retrieved July 24, 2012, from http://www.hollywoodreporter.com/news/roundtable-casting-directors-145676.

Russo, Alex, 2010, *Points on the Dial: Golden Age Radio beyond the Networks*, Duke University Press, Durham, NC.

Rutherford, Kevin, 2010, "Let's Play: Vernacular Video Game Criticism and the Composition Classroom," conference presentation, Meaningful Play, East Lansing, MI, October 21. Retrieved July 26, 2012, from http://meaningfulplay.msu.edu/proceedings2010/abstract.php?paperid=58.

Ryan, Bill, 1992, *Making Capital from Culture*, Walter de Gruyter, Berlin/New York.

Ryan, John, 1985, *The Production of Culture in the Music Industry: The ASCAP-BMI Controversy*, University Press of America, New York.

Ryan, Maureen, 2012, "Dan Harmon Fired from 'Community': How TV Executives Britta'd It," *Huffington Post*, May 19. Retrieved July 17, 2012, from http://www.huffingtonpost.com/maureen-ryan/dan-harmon-fired-community_b_1529588.html

Salaman, Graeme, 1997, "Culturing Production," in Paul du Gay, ed., *Production of Culture/Cultures of Production*, Sage, London, 235–84.

"Sales Clinic: Independents Plan Outlined," 1949, *Broadcasting*, April 18, 29.

Sanderson, Jimmy, 2008, "The Blog Is Serving Its Purpose: Self-Presentation Strategies on 38pitches.com," *Journal of Computer-Mediated Communication* 13 (4), 912–36.

Sanford, Carol, 2011, *The Responsible Business: Reimagining Sustainability and Success*, Jossey-Bass, San Francisco.

Sanjek, David, and Russell Sanjek, 1991, *American Popular Music Business in the 20th Century*, Oxford University Press, New York.

Sarris, Andrew, 1996, *The American Cinema: Directors And Directions 1929–1968*, Da Capo Press, Boston.

Satherley, Art, 1969, interview, Ed Kahn Collection, June 14, Southern Folklife Collection, University of North Carolina, Chapel Hill, NC.

——, 1971, interview, Ed Kahn Collection, June 12, Southern Folklife Collection, University of North Carolina, Chapel Hill, NC.

Schapiro, Mark, 1991, "Lust-Greed-Sex-Power: Translatable Anywhere," *New York Times*, June 2, B29.

Schlesinger, Philip, 1978, *Putting "Reality" Together: BBC News*, Constable, London.

———, 2010, "'The Most Creative Organization in the World'? The BBC, 'Creativity' and Managerial Style," *International Journal of Cultural Policy* 16 (3), 271–85.

Schwoch, James, 1990, "Selling the Sight/Site of Sound: Broadcast Advertising and the Transition from Radio to Television," *Cinema Journal* 30 (1), 55–66.

Scott, Allen J., 2005. *On Hollywood: The Place, The Industry*, Oxford University Press, Oxford.

Scott, Vernon, 1987, "Everyone, at Times, Loves a Casting Director," *UPI Hollywood Reporter*, August 15, BC cycle.

———, 1988, "Casting Directors Give Movies Their 'Personality,'" *UPI Hollywood Reporter*, June 3, BC cycle.

Seipp, Catherine, 2003, "Casting Directors Can Make You a Star," *UPI Press International*, June 18. Retrieved January 1, 2014, from http://www.upi.com/Odd_News/2003/06/18/Casting-directors-can-make-you-a-star/UPI-86031055948029/

Senft, Theresa M., 2008, *Camgirls: Celebrity & Community in the Age of Social Networks*, Peter Lang, New York.

Shepard, Richard, 1956, "Stations Urged to Cut B.M.I. Ties," *New York Times*, October 1, 31.

Shewey, Don, 1982, "They Comb New York to Give Its Movies a Special Look," *New York Times*, April 11, Late City Final, 19.

Skeggs, Beverly, 2009, "The Moral Economy of Person Production: The Class Relations of Self-Performance on Reality Television," *Sociological Review*, 57 (4), 625–44.

Snider, Mike, 2011, "Felicia Day Breathes Fire into 'Dragon Age' Series," *USA Today*, February 15. Retrieved July 26, 2012, from http://www.usatoday.com/life/lifestyle/2011-02-15-felicia15_ST_N.htm.

Socolow, Michael, 2002, "Questioning Advertising's Influence over American Radio: The Blue Book Controversy of 1945–1947," *Journal of Radio Studies* 9 (2), 282–302.

Søndergaard, Henrik, 1999, "Some Reflections on Public Service Broadcasting," *Nordicom* 20 (1), 21–28. Retrieved April 6, 2011, from www.nordicom.gu.se/common/publ_pdf/33_sondergaard.pdf.

Stanford University, 2010. "the d.school: The Hasso Plattner Institute of Design at Stanford." Retrieved July 10, 2012, from http://dschool.stanford.edu/wp-content/uploads/2010/09/dschool-fact-sheet1.pdf.

"Station Managers Urge Changes in Code," 1947, *Broadcasting* September 29, 32.

Steen, Mike, 1974, *Hollywood Speak! An Oral History*, J. P. Putnam and Sons, New York.

Sterne, Jonathan, 1999, "Television under Construction: American Television and the Problem of Distribution," *Media, Culture, & Society* 21 (4), 503–30.

Sterling, Christopher H., and John M. Kittross, 1978, *Stay Tuned: A Concise History of American Broadcasting*, Wadsworth Publishing Company, Belmont, CA.

Stoler, Ann Laura, 1995, *Race and the Education of Desire: Foucault's History of Sexuality and the Colonial Order of Things*, Duke University Press, Durham, NC, and London.

Strange, Niki, 2011, "Multiplatforming Public Service: The BBC's 'Bundled Project,'" in James Bennett and Niki Strange, eds., *Television as Digital Media*, Duke University Press, Durham, NC, 132–57.

Straubhaar, Joseph, 2003, "Choosing National TV: Cultural Capital, Language, and Cultural Proximity in Brazil," in Michael G. Elasmar, ed., *The Impact of International Television: A Paradigm Shift*, Taylor & Francis, Mahwah, NJ, 75–105.

———, 2007, *World Television: From Global to Local*, Sage, Los Angeles.

Strom, Sharon Hartman, 1992, *Beyond the Typewriter: Gender, Class and the Origins of Modern American Office Work, 1900–30*, University of Illinois Press, Chicago.

Sutton, Allan, 2005, *Pseudonyms on American Records (1892–1948), A Guide to False Names and Label Errors*, (2nd rev. and exp.. ed., Mainspring Press, Denver, CO.

———, 2008, *Recording the Twenties: The Evolution of the American Recording Industry, 1920–1929*, Mainspring Press, Denver, CO.

Sylvie, George, et al. 2008, *Media Management: A Casebook Approach*, Routledge, New York.

Tannen, Deborah, 1994, "The Sex-Linked Framing of Talk at Work," *Gender and Discourse*, Oxford University Press, Oxford, 195–212.

Tartikoff, Brandon, and Charles Leerhsen, 1992, *The Last Great Ride*, Turtle Bay Books, New York.

Teather, David, 2001, "Working with Dinosaurs," *Media Guardian*, February 12. Retrieved August 8, 2005, from http://media.guardian.co.uk/0,3858,4134854-105337,00.html.

Théberge, Paul, 2005, "Everyday Fandom: Fan Clubs, Blogging, and the Quotidian Rhythms of the Internet," *Canadian Journal of Communication* 30 (4), 485–502.

Thompson, Ann Bahr, 2003, "Brand Positioning and Brand Creation," in Rita Clifton and John Simmons,eds., *Brands and Branding*, Bloomberg Press, Princeton, NJ, 79–96.

Thompson, Mark, 2004, "Mark Thompson Celebrates the Official Opening of a New State-of-the Art BBC Building in Hull." Retrieved December 15, 2011, from http://www.bbc.co.uk/pressoffice/pressreleases/stories/2004/10_october/21/hull.shtml.

———, 2006a, "BBC Creative Future," *Guardian*, April 25. Retrieved April 14, 2011, from http://www.guardian.co.uk/media/2006/apr/25/bbc.broadcasting.

———, 2006b, "Creative Future: The BBC Programmes and Content in an On-Demand World," Royal Television Society Fleming Memorial Lecture..Retrieved February 14, 2007, from http://www.bbc.co.uk/pressoffice/speeches/stories/thompson_fleming.shtml.

Tinic, Serra, 2005, *On Location: Canada's Television Industry in a Global Market*, University of Toronto Press, Toronto.

Todd, Tony, 2009, "Meanings and Authorships in Dune," *Film-Philosophy*, 13 (1), 68–90.

"Transformation Scene in World Television," 1992, *Screen Digest*, February, 33–40.

Turow, Joseph, 1978. "Casting for TV Parts: The Anatomy of Social Typing," *Journal of Communication* 4 (December), 18–24.

———, 1981, "Unconventional Programs on Commercial Television: An Organizational Perspective," in C. Whitney and J. Ettema, eds., *Individuals in Mass Media Organizations*, Sage Publications, Beverly Hills, CA, 107–30.

———, 1985, "The Influence of Pressure Groups on Television Entertainment: A Framework for Analysis," in W. Rowland and B. Watkins, eds., *Interpreting Television*, Sage Publications, Beverly Hills, CA, 142–64.

———, 1992, *Media Systems in Society: Understanding Industries, Strategies, and Power*, Longman, New York.

Tuchman, Gaye, 1978, *Making News: A Study in the Construction of Reality*, Free Press, New York.

"Twitter Enabled Negative Word-of-Mouth to Instantly Affect Bruno at the Box Office" 2009, *Buzz Study*, July 15. Retrieved July 10, 2012, from http://infegy.com/buzz-study/twitter-enabled-negative-word-of-mouth-to-instantly-affect-bruno-at-the-box-office/.

Untitled Full-Page Anti-Union Ad, 1980. *Daily Variety*, March 25, 32

Vickers, Amy, 1991, "BBC's Highfield to Make All Shows Interactive," *The Guardian*, March 13. http://www.theguardian.com/media/2001/mar/13/broadcasting.bbc2.

Vogel, Robert, 1991, "Robert Vogel Oral History," interviewed by Barbara Hall, Margaret Herrick Library, Beverly Hills, CA.

Walker, Frank, 1962, interview, Mike Seeger Collection, June 9, Southern Folklife Collection, University of North Carolina, Chapel Hill.

Walkerdine, Valerie, 2003, "Reclassifying Upward Mobility: Femininity and the Neo-Liberal Subject," *Gender and Education*, 15 (3), 237–47.

Wallace, Amy, 2010, "Violence, Nudity, Adult Content," *GQ*, November . Retrieved July 25, 2012, from http://www.gq.com/news-politics/newsmakers/201011/chris-albrecht-vegas-hbo-starz.

Weber, Max, 1924/1947, *The Theory of Social and Economic Organization*, A.M. Henderson and Talcott Parsons trans., Free Press, New York.

Wheaton, Wil, 2011, "if you cut me, i will bleed," *WWdN: In Exile*, July 25. Retrieved January 31, 2012, from http://wilwheaton.typepad.com/wwdnbackup/2011/07/if-you-cut-me-i-will-bleed.html.

White, Michele, 2006, "Television and Internet Differences by Design: Rendering Liveness, Presence, and Lived Space," *Convergence: The Journal of Research into New Media Technologies* 12 (3), 341–55.

"Widespread Payola Hurting Disk-Jockey Shows, Arnold Warns Programmers' Clinic," 1950, *Billboard*, February 4, 4.

Wojcik, Pamela Robertson, 2003, "Typecasting," *Criticism*, 45 (2) (Spring), 227–37.

Wolfe, Charles, 2005, "The Legend that Peer Built: Reappraising the Bristol Sessions," in Charles K. Wolfe and Ted Olson, eds., *The Bristol Sessions: Writing about the Big Bang of Country Music*, McFarland Press, Jefferson, NC, 17–39.

Wolfe, Charles K., and Ted Olson, 2005, eds., *The Bristol Sessions: Writing about the Big Bang of Country Music*, McFarland Press, Jefferson, NC.

Wollen, Peter, 1972, *Signs and Meaning in the Cinema*, Secker & Warburg, London.

Yellin, Emily, 2009, *Your Call Is (not that) Important to Us: Customer Service and What It Reveals about Our World and Our Lives*, Free Press, New York.

Young, Alma, 1977, "Alma Young Oral History," interviewed by Anthony Slide and Robert Gitt, Margaret Herrick Library, Beverly Hills, CA.

Young, Jeffrey R., 2007, "The Mud-Wrestling Media Maven from MIT," *The Chronicle of Higher Education* 54 (3), B20–25.

Zafirau, Stephen, 2007, "Reputation Work in Selling Film and Television: Life in the Hollywood Talent Industry," *Qualitative Sociology* 31 (2), 99–127.

Zoellner, Ann, 2009, "Professional Ideology and Program Conventions: Documentary Development in Independent British Television Production," *Mass Communication and Society*, 12 (4), 503–36.

Zwonitzer, Mark, and Charles Hirschberg, 2004, *Will You Miss Me When I'm Gone?: The Carter Family and Their Legacy in American Music*, Simon & Schuster, New York.

KYLE BARNETT is Associate Professor in the School of Communication at Bellarmine University. His current research focuses on cultural production in the U.S. recording industry between 1920 and 1935. Publications include "The Selznick Studio, 'Spellbound,' and the Marketing of Film Music" in *Music, Sound, and the Moving Image* and "The Recording Industry's Role in Media History," in *Convergence Media History*.

JAMES BENNETT is Senior Lecturer in Television Studies at Royal Holloway, University of London. He is the Principle Investigator on a two-year AHRC Research Project (AH-H018522-1) examining the relationship of multiplatform production, public service broadcasters, and the independent sector. He is the author of *Television Personalities: Stardom and the Small Screen* and the co-editor with Niki Strange of *Television as Digital Media*.

COURTNEY BRANNON DONOGHUE is Assistant Professor in the Department of English and Cinema Studies Program at Oakland University. She has publications on the Brazilian film industry and Globo Filmes, *Ugly Betty* and transnational telenovela flows, and digital piracy in Spanish cinema. She is currently working on a book exploring the local language production strategy developed by Sony and its peers during the Conglomerate Hollywood era.

ELIZABETH ELLCESSOR is Assistant Professor in the Department of Communication and Culture at Indiana University. Her research interests include digital media, disability studies, star studies, and convergences between digital media and older media forms. Broadly, her work focuses on the limitations to technical use and personal identity that are encountered in digital media, and thus the way that these tools themselves shape the nature and diversity of participation.

ELIZABETH EVANS is a Lecturer in Film and Television Studies at the University of Nottingham. Her research focuses on the film and television audiences, in particular in relation to the emergence of new technologies. She is the author of *Transmedia Television: Audiences, New Media and Daily Life* and has published in *Media, Culture and Society* and *Participations*.

SAM FORD is Director of Audience Engagement with Peppercomm Strategic Communications, a research affiliate with the MIT Program in Comparative Media Studies, a weekly contributor to *Fast Company*, and a lecturer with Western Kentucky University's Popular Culture Studies Program. He is co-author with Henry Jenkins and Joshua Green of *Spreadable Media*, and co-editor with Abigail De Kosnik and C. Lee Harrington of *The Survival of the Soap Opera*. Ford has written for *BusinessWeek*, *The Huffington Post*, *The Christian Science Monitor*, *Portfolio*, *Chief Marketer*, and a range of other publications.

TIMOTHY HAVENS is Associate Professor of Communication Studies and African American Studies at the University of Iowa and a former Senior Fulbright Scholar to Hungary. He is the author of *Global Television Marketplace* and *Black Television Travels: Media Globalization and Contemporary Racial Discourse*, and co-author with Amanda D. Lotz of *Understanding Media Industries*. His published research has also appeared in *Communication, Culture & Critique*; *Critical Studies in Media Communication*; *Media, Culture & Society*; *The Journal of Broadcasting and Electronic Media*; *Gazette*; and *The Global Media Journal*.

ERIN HILL is a Ph.D. Candidate in Cinema and Media Studies at UCLA. She is currently completing work on feminized labor sectors in studio-era film production and their relation to gendered media production today. Erin is co-founder of *Mediascape*, UCLA's online media studies journal, and her work has been published in the print anthologies *Reading Deadwood, Production Studies,* and *The Production Studies Reader.* She also freelances as a story analyst for film production companies and writes about her experiences as a media academic/production worker at filmindustrybloggers.com and erinthill.wordpress. com.

DEREK JOHNSON is Associate Professor of Media and Cultural Studies at the University of Wisconsin, Madison. He is the author of *Media Franchising: Creative License and Collaboration in the Culture Industries* and the co-editor of *A Companion to Media Authorship.*

DEREK KOMPARE is Associate Professor of Film and Media Arts in the Meadows School of the Arts at Southern Methodist University. His research interests center on media formations, i.e., the cultural and industrial factors that generate particular media forms and relationships. He is the author of *Rerun Nation: How Repeats Invented American Television, CSI,* and several articles in journals and anthologies on television history and form.

AMANDA D. LOTZ is Associate Professor of Communication Studies at the University of Michigan. She is the author of *The Television Will Be Revolutionized* and *Redesigning Women: Television after the Network Era,* and editor of *Beyond Prime Time: Television Programming in the Post-Network Era.* She is co-author, with Timothy Havens, of *Understanding Media Industries* and, with Jonathan Gray, of *Television Studies.*

LAURIE OUELLETTE is Associate Professor in the Department of Communication Studies at the University of Minnesota. She is co-author of *Better Living through Reality TV: Television and Post-Welfare Citizenship* and co-editor of *Reality TV: Remaking Television Culture.*

ALEXANDER RUSSO is Associate Professor of Media Studies at the Catholic University of America in Washington, D.C. He is the author of *Points on the Dial: Golden Age Radio beyond the Networks.* He has also published on a variety of radio and television topics in *The Historical Journal of Film Radio and Television* and *The Velvet Light Trap* as well as the anthologies *Down to Earth: Geopolitics, Systems, Domains, and*

Cultures of Satellites, The Radio Reader: Essays on the Cultural History of Radio, and *Urban Procedural: The Wire and the Neoliberal City.*

AVI SANTO is Associate Professor in the Department of Communication and Theatre Arts and Director of the Institute for the Humanities at Old Dominion University. His research focuses primarily on the historical development of character licensing and brand extension. His published works can be found in *Cinema Journal, Critical Studies in Media Communication, Framework, Journal of Consumer Culture,* and *Popular Communication.* His monograph, *Selling the Silver Bullet: The Lone Ranger, Incorporated and Character Brand Licensing, 1933–2010,* is forthcoming from University of Texas Press.

NIKI STRANGE is a Research Fellow at the University of Sussex and the founder of Strange Digital, a company providing research and strategy consulting for digital businesses and the culture, education, and public sectors. She is co-editor with James Bennett of *Television as Digital Media.*

JUSTIN WYATT is Vice President, Consumer Insights and Research at CMT/MTV Networks/Viacom. He has previously held primary research positions at NBCUniversal, ABC TV Network, and Frank N. Magid Associates. He is the author of *High Concept: Movies and Marketing in Hollywood* and the co-editor of *Contemporary American Independent Film: From the Margins to the Mainstream.*

Printed and bound by CPI Group (UK) Ltd, Croydon, CR0 4YY

16/04/2025

14658441-0002